Ret... ☑ P9-CRH-113
Review Copy.............................
Complimentary Copy..............
Desk Copy.............................
Exam Copy.............................

LESBIANS

IN CANADA

Retail Price
Review Copy
Complimentary Copy
Desk Copy
Exam Copy

LESBIANS
IN CANADA

Edited by Sharon Dale Stone

between the lines

© 1990 Sharon Dale Stone

Published by
Between The Lines,
394 Euclid Ave.,
Toronto, Ontario M6G 2S9

Cover illustration and design by Pamela Pfohl

Typeset by Mary Scally and The Coach House Press

Printed in Canada

Between The Lines receives financial assistance
from the Canada Council, the Ontario Arts Council,
and the Department of Communications.

CANADIAN CATALOGUING IN PUBLICATION DATA

Main entry under title:
    Lesbians in Canada

ISBN 0-921284-28-4 (bound)
ISBN 0-921284-29-2 (pbk.)

1. Lesbians – Canada.   I. Stone, Sharon Dale, 1955-

HQ75.6.C3L48 1990   306.7´663´0971   C89-090575-4

Contents

Acknowledgements

WITHOUT THE encouragement and support I received from others, I would never have dared to put together a book about lesbians. I had wanted to do this for years, but did not actually take this project seriously until Livy Visano assured me that editing an anthology did not take much work (he was wrong!), and encouraged me to get going on it. For believing I could do it in the first place, I am grateful to him.

In the early stages of putting this together and editing articles I benefited from discussions with Joanne Doucette. In the latter stages of the project I owe special thanks to Frank Harding, who served as my editorial critic and sounding board. I also owe special thanks to Carolyn Gammon, who made extensive and helpful comments on the introduction and the article on lesbians in Newfoundland. The enthusiasm of the contributors was, of course, crucial; the book is as much a product of their labour as mine. I thank all of them for believing in this project enough to contribute to it. Also for believing in this project when many others would not touch it with a ten-foot pole, I thank the people at Between The Lines and in particular, Robert Clarke, Jamie Swift, and Michael Kaufman. Lorna Weir, Alice de Wolff, and Barry Adam also provided much needed encouragement and made helpful suggestions about the manuscript. The Kimeta Society of Toronto provided a small grant in aid of the book's publication, for which we are most grateful. Finally, I am grateful to the Ontario Arts Council for granting financial assistance for my writing.

Micheline Grimard-Leduc's article "The Mind-Drifting Islands" was originally published in French in *l'île des amantes* (Micheline Grimard-Leduc, Montreal, 1982). It was also published in English in the journal *Trivia*, No. 8 (1986) and in *For Lesbians Only: A Separatist Anthology* edited by Sarah Lucia Hoagland and Julia Penelope (London: Onlywomen Press, 1988). "Man Royals and Sodomites" by Makeda Silvera was previously published in *Fireweed: A Feminist Quarterly*, Issue 28 (Spring 1989) and in *Sight Specific: Lesbians and Representation* (Toronto: A Space, 1988).

S.D.S.

Introduction

Defining the Context

Sharon Dale Stone

LESBIANS MAKE UP a significant proportion of the Canadian population, but have had very little written about them. For the most part they are hidden from public view and much misunderstood. This book was compiled to bring Canadian lesbians into public view, to correct stereotypes and assumptions, and to present lesbianism as a viable alternative to heterosexuality.

It is not always understood, for instance, that lesbians are not similar to homosexual men. Lesbians are commonly discussed in conjunction with gay men and are often assumed to be merely gay men's female counterparts. Just as many women's studies scholars argue that most of what passes as knowledge about "mankind" is actually about men and ignores women, so many who discuss homosexuality typically speak of the male gay experience to the exclusion of the lesbian experience.

Lesbians are *women*. This point is crucial for understanding lesbian existence within a heterosexual, patriarchal context. As women, lesbians do not have access to male privilege. No matter how much lesbians might reject traditional notions of femininity (and not all do), they do not have the same access to well-paying jobs that men have, are frequently subjected to sexual harassment, and are as likely to be raped as a heterosexual woman. These realities constitute some of the differences between lesbians and gay men. They make the experience of being lesbian qualitatively different from the experience of being a gay man. Lesbians, in short, are as

9

different from gay men as heterosexual women are different from heterosexual men.

Most girls grow up in an environment that assumes heterosexuality as both the natural and preferred mode of sexual expression. This is what is meant when critics say heterosexuality has been institutionalized.[1] Girls are not likely to hear anything positive about lesbianism – if they ever hear of it at all. The dominant culture largely erases evidence of lesbian existence or, when it cannot be ignored, presents lesbianism as either: a) a deviant way of life (abnormal, perverted, pitiable, abhorrent); or b) "kinky" sexual behaviour that is harmless so long as the women involved remain available for the pleasure of men.[2]

Too many girls have grown up and continue to grow up believing that unless they find a man to marry, they are destined to become lonely "old maids."[3] Girls do not need to be told this explicitly for the message to sink in – though the message often *is* explicit. They get the message readily enough from popular books, movies, TV programs. They get it from as simple an activity as playing the children's card game "Old Maid." No one wants the old maid. It is small wonder that most women, including many lesbians, grow up to marry a man and produce children. Not only is this what women are taught to do, but this prescription is also presented to them as the only way to find happiness and fulfilment (Catholic girls also have the option of becoming nuns).[4]

In contemporary psychoanalytic theory, there is the implicit recognition that, at least for women, heterosexuality is learned behaviour.[5] Essentially, this complex insight acknowledges the primacy of the mother / daughter bond and the corresponding secondary nature of girls' and women's attachments to men. At puberty, girls are expected to redirect their interest away from women. That so many women in fact do this is often taken as evidence that heterosexuality is "innate." Given the evidence, this is not a logical conclusion. There are, as contemporary theorists such as Adrienne Rich and Janice Raymond have separately pointed out, many practical reasons for assuming a heterosexual way of life – reasons that have nothing to do with sexual attraction.

Historically, women and men have tended to marry, not for reasons of romantic love, but for economic and other practical reasons (for example, for social standing, to have legitimate children). This is not to say that women and men never fell in love with each other.

History books are filled with examples of heterosexual romance. Yet the idea that love and marriage go together is relatively recent. For the upper classes, marriage has traditionally represented the opportunity to increase family fortunes and solidify family ties, and the dictates of the sexual division of labour have meant that women and men in all classes have needed to form unions for economic survival.[6]

The idea of companionate marriage – a union based on friendship and sexual satisfaction – did not become a common goal until the 1920s. Prior to that, few people really believed that women and men could find total fulfilment together. The prevailing ideology held that women and men belonged to separate spheres. Women's sphere was the private world of domesticity; men's sphere was the public world outside the home (this ideology has far from disappeared).

Much has been written recently on the Victorian belief that the sexes did not have much in common with each other, and on the implications of that belief. In particular, Carroll Smith-Rosenberg has argued that intimate and loving friendships between women were casually accepted in eighteenth- and nineteenth-century American society.[7] It was only towards the end of the nineteenth century that love between women began to be seen as suspect, or deviant. Lillian Faderman provides convincing evidence that the women's movement, along with women's growing economic independence, figured prominently in the redefinition of passionate love affairs between women as sick. For the first time in modern history, unprecedented numbers of women were able to make their way in the world without being tied to men.[8] Christina Simmons makes a similar argument concerning the emergence of the twentieth-century perception of lesbianism as a threat to be guarded against.[9]

Putting Women First
The word "lesbian" has become a scare word, to be hurled at any woman who does not conform to conventional notions of femininity. These conventional notions include the idea that women exist for the pleasure of men – not simply for men's sexual pleasure, but also to nurture men, bolster their egos, and raise their progeny. It is a word that is used to divide women from each other, to keep them from discovering that it is possible to find happiness and fulfilment without men. Feminists in particular are commonly suspected of being lesbians, because feminists believe, among other things, that

women *matter*. This idea radically challenges the patriarchal under-pinnings of society. The suspicion that feminists are "really" les-bians lies behind the fear many women have of being seen as femin-ist. Thus, many women will preface statements such as "I believe in equal rights for women" with *I'm not a feminist, but ...*". By quali-fying a feminist statement in this manner, women are able to hold feminist beliefs yet continue to see themselves and be seen by others in conventional society as "normal" – not lesbian man-haters.

It is significant that lesbians are so commonly perceived as man-haters. This view dramatically underscores the misogynist founda-tion of conventional society.[10] Only a woman-hating society could assume that women who love other women must therefore hate men.[11] It seems to be stretching credulity for many people to think that men could be irrelevant for some women. The love that lesbians have for other women rarely has much to do with their feelings towards men. Lesbians are women who love other women.

The Scope of this Collection

A single collection such as this cannot address all areas of lesbian studies or all issues of contemporary debate. To adequately discuss all topics relevant to lesbian studies and the ethics involved would require not one volume, but a library of volumes.[12]

This collection grew from my own consciousness as a lesbian, a feminist, and an activist. Also, as an academic, I was dissatisfied with the lack of easily accessible information on this subject. There exists a growing amount of written material about lesbians, but for the most part, this material is not specifically about Canadian les-bians. To read about Canadian lesbians means sifting through a vari-ety of newsletters, magazines, newspapers, and journals.[13] As well, there is an overwhelming tendency in books about lesbians to gloss over differences among lesbians. As Susan Krieger has pointed out, research disproportionately reflects "the white, well-educated, artic-ulate, youthful, middle-class lesbian who has some commitment to feminist ideology."[14] Lesbians are a minority group, but there are also minorities within this minority group. The fact of our lesbian-ism does not make us all essentially the same.

Canada is a vast country, with different regions offering different social and economic conditions. There are two official languages; many Canadians claim neither of them as their native tongue. Whites form a majority in this country, yet there are also significant numbers of people from other racial backgrounds. Many of them – not only Native People and Inuit, but also Blacks and Asians – have been in Canada longer than some whites. This truth is overlooked in the common assumption that anyone with black skin or Asian features was not born in Canada. As well, there are important class divisions in Canada, which affect not only social and economic opportunities, but also personal consciousness.

I began with the intention of including chapters that would address all of the above-noted divisions. Unfortunately, I was unable to obtain articles focusing on topics such as working-class lesbian life, francophone lesbians, bars and bar culture, or butch / femme identities. That these differences among lesbians are not discussed at length here should not be taken to mean that they are unimportant.

What I have ended up with is, admittedly, a small sampling of lesbian life in Canada but I hope the collection suggests at least some of the diversity among lesbians and provides a starting point for further explorations.

The focus in this anthology is on the experiential. Most articles are based on interview data, and spend more time giving voice to those interviewed than analyzing what was said. Readers looking for unrelenting analysis and theory will by and large be disappointed. Yet the scholarship is far from sloppy. The articles reflect a respect for those who were spoken with, in an attempt to show how *they* experience their lives. Little has been written elsewhere about lesbians in Canada. This makes it all the more important that Canadian lesbians be allowed to speak for themselves.

Although each contribution to this volume is unique, there are common threads that tie them together. For example, one topic explicitly taken up in several articles – and which crosses through the three parts of the book – is formal education. This emphasis reflects the significance of institutionalized education in the lives of most lesbians, whether or not they have a career in education. All of us have contact with the education system early in life (and increasingly, later in life as well), and this contact usually has a lasting impact. With rare exceptions, lesbianism is never mentioned – especially not in elementary or high school. This lack of acknowledgement of lesbianism as a viable way of life shapes the consciousness of us all.

Motherhood is another topic taken up repeatedly. Two articles are about lesbian mothers, and many other articles discuss lesbian mothers. This may surprise some readers, since it is commonly assumed that lesbians do not reproduce. Lesbianism, however, does not render a woman infertile. Lesbians often give birth to children as a result of heterosexual intercourse and, increasingly, as a result of artificial insemination. Motherhood is a female experience, not simply a heterosexual experience.

Part I: A Diversity of Lesbian Experiences

Lesbians really are everywhere. Contrary to popular stereotypes, lesbians are an extremely heterogeneous lot – as diverse as the general population. The articles in the first part of this book shed light on some of the differences among lesbians, as lesbians living in various situations talk about their experiences.

How many lesbians have been warned that their failure to marry will lead them to a lonely old age?[15] Old age is a prospect that we learn to fear in western culture for many reasons, as Jeanette Auger points out. Still, many old lesbians have defied societal expectations and been happy. Auger presents us with the words of old lesbians themselves, as they talk about their lives. Her article makes it clear that, rather than "triple trouble," there are lesbians who experience their old age as a time of "tremendous thrill."[16]

Women raising children while not living with men are thought of as "single" mothers. For heterosexual mothers this term may be appropriate. For lesbian mothers the term is often inappropriate. Many lesbian mothers, as Dian Day shows, live with lovers who act as co-parents. Drawing on her own experience as well as interviews with other lesbian mothers in Nova Scotia, Day highlights their concerns. She draws attention to the unique problems lesbian mothers may face, while noting that they also have many concerns that are common to all mothers.

In "Man Royals and Sodomites," Makeda Silvera writes about racism and heterosexism, drawing on her own experiences as a Black lesbian. She writes poignantly of the strong women who were part of her childhood in Jamaica, and of how she learned only later that some of them were lesbians. Just as their stories were silenced in Jamaica, Silvera discusses the silencing of Afro-Caribbean lesbians in Canada, and their invisibility. She shares with us her dream for all lesbians and gays of colour: a day when "being invisible is no longer."

The lesbians that Joanne Doucette interviewed were either visibly or invisibly disabled, and she shatters some myths about them in her article. Disabled lesbians, as she points out, "face at least triple oppression – as disabled people, as women and as lesbians." If, in addition, they face racist oppression – as do many in Doucette's sample – they are even less welcome in mainstream society. The voices in her article are mostly angry voices: there is anger at patronizing assumptions about disabled people in general, and anger because some disabled people will not accept their lesbianism while other lesbians seem to be afraid of their disability. Disabled lesbians, Doucette argues, are ultimate outsiders, and this puts them in the unique position of being able to create "startling new visions of how the world could be."

The next two articles are about the work experiences of lesbians who are in a relatively privileged position, in the sense that they are able to work in middle-class professions. As Janice Ristock maintains, however, life as a lesbian social service worker can carry its own set of difficulties. Only one of the six workers Ristock talked to was unselective in telling people about her lesbianism. The others felt too vulnerable to be completely open about themselves. As one of them said, "I have to present a façade and I'm not able to relax about who I am." All of them also volunteered at a lesbian and gay counselling centre but as Ristock reveals they also ran into problems in that environment.

Considering that even the suggestion of allowing homosexuals to be ministers has prompted an exodus from the United Church, it is hardly surprising that public school teachers are careful about keeping their lesbianism a secret. If adults do not want homosexuals preaching to them, they are even less likely to want lesbians instructing their children. As Didi Khayatt says in her article, even in provinces where sexual orientation is protected by law, "It is not particularly safe for a lesbian teacher to come out if she intends to stay in teaching." Drawing on her interviews with lesbian teachers, Khayatt explores various methods they use to protect their careers, while maintaining personal integrity.

The risk of being visible comes up again in the last chapter of Part I, in the results of a survey of lesbians in St. John's, Newfoundland. This article, which I wrote in co-operation with the Women's Survey Group, touches on issues that many Canadian lesbians struggle with, no matter where they live, including relationships with family members, the availability of positive information about lesbians, attitudes towards bisexuality, and attitudes towards feminism. At the same time, we point out the unique features of lesbian life in St. John's.

Part II: Problems and Possibilities in a Lesbophobic Society[17]
Homophobia connotes fear and hatred of homosexuals in general, while lesbophobia refers to fear and hatred of lesbians in particular. The term "lesbophobic" is not a common one, but is used to emphasize that lesbians, as women, are subjected to sexist oppression in addition to heterosexist oppression. It is also used to emphasize that lesbians are viewed and treated very differently from gay men. In many respects, lesbians are much more threatening to the social order than gay men. This remains true despite widespread fear of Acquired Immune Deficiency Syndrome (AIDS) – erroneously referred to by many as the "gay plague."[18] Patriarchal society is phallocentric – organized by and for men. It is built on the assumption that women exist to serve men. Lesbians, simply by existing, flagrantly challenge this assumption. Lesbians, as already noted, are women who exist for themselves and other women, and lesbianism is the ultimate expression of female autonomy from men. It is for this reason that lesbianism represents a profound threat to the patriarchal order – a threat that is qualitatively different from the threat that gay men are seen as representing.

In this section contributions focus on some of the problems facing lesbians in mainstream Canadian society. They also encourage us to consider what life could be like without the obstacles of prejudice or discrimination.

Think, for example, of how different life could be for lesbians if they were legally protected from discrimination based on sexual orientation. Of course, such legal protection would not be able to prevent all discrimination, just as people of colour continue to experience racist discrimination despite laws against it. Yet laws against discrimination based on sexual orientation could potentially make life a lot easier for lesbians. Mary Eaton discusses this issue in a fascinating review of how current Canadian law affects lesbians. She also looks at the new possibilities for legal parity that came into being with the entrenchment of Section 15 of the Charter of Rights and Freedoms. There is room for hope but as Eaton concludes, "The litigation of lesbian difference will likely be a long hard struggle."
Becki Ross continues the discussion of lesbians and the law by

giving an account of how she experienced the debate on Bill 7 in the Ontario legislature (the bill to include sexual orientation in the Human Rights Code). Ross does not suggest that the Ontario debate was similar to debates in other parts of Canada. Nor does she pretend to be speaking for other lesbians. Rather, she tells us how she felt as she watched a group of people cavalierly summarize and dismiss her life under the category homosexual. Ross's account is important because it forces an abstract discussion onto the plane of lived experience. From her standpoint as a lesbian, she brings to light features of the struggle for legal rights that are routinely censored by the mainstream media, and suggests the implications of the passage of Bill 7 for the everyday lives of lesbians.

One of the consequences of lesbophobia is that most people are able to voice ready-made arguments opposing lesbianism. There are probably few lesbians who have not come up against arguments about nature and morality; such discussion helps to keep lesbophobia alive, and philosophical statements discrediting lesbianism are an implicit part of mainstream Canadian culture. Their pervasiveness represents a huge stumbling block in the struggle to legitimate lesbianism as a positive life choice. In "Aristotle, Sex, and a Three-Legged Dog," Joan Blackwood offers a philosophical perspective on lesbian sexuality. Starting from the assumption that women do not exist solely as objects of men's desires, she confronts the common debates about both nature and morality, providing a challenge that forms a welcome corrective.

Universities are commonly upheld as institutions committed to the production and teaching of pure (that is, neutral, unbiased) knowledge. Jeri Wine questions the validity of this assumption by pointing to the almost total silence surrounding the subject of lesbianism. Drawing on her interviews with lesbians in places of "higher learning," Wine illuminates problems created by heterosexism — problems that extend beyond the walls of the "ivory tower." At the same time she invites us to consider the unique possibilities that the academic setting provides for the flourishing of knowledge that is not tainted with heterosexism.

Micheline Grimard-Leduc, in the final chapter of Part II, identifies the psychic harm done to lesbians by lesbophobic society and presents a vision of lesbian autonomy. Grimard-Leduc's writing is inspired by a tradition known in Quebec as radical lesbianism — a political position similar to what anglophones call lesbian separatism.[19] She is not alone in her conviction that lesbians can draw strength from remembering their proud heritage. Grimard-Leduc celebrates the ability of lesbians to overcome the barriers constructed by male society and create their own reality.

Part III: Lesbians Organizing for Survival

The third part of *Lesbians in Canada* looks at how lesbians are organizing to fight for their rights and to create an atmosphere of acceptance.

Especially since the 1970s, and the renewed energy of the women's liberation movement, more and more lesbians have been coming out of the closet and learning to take pride in a lesbian identity. This is as true in Canada as in the United States and, indeed, anywhere else in the western world.[20] A lesbian liberation movement is growing, and it is often quite distinct from either gay liberation or women's liberation. Although there are still many lesbians who feel safer in the closet and perhaps secretly believe that there is something wrong with them, there are countless other lesbians who loudly proclaim and rejoice in their love for women.

Of lesbians who are involved in the struggle for liberation, some prefer to work and identify with the gay liberation movement, because they "see, feel and understand the need to end the suppression of their homosexuality."[21] The gay liberation movement is sometimes simplistically perceived as concerned with nothing more than assimilating gay men into the existing social structure; but as with any other social movement, it is actually many-faceted. Although the gay liberation movement is male-dominated, many of those involved in it are committed to working to end all forms of oppression, based on an analysis that extends to include a feminist analysis of the oppression of women.[22]

Other lesbians prefer to work and identify with the women's liberation movement, believing that their fate as lesbians is inextricably tied to the fate of all women.[23] Many of these lesbians found the courage to come out within the context of feminism, and identify strongly as feminists. In the women's liberation movement lesbians do not have to deal with sexist oppression. They do, however, have to deal with lesbophobia on the part of heterosexual women.

Other lesbians believe that lesbian oppression is not adequately addressed by either gay liberation or women's liberation, and prefer to organize separately from both men and heterosexual women. Many of these lesbians identify as lesbian-feminists, to emphasize a connection to all women, and many of them identify as lesbian separatists, to emphasize the connection they feel to lesbians everywhere and the strength they get from being with other lesbians.

In "A Test of Unity," Julia Creet gives an historical account of a group of lesbians who began organizing for lesbian rights in 1974. The Lesbian Caucus of the British Columbia Federation of Women (BCFW) was formed because lesbians realized that they could not rely on heterosexual women to address their concerns as a matter of course. Quoting from original documents as well as from her interviews with those involved in the Lesbian Caucus, Creet traces the emergence of lesbian-feminist consciousness and the conflicts surrounding the issue of lesbianism in the British Columbia women's movement.

Four years after the Lesbian Caucus began organizing in British Columbia, lesbian mothers founded their own organization in Toronto. As I discuss in chapter 14, the Lesbian Mothers' Defence Fund (LMDF) spent close to ten years breaking the silence about the existence of lesbian mothers and defending their rights. In the words of those involved with LMDF, we learn what the organization meant to mothers and non-mothers alike.

The final two articles are written by lesbians who are passionately concerned about creating a space for lesbians in society. The authors are visionary, and it is appropriate to end this collection with a discussion of how lesbians are working to make Canadian society a more congenial place for lesbians. Carolyn Gammon and other members of the Lesbian Studies Coalition at Concordia University in Montreal write about why they are involved in the struggle to validate a lesbian perspective in education. Although each author says it differently, all of them are angry with the heterosexist nature of the curriculum that has confronted them at all levels of schooling. They believe "It's high time to make a consolidated attack on the heterosexism in our Canadian universities."

In the last chapter, Carmen Paquette offers a retrospective look at lesbian organizing in Ottawa, and talks about why she is involved in organizing lesbians for political action there and across Canada. In so doing, she touches on a variety of issues relevant to lesbian organizing. She closes by asking, "How Far Have We Come?" and says "There are still many gaps." Some of the gaps in our knowledge about Canadian lesbians have been filled through other publications; many more gaps have yet to be filled. This collection, I hope, represents a beginning.

Notes

1. On heterosexuality as an institution, see "Not for Lesbians Only" and "Learning from Lesbian Separatism" in Charlotte Bunch, *Passionate Politics: Feminist Theory in Action* (New York: St. Martin's Press, 1987); Adrienne Rich, "Compulsory Heterosexuality and Lesbian Existence," in *Signs: Journal of Women in Culture and Society*, Vol. 5 (Summer 1980), pp. 631-657; Janice Raymond, *A Passion for Friends: Toward a Philosophy of Female Affection* (London: The Women's Press, 1986).

2. Lesbianism is conspicuously absent from high-school curricula, and if lesbianism is discussed at all in university courses it is generally in abnormal psychology or sociology of deviance courses; even then, only male homosexuality is usually mentioned.

3. There is a great deal of evidence that never-married old women lead happy and fulfilling lives, including busy social lives. See, for example, Barbara Levy Simon, *Never Married Women* (Philadelphia: Temple University Press, 1987); and Jeanette Auger's chapter in this book. On the attitudes of contemporary Canadian teenage girls, see Myrna Kostash, *No Kidding: Inside the World of Teenage Girls* (Toronto: McClelland and Stewart, 1987).

4. See Rosemary Curb and Nancy Manahan (eds.), *Lesbian Nuns: Breaking Silence* (Tallahassee, Fl.: Naiad, 1985). The book includes Canadian contributions.

5. For example, the work of Nancy Chodorow, *The Reproduction of Mothering* (Berkeley, Cal.: University of California Press, 1978); and Dorothy Dinnerstein, *The Mermaid and the Minotaur: Sexual Arrangements and the Human Malaise* (New York: Harper & Row, 1976).

6. See Lawrence Stone, *The Family, Sex and Marriage* (New York: Harper & Row, 1977).

7. Carroll Smith-Rosenberg, "The Female World of Love and Ritual: Relations between Women in Nineteenth-Century America," in *Signs: Journal of Women in Culture and Society*, Vol. 1 (Autumn 1975), pp. 1-29. There is every reason to assume that relations within and between the sexes were similar in early Canadian society.

8. Lillian Faderman, *Surpassing the Love of Men: Romantic Friendship and Love between Women from the Renaissance to the Present* (New York: William Morrow, 1981); also her article "The Morbidification of Love between Women by 19th-Century Sexologists," in *Journal of Homosexuality*, Vol. 4 (Fall 1978), pp. 73-89.

9. Christina Simmons, "Companionate Marriage and the Lesbian Threat," in *Frontiers: A Journal of Women's Studies*, Vol. 4 (Lesbian History Issue, Fall 1979), pp. 54-59.

10. See, for example, Andrea Dworkin, *Woman Hating* (New York: E.P. Dutton, 1974); also Marilyn Frye, *The Politics of Reality: Essays in Feminist Theory* (Freedom, Cal.: The Crossing Press, 1983).

11. This is not to say that there are no lesbians who hate men. It must be remembered, though, that there are many heterosexual women who also hate men. That lesbians are singled out and stereotyped as man-haters is an indication of the lengths to which conventional society will go to keep women in line.

12. Not only have lesbians been writing about themselves and for themselves outside an academic context in an ever-increasing number of newsletters, magazines, and journals, but also academics sympathetic to feminism have begun to publish scholarly works about lesbians – works that do not begin with the assumption that lesbianism is a deviant preoccupation needing to be explained. References to such works are scattered throughout this introduction.

13. An important exception is the Lesbian Issue of *Resources for Feminist Research*, Vol. xii, No. 1 (March 1983), a compilation of writing and research by Canadian lesbians.

14. Susan Krieger, "Lesbian Identity and Community: Recent Social Science Literature," in *Signs: Journal of Women in Culture and Society*, Vol. 8 (Autumn 1982), pp. 91-108, p. 96. It is heartening to see, however, that recent books are beginning to address differences among lesbians. Particularly valuable is the book edited by the Boston Lesbian Psychologies Collective, *Lesbian Psychologies* (Urbana and Chicago: University of Illinois Press, 1987). See also the collection edited by Trudy Darty and Sandee Potter, *Women-Identified Women* (Palo Alto, Cal.: Mayfield Publishing, 1984).

15. As Janice Raymond notes on p. 3 in *A Passion for Friends*, "The perception is that women without men are women without company or companionship."

16. In our culture to be old and female is to experience what Judith Posner calls the "double whammy" in "Old and Female: The Double Whammy," in *Essence*, Vol. 2, No. 1 (1977), pp. 41-48. If we follow this line of thinking we can suppose that old lesbians may experience "triple trouble" – discrimination based on age, sex, and sexual orientation.

17. The title of this part was inspired by the work of Jeri Dawn Wine. See her contribution in this volume.

18. Lesbians are the least likely group of people to contract AIDS from a sexual partner. See Mary Louise Adams's discussion with Cindy Patton, "Lesbians, straight women and safer sex," in *Rites*, Vol. 5 (April 1989), p. 11.

19. For a discussion of radical lesbianism and lesbian separatism, see *Amazones d'hier lesbiennes d'aujourd'hui*, Vol. 4 (May 1986); also Sarah Lucia Hoagland and Julia Penelope (eds.), *For Lesbians Only: A Separatist Anthology* (London: Onlywomen Press, 1988), which has several Canadian contributions.

20. Increasingly, lesbians are also organizing in other parts of the world. See the International Lesbian and Gay Association's *Second ILGA Pink Book* (Utrecht: Interfacultaire Werkgroep Homostudies, 1988).

21. Chris Bearchell, "Why I Am a Gay Liberationist," in *Resources for Feminist Research*, Vol. XII, No. 1 (March 1983), pp. 57-60.

22. See the pamphlet published by Gay Liberation Against the Right Everywhere, *Gay Men and Feminism: A Discussion* (Toronto, 1982). Available at the Canadian Gay Movement Archives, Toronto.

23. It is also safer for lesbians to be active in women's organizations as opposed to explicitly lesbian and gay organizations. See the chapter here, "Lesbian Life in a Small Centre."

Part I
A Diversity of Lesbian Experiences

I

Lesbians and Aging

Triple Trouble or Tremendous Thrill

Jeanette A. Auger

DID YOU SEE the commercial on television the other day about the two old lesbians discussing where to vacation on their retirement pensions?[1] What about that movie where the two old women who had been best friends for over thirty years fall in love and become lesbians at sixty-eight and seventy-two respectively? Or that new book on how to deal with the loss of a lesbian lover of twenty-five years when you are sixty-eight and live in a conservative rural town in Canada where no one knows about your sexuality?

Of course you have not come across any of these images of old lesbians in Canadian popular culture, or anywhere else; but you may well know of or have personally experienced any of these scenarios. In general, old lesbians are thought to be non-existent, not only by the media but often also by the lesbian community. In the feminist academic press there is little or no mention of lesbian elders, and the gerontological world seems oblivious to the sexuality of old people in general, let alone that of old lesbians. When articles on sexuality do appear in noted journals like *The Gerontologist*, they are about heterosexual practices or, and these are rare occurrences, homosexual men. Lesbians who are old are thus in triple jeopardy, as they represent at least three oppressed groups in North American culture. They are not young, they do not enjoy the privilege of patriarchal masculinity, and they do not receive the social rewards of heterosexuality. Those who are not white suffer yet another stigma, as do those who are differently abled.

The demographics of aging reveal that some 11 per cent of Canadian people are sixty-five and older. Of this group, 58 per cent are female. Using the Masters and Johnson and Kinsey reports on sexuality, we can conservatively assume that one in ten of these women are lesbian. Theoretically, we are speaking of some 156,000 women aged over sixty-five.[2] In the census, however, there is no category of "lesbian" under the marital status section. Presumably, many of us fall under the "single" category, while others are subsumed under the categories of "married," "widowed," or "divorced." Many lesbians "come out" after age fifty, often from heterosexual marriages of long duration, or in later life after they have been widowed. Lesbian women are thus hidden within the official demographics of Canadian culture.

Lesbians who are old are hidden or invisible partly because there is a lack of research on them. Also, it is often difficult to identify older "lesbians" in the first place. For example, in working with and for seniors, I heard about "possible" older lesbians mostly by accident. The older lesbians I have talked to speak of their own isolation within lesbian and heterosexual cultures. They also speak of the many pleasures and benefits of growing old without the societal expectations and pressures placed on heterosexual women.[3]

In 1983 I interviewed women who were never married, including a seventy-four-year-old woman in Vancouver:

Me: When you lived for twenty-three years with your friend, did you ever speak of yourselves as lesbians?
J: Oh, we were not lesbians truly. We were intimate in every sense of the word, but we were certainly not lesbians.
Me: I assumed that when you said that you were gay that you meant that you were lesbians.
J: No, I said that we were gay – happy and gay. Lesbians dress like men; they do men's work and act like men. We were just women who loved each other and were happy with that.

A friend in Vancouver who runs a support network for women who are divorced or widowed told me about a telephone conversation with an eighty-year-old woman:

Caller: I want to know where I can get a nice clean girl to replace my P who has died.

Friend: Have you tried some of the lesbian resources in the community? Or, perhaps the feminist bookstore would know who you could contact about meeting other lesbian women.
Caller: I don't want nothing to do with them libbers or lesbian types. I just want a nice clean girl to replace my P. None of these club types or "feminists" saying we should all act like women as if we didn't know that we was women. We just like to have short hair and wear men's clothes.

Research, as well as everyday life, suggests that some older lesbians, believing in rigid sex roles (the so-called "butch" and "femme"), identify more with heterosexual men than with feminist lesbians. Some older lesbians feel themselves judged by their feminist sisters on this issue. In these examples, the women did not identify themselves as lesbians for different reasons. The first woman objected to those lesbians who "look and act like men"; the second objected to those who *did not* look and act like men.

In 1982 I conducted research in care facilities in British Columbia. On one visit to a friend, we were in the dining room of a multi-level care facility. Established residents sat at tables for four, while newer ones sat alone until the staff formed a regular group for them. We heard the following conversation:

G: See that woman over there, she's one of "them," you know.
J: One of what?
G: You know, them queers. People who like bread on bread with the same filling in the middle.
J: Do you mean that she is a lesbian? How do you know that?
G: Yeah, that's right. The orderly told me who cleans up the rooms. She said she lived with another one for a real long time. The other one up and dies and now she's in here.
J: It must be terrible to lose someone you are so close to after so long.
G: Well, I don't think that sort should be allowed to live in places like this. It's one thing to lose a husband — that's proper — but that sort of thing is not.

I later talked with the orderly who had passed on the information about the resident. She informed me that, "Nowadays, two women don't live together that long unless they are up to something." She said that she had told some of the other residents to "be careful" around this woman, because you "never know about them queers." When I pointed out that lesbian women are as selective about who they want to be involved with as anyone else, the orderly still felt it her "duty" to let people know "what was going on" (even though she clearly did not know).

These illustrations make visible some of the experiences of women who are reluctant to identify themselves as lesbians because of myths and the assumptions of others about who they think lesbians might be.

When dealing with a topic as complex as lesbianism, it is important to recognize that there is no such thing as a "typical lesbian." Lesbianism is not merely a set of behaviours based on the preference of one sex over another. For many, lesbianism is also a political and emotional stance in the world, which creates an ideological base allowing lesbians to define themselves, regardless of age. By identifying some of the issues related to lesbians and aging, we can recognize the diversity in lesbian experience.

Fear of Aging

We are all growing older, and have been since the day we were born. Aging affects every one of us, whether twenty-five or sixty-five. In our culture, old age is seen as a negative experience – as something to dread. The media bombards us with images of women who look to be at most forty, yet they "hide wrinkles" with Oil of Olay, remove "age spots" on their hands with Porcelana, and hide "that ugly grey" with Lady Grecian formula. Old age is not presented as something to celebrate or look forward to. A thirty-year-old lesbian at a workshop on aging remarked:

> It's neat that you sort of sell this old age thing as good, but I don't want to get old. I would hate to have wrinkles and withered skin. I couldn't bear the thought of being with an old woman. She would feel so flabby to me.

Not only do some older lesbians fear their own aging, but they receive little support from their communities in seeing old age as a positive experience.

The experiences of women who are old today are probably different than they will be for those of us still teenagers, or, as I am, approaching middle-age. At a lesbian workshop on aging, the group members were asked when they first thought of themselves as "old." Some said "forty," some "fifty." Others related a sense of growing old based on particular life experiences, as did this fifty-eight-year-old:

> My lover and I split up, and suddenly I realized that no one in the world knew about us. I was alone on the farm and I had really bad arthritis and probably couldn't manage without her. Then I realized: Shit, I'm *old.*

It becomes apparent that old age is relative – a state of mind we seldom invoke, unless life happenings cause us to take stock of ourselves.

Coming Out or Staying In

Lesbians who are "out of the closet" experience aging differently from those who are still "in." The woman last quoted said that her rural community did not know about her sexuality. Therefore, neighbours, family, and friends could not be supportive. This experience was shared by many older lesbians I spoke with. They were concerned not only with coming out to friends, family, colleagues, and medical and service providers, but also with coming out to their children and grandchildren, and sometimes to spouses.

Related to this is the issue of when we recognize our own lesbianism, and what we choose to do with the knowledge. Many reject their feelings for other women because of the negative stereotypes associated with being gay; others because of the social stigma attached to those who choose to be open about their sexual preference. Some women are already in heterosexual marriages by the time they recognize their sexuality, and do not want to lose the rewards that heterosexual privilege provides, or risk losing their children if their husband is not supportive of their sexuality. Some older women have been lesbians as long as they can remember, while others came out in later life. Some, such as Gwen, the mother of a fifty-year-old daughter, came out in their late seventies:

> I kept going to these A.A. meetings and there were some wonderful women there. When Louise [her daughter] told me that she was gay I thought about it quite a lot. I have also loved

women, liked them better than men. Now, I just wish that there was someone I could meet so that I could have a lesbian relationship. I have given it a lot of thought and I am ready for that thrill. No one cares about little old ladies of seventy anyway, so I should be able to get away with it until I die.

Many of the older lesbians I spoke with came out when there was no gay liberation, no political lesbian literature or movies to speak of, and no women's movement to raise awareness of sexual issues. Some of them talked about how hard it was to come out to family members, especially to children and grandchildren, as well as to their own parents, without any support systems in place. Often, many reported having very few kinship networks left, because family members just could not accept their sexuality. Older lesbians often said they had never heard the word "lesbian" and believed they were the only women in the world to love women.

There are obvious reasons, then, why some older lesbians prefer not to identify with younger lesbians. Why would they want to, when being old or lesbian is seen only in negative terms?

Geography and Support Systems

Rural and urban settings affect the lives of older lesbians. In most urban settings in Canada there are lesbian networks, which allow lesbians to socialize and get together for meals, dances, conferences, and so on. In addition to networks for emotional support, urban environments usually offer some services geared especially to lesbians. In large metropolitan areas we are more likely to find lesbian or lesbian-positive doctors, lawyers, and dentists. As a seventy-three-year-old lesbian noted:

> When I found out that I had cancer I made sure to phone my friend who is a nurse at the cancer clinic. I asked her to put me in touch with a lesbian doctor so that I could be honest about my lifestyle. She was just great. My lover was allowed to be in my room anytime and the doctor discussed everything with her. It wasn't like when we lived in that village in Quebec, there was nowhere to turn if you were sick and the neighbours would have died if they knew we were gay.

Regarding institutionalization, older lesbians from small rural areas have very little choice about where they will spend the rest of their lives. Most likely they will be relocated to another town or village that has an appropriate care facility. Even when such a facility exists locally, staff members are unlikely to be sympathetic or knowledge-able about lesbian lifestyles. When a woman has lived for most of her life in the same community, this relocation can be traumatic and severe. If she has a partner, separation can place an additional burden on both women.

Several lesbian groups across Canada have discussed the idea of setting up either lesbian homes for the aged or communities where lesbians can grow old in a co-operative project, allowing women of all ages to live together — some with their children of both sexes, others without children or with daughters only. In this plan, lesbian doctors, nurses, and other caregivers would live in, or be available to these communities so that they would be fairly self-sufficient in pro-viding health care for older group members. To my knowledge, no such community yet exists, but it is surely just a matter of time before we begin to realize our visions.

Relationships

Older lesbians are concerned about being in or out of relationships, and how that becomes different as they grow older. Those who have been in long-term relationships that suddenly come to an end often say that the feeling of loss is far greater than anything they experi-enced in their younger years. A sixty-two-year-old said:

> When D said she wanted out of the relationship, to be with a younger woman, I was really devastated. I knew that things hadn't been going all that well for a while, but I really thought that after twenty-two years we would stay together forever. When I was younger I thought I was pretty cute and other women liked me a lot. I can't imagine who would want me now or where the hell I would ever meet anyone in this place. Every-one I know has been the lover of someone else. That's the trouble with living in a small community.

Women are thought to be asexual as they grow older. The double standard dictates that men are sexy and more mature in old age. Their facial lines are said to express attractiveness and experience; ours are "wrinkles" we are supposed to hide with cosmetics. There-fore, old women are sexless and ugly. This stereotype flows into the lesbian community: we are all socialized by the same system to be women, regardless of our sexuality.

Monogamy is also invoked frequently by older lesbians, who seem to prefer having one mate over open relationships, whether they are currently in a relationship or attempting to find a partner. A fifty-eight-year-old lesbian succinctly stated the most frequently provided reason:

> We went to one of those feminist do's and this psychologist who was a lesbian was saying that open relationships were the new trend among gay women she sees. F and I have been together eighteen years now, and we like each other better than anyone else we know. We don't want or need to be with anyone else. When you get older you need more stability in your life. I've had my flings – I know what it is like to love other women, but I want to be settled down and get on with what's left of our lives together, so that when either one of us is gone the other will have wonderful memories to look back on, without the worry of whether or not we need to have an open relationship.

Menopause

Lesbians who become sexually dissatisfied or bored with their partners, especially those in long-term monogamous relationships, sometimes use menopause as an "excuse" for not wanting to have sex anymore. One older lesbian in a workshop on lesbian issues explained the situation as follows:

> When I started menopause it was somewhat of a relief because then I could say that was why I didn't want to have sex anymore. I guess we just got too used to each other or something. We are still together and are very intimate. Maybe sex just isn't as important when you are older.

Another said:

> Sex never really was a big deal for us. I didn't like it all that much in the beginning but M did. With menopause I had some pain. I was sort of itchy all the time and so that seemed like a good time to stop having sex. Other than that our relationship is perfect for me, although I do think that M would still like to have sex more often.

This rationale has also been cited by many heterosexual women in various studies on menopause. Lesbian and heterosexual women alike are vulnerable to the myth that after menopause they are no longer sexual or attractive. There is no bio-medical evidence to support the idea that hormonal changes during menopause affect sexual desire, attractiveness, or sexual capacity. Women can be as sexually active, or not, during and after menopause as they were before. Another myth is that we need to be sexual to remain in relationships, but this is clearly not so. There are many ways to be close and intimate with others.

The demographics of aging are based primarily on chronology. Medical research and common-sense experience tell us that certain physiological and social changes do occur as we grow older. What matters is how we deal with these changes. Many in our society view menopause as the end of female desire, attractiveness, and sexual activity. Biologically, it is simply the end of childbearing possibilities.

The assumption is sometimes made that lesbians are less affected by menopause than heterosexual women, due to the notion that we are not interested in reproduction. This assumption ignores the reality that many lesbians are mothers, and that many wanted to conceive but could not for medical, economic, political, or logistical reasons.

Another assumption is that because we are lesbians, we are more reflective, thoughtful, open, sensitive, and aware. Because of these positive attributes, we are not expected to have the same problems with retirement and menopause as our heterosexual sisters. However, we are socialized first to be women – not lesbians – so we carry around many of the same cultural self-expectations and values about what we are "supposed to do."

Many women identify as heterosexual prior to becoming lesbians. The notion that women reach their fullest potential only through childbirth and childrearing may still be subtly at work. Choosing to relate to other women sexually does not necessarily preclude the desire to bear a child. Just as for heterosexual women, for lesbians who want to have a child menopause marks the regretted end of that possibility.

The Aging Experience Personalized
We age all of our lives, not just on our sixty-fifth birthday when we are magically eligible for government assistance based on

chronology. How we experience our aging and how we learn to deal with issues in our lives throughout the life cycle affect how we cope with aging. If we have unfinished business, unresolved conflicts, unspoken fears, resentments, or anger while young, and do not deal with them, we are bound to carry them on to old age. It is helpful if we can resolve them while young, through therapy, dreams, fantasy, journals, or – if possible – in real life. Who we are while young can be who we become as older selves. One of the saddest thoughts I am often left with by older lesbians is the notion of unfinished business or unresolved issues: what I call the "if only's."

On the other hand, if we do not, when we are old, focus on what might have been, we could have the same attitude as a friend who was celebrating her seventieth birthday. She marvelled at how lucky she was to be in good health, in a relationship in which she could grow and flourish, and among lesbian friends she loved and admired. Someone asked her what it was like to be an aging lesbian, and whether she experienced it as a triple problem. She replied:

> Never – I am as happy now as I ever was in my life. This is a tremendous thrill. To love and be loved by women is well worth living for. I just wish that all lesbians could learn from their loving as I have done.

Notes

1. This article is dedicated to my partner. I hope that we grow old together walking up green hills overlooking the ocean, and that we will feel free like seagulls sailing over the sand.

2. Based on a population of twenty-five million, approximately 11 per cent of which is aged sixty-five plus, 58 per cent of which is female, 10 per cent of which is lesbian.

3. The material for this article is informed by and based on personal experience, literature, and research interviews from 1982 to the present with care providers and older lesbians in institutions and workshops.

2

Lesbian / Mother

Dian Day

MANY OF OUR issues as lesbian mothers are not fundamentally different from the issues of heterosexual mothers.[1] As mothers we face the same hardships as straight women raising children. If we are single, or have partners who do not wish to share parenting, we encounter the same discrimination in jobs and housing, and the same difficulties in making ends meet and coping alone with the stress of motherhood. If we have partners who view our children as unwelcome baggage, we deal with the same jealousies, insecurities, and tensions as many straight couples. If we have partners whom we agreed or contracted to parent with, we have the same struggle in balancing the relationship, and experience the same exhaustion and frustration of adjusting to children in our lives.

There are, however, differences that serve to change the experience in a significant way. To be both lesbian and mother is often more difficult, requires a more conscious decision-making process, and is more stressful. Many lesbian mothers have to face daily the uncertainty of custody issues. If they are out of the closet, lesbians recognize that they may be declared unfit mothers, solely on the basis of their sexuality. They may choose not to come out, especially to ex-spouses and children, precisely for this reason. Also, the choice about whether to have children is a much more complicated matter for lesbians. The difficulties of getting pregnant or adopting children in the first place are enough to discourage many from attempting motherhood. Decisions concerning whether to come out to children,

and how, and when, may mean we are less likely to take our relationships with our children for granted, and more likely to worry
consciously about how our children will feel about us in the face of a
homophobic culture. Even finding a babysitter takes on an added
dimension for lesbian mothers.

> Every time we move and have to find new babysitters, I go
> through this paranoia about whether or not she'll come back
> after the first time. It's obvious there's only one bed. I have to
> squash the urge I always have to hide the lesbian books, the
> love notes, and the picture of us kissing.[2]

Finally, motherhood often carries a stigma in lesbian culture.
Motherhood for straight women is a fulfilment of a social role expec-
tation, while motherhood for lesbians is seen as an antithesis. It is
not generally supported in either heterosexual or lesbian culture.

> Gay friends think I am crazy to be in a relationship with a
> woman with kids. Some think it is because I always wanted to
> have them myself and am now in a sense surrogate parenting to
> make up for that. Others think I needed a "family" life and now
> I have one. Others cannot understand how I could change my
> lifestyle so completely and attribute it to not having had a
> "proper" relationship previously, even though when I was in a
> fifteen-year relationship my lover and I were held up on a ped-
> estal as the most appropriate couple.

Real Lesbians

Real lesbians don't have children. This is proclaimed with equal
loudness by both straight women (and men) and "real" lesbians. Real
lesbians have never been fucked (perhaps rape is an exception). Real
lesbians have never had sperm inside their bodies. The thought of
sperm makes them sick. Real lesbians are not interested in children
– especially male children. Real lesbians find children boring and
tedious. Real lesbians have much more important work to do.

For lesbians who manage to unravel the puzzle of their sexuality
only after producing a child, or several children, there is very little
support (after all, if we were real lesbians, we would have had abor-
tions). Lesbian women who once identified as heterosexual can

easily forget that they were ever with men, except for those who had children with them. These children are a visible reminder of a changed sexuality and a past that may be threatening to our selves, our partners, and our community.

This "real lesbian" hierarchy oppresses lesbians in three ways: 1)it negates the wish of some lesbians for a child; 2) it negates that we were all socialized *as women*; and 3) it negates the choices and experiences in our lives before coming out.

Getting Pregnant – Getting Children

Many of us did not choose to have children in any real sense. We had children while we were in heterosexual relationships, using faulty birth control or no birth control. Some of us had children because we thought we were straight and we were married, and that's what straight married women did. Some of us had children in attempting to deny or compensate for our sexuality – we thought motherhood would cure us. Some of us acknowledged our sexuality, and then worked through the complicated procedure of getting pregnant, with or without a partner. Some of us found ourselves step-parents in a "package deal" when we fell in love with a woman who was already a mother.

> As with most parenting situations I acquired my children by accident. Not because my male lover's sperm penetrated one of my eggs, but because the woman I love's soul entered mine in a way that made me want to commit myself to her, and, as a by-product, to her children. Clearly, though, I did not freely choose to have children. I was in a sense choiceless in that no other suitable options seemed available to me. In this way, I share a world in common with most women. What I do not share with them is the social sanctions, the permission and approval if you will for making that choiceless choice. I receive no legal, financial or political benefits for parenting. If anything, I receive social disapproval in both subtle and implicit ways.

The number of lesbians who actively choose motherhood may be equal to the number of heterosexuals who do so. Most heterosexuals create babies as a result of accident or pronatalism, rather than by true choice. Pronatalism is not a factor in lesbian relationships in the same way, except perhaps when a woman uses motherhood as an indication, to herself and the heterosexual world, of some "normalcy." Heterosexuals have children primarily as a result of continued heterosexual sexual activity. Such "accidents" simply cannot occur within lesbian relationships.

Having children after coming out usually involves complicated decision-making and planning, because motherhood is not taken for granted in lesbian culture, the way it is for straight women. We actually have to think about how we are going to do it. It is not a simple matter of egg meets sperm; it is, "Should I pick somebody up at a bar, should I ask a friend or the friend of a friend, should I ask a gay friend, do any of these men have AIDS, can I ask him to get tested, should I have intercourse, should I use a turkey baster, should I go to the infertility clinic and try to get in,[3] or should I forget the whole idea?" It is likely to be a lonely and unsupported enterprise, especially if we choose to parent alone.

> My doctor, a lesbian, assumed I would want an abortion. My ex-lover told me to get an abortion. The father of the baby – I told him when I was three months pregnant – told me to get an abortion. I told my mother when I was five months pregnant. She said, "You've been telling me that you're gay since you were seventeen, and now you're telling me you're pregnant!" She tried to get me to say I would give the baby up for adoption. I didn't tell my father until I went into the hospital a week before the baby was born. It was the hardest time in my whole life. Nobody was there for me.

While many of us have actually chosen to have children *as lesbians*, most of us became mothers through accidental or planned pregnancies with men we were in relationships with. We "chose" to have children for the same reasons as many heterosexual women: to enrich our lives; to pacify our husbands; to give our mothers a grandchild; to have someone look after us in old age. This should not be surprising, as many of us thought we *were* heterosexual women.

> I didn't actually *choose* my children, didn't choose to have them in any real sense, until after I left my male partner. At that time I seriously considered leaving one or both of them with him. After several months of them going back and forth from my house to his, it became clear to me that I would not

choose to be without them. A large part of me was a mother and I was unable and unwilling to give that up.

According to the heterosexual "norm," the child is biologically related to both parents. This is (at present) impossible in lesbian relationships, where one mother makes a biological connection with a male "third party," anonymous or known. The other mother has no biological – and therefore no legal – connection to the child.

It annoys me that legally I have no claim on sharing the kids' lives, that their father would be more entitled to living with them than me, that it would be as if our relationship never happened should their mother die. Although this situation is unlikely, it is still nonetheless present in the psychological realm of our lives.

Lesbians who choose to parent together need a legal contract in case of a separation or the death of the biological mother. Within co-mother relationships, lesbians need to resolve the issue of "ownership" in terms of this biological connection.

When we first got together, it was a big issue for her that they were biologically "my" kids, and that I had made them with a man. She didn't feel she could ever love them the way I did. I wasn't very supportive; I didn't think of them as my property and couldn't see what the fuss was about.

Male Children

Lesbian mothers of male children face not only added pressures from the heterosexual world to provide male role models for their children, but also have to deal with exclusion or ostracism from the lesbian community. While most lesbian-feminist events now include childcare, male children over a certain age are often excluded. Sometimes this "acceptable" age limit is as young as two or three years old. Lesbians report feeling at best unwelcome if they bring sons to social gatherings; at worst, they are often not invited themselves.

This is a difficult issue to resolve. If, as political lesbians, we choose to live without men, but rear sons, we put ourselves in a situation that of necessity requires compromise. Many lesbians feel that raising sons – the devoting of eighteen or so years of mothering energy to a boy/man – would compromise their politics. Many choose not to conceive, because at present there is no guarantee of obtaining a daughter. On the other hand, those who do have sons certainly love them no less than daughters, and as lesbian mothers they face the often more difficult task of battling male sex-role stereotypes, with less support.

Lesbians with male children are much more likely to feel public disapproval for being without a male partner and, as a result of this pressure, much more likely to buy into the myth that "a boy needs a man." None of the lesbians I spoke with who had only female children said that they received comments about male role models, while almost all of the mothers of sons did. These comments came from complete strangers who were unaware of the mother's sexuality, as well as from insensitive friends and family members.

> He's a very charming baby. People come up to me and say things like, "Oh, his father must be so proud of him." My mother says, "Now that you have a son you have to get married." My brother-in-law, who knows I am a lesbian, says things like, "Do you have sex in front of your son?" It really hurts. I try to forget it. Especially because the baby is a boy, people think he really needs a man. I feel like I have to make it up to him for not having a father.

Keeping the Children

Custody litigation in lesbian motherhood is the major concern in the existing literature. While this is certainly a central theme for lesbian mothers themselves, academic research thus far has focused on attempting to prove whether lesbians are "fit" mothers, and if they differ from heterosexual mothers in any significant way. The stress of constantly dealing with custody fears and the resultant coping strategies are more to the point for lesbian mothers than studies comparing them to straight women.

Decisions concerning whether to come out, to whom, where to live, whether to live with a lover, whether to be involved politically, whether to publish, and many other aspects of lesbian daily life, are affected by fear of custody loss. The repercussions of trying to keep certain information secret in order to retain custody cannot be underestimated. Lesbian mothers must seriously assess the risks of coming out versus staying in vis-à-vis their ex-partners. Many do not tell the children's father about their sexuality, fearing the information will be used to have them declared "unfit" mothers, and that, therefore, they will lose custody of the children. Another risk is that, after custody is decided in the courts, the case may be reopened if new evidence is brought forward or circumstances change. Should the father later find out about the mother's sexual orientation, he would have grounds for reopening the case. When the father has visitation rights or joint custody, the children – who may be charged with keeping their mother's lesbianism secret – have a difficult burden to bear. Sometimes children are not told of their mother's sexuality in case they inadvertently let the secret out.

> If there was no ex-husband in the picture, I think I would be far more open. What if he decides to go for custody? Although I might be the model mother I don't want to have to go to court. He would probably look at this [her lesbianism] as a wonderful opportunity. He could take me to court on the basis of my sexuality, and that's the only basis he has ... I don't want to put my kids through something like that, or my partner.

For lesbians whose ex-partners know about their sexuality, there is another set of issues. Ex-husbands are often violently angry when they learn of a former partner's lesbianism, and many lesbians feel men pursue custody for revenge, not because they genuinely care for their children. Lesbians and their partners often feel vulnerable to this revenge in other ways as well. They fear that vindictive complaints may be made to landlords, employers, or social service workers. Some give in without fighting because of the very real risk of losing custody of their children should the case go to court. There is often an out-of-court, unofficial trade-off: she gets the kids, but no child support or fair division of jointly-owned property. Many lesbians also have to deal with the realization that the man they spent (sometimes) years of their lives with is no longer behaving rationally. We then have to choose between operating in the children's best interest to maximize their contact with the father, or operating in our own best interest to minimize contact that is stressful and may lead to a custody challenge.

> I'm really torn between wanting him to see the kids more for their sake, and wanting him to disappear from their lives

totally. I know that the longer he goes without seeing them, I become less and less in jeopardy of losing a court case if he later changes his mind about custody.

The overwhelming strategy of the courts (although this is slowly changing), has been to deny lesbians custody of their children, as a punishment for lesbianism. The "learned judges" use three main arguments to support this violation of basic human rights. They argue that the child will: 1) grow up sexually abused (if a girl) or rejected (if a boy); 2) grow up stigmatized by her / his peers because of the mother's sexuality; and 3) be more likely to grow up gay. Lesbians have been asked in court whether they have sex in front of their children, whether the children's friends know, and whether they want their children to be homosexual.

The issue of our children's sexuality is rarely discussed in a non-homophobic manner. In the courts the line is that we may be allowed to keep our children, as long as we do not attempt to influence them towards replicating our lifestyle. Lesbians can only keep their children as long as they do not raise gay (read abnormal) children. If we are proud of ourselves as lesbians, however, we are likely, along with other parents who have a positive self-image, to have no qualms should our children become like us.

I sometimes feel guilty when I acknowledge that I want my daughter to be a lesbian. I think then that all this stuff I tell her about having a choice is just a line. The truth is, I *would* prefer she was lesbian. Then, I think, hell, did my mother ever say to me even so much as, "I'd prefer you were straight, dear, but I'll still love you if you choose otherwise?"

Sharing Parenting with our Partners

In much of the academic literature, lesbian mothers are assumed to be single, regardless of whether they have a partner who shares parenting. This is a case of applying a heterosexual model to homosexual culture, and it does not work. If a heterosexual mother is not living with a man, she is assumed to be single. If a lesbian mother is not living with a man, she is also assumed to be single. Consequently, many studies have been conducted comparing a sample of single heterosexual mothers to a sample of lesbian mothers, some of whom are single, and some of whom are in relationships with a female co-parent. The struggles we have in sharing parenting with a lover when there are no rules remain undocumented.

> She felt awkward with the baby. She's never been around babies before – neither had I before he was born. Having sex was miserable. His crib was right at the bottom of my bed. I was breastfeeding too. She loves him now though – she barks at him like a mother. Maybe next spring we'll move in together. I am being very cautious – I don't want him to go through any more hurt than he'll have already having a lesbian mother.

Lesbians without partners often put the possibility of a committed relationship on hold until the children are grown. This may be because we cannot find lesbians who are willing to accept our children as part of a relationship with us, or because after the demands of childrearing, we find we have no extra energy for an additional person in our lives.

> Now I am a single parent. I have to ask my partner to keep an eye open, give a bath, read a story. It results in resentments. She doesn't like it. I don't like it that she doesn't like it. I want her to co-parent. She wants him to win the custody case. I feel like I do all the work. She feels like she didn't choose this – she wants me, not them. She feels like they always come first, but she wants to come first. I have to admit that they come first. I temper the way she is with them, I temper the way they are with her. I am a go-between. I make excuses for my children to her. I say, they are tired, they are hungry, they are very little, don't be so hard on them. A lot has happened for them recently – many changes. She wants them to be perfect, not to pee on the porch, not to talk too loudly, not to want more ice-cream. She resents the way they interfere with her life. I think, what is this resentment doing to them? Is it fair? Why did I think I could do this? I remember I did not mean to. I fell in love. It was like coming home.

Getting Support

The lesbian mother groups that are springing up in many urban areas are still absent in rural communities. Here in the Maritimes, lesbians from city and country alike express an often overwhelming sense of isolation from others who share their concerns as lesbian / mother. Even if one of us is going through a custody battle, our partner – if we have one – often cannot give enough because she herself needs support in this situation.

> There has to be something for women like me. I wasn't popular before [I got pregnant] but I thought I had friends.... I don't have very much in common with lesbians who don't have children. I definitely wish I had some lesbian friends who are mothers. I want to talk about my son's new tooth. I want to share his falls and good times.

Parenting can help us renew a connection to other women which is sometimes lost when we come out as lesbians.

> In spite of non-support, or to put it more positively, confusion, on the part of friends and family, there are benefits to lesbian parenting. Some have to do completely with enabling one to pass in a heterosexual world – if you have kids, whether out of your body or not, then maybe you aren't that different. Having kids somehow puts us into another realm of being able to understand heterosexual experience, thus making us more legitimate, more empathetic. Women friends and colleagues who had problems with my being gay before now say things like, "Welcome to the world of parenting," or, "Isn't having kids a pain / joy?", "Bet you didn't know what having kids was really like before, eh?" These sorts of statements thus put me into a world of women sharing. Now I am more acceptable, more one of "us."

Some lesbians are adamant that they are no different from other mothers, and feel no personal need for a lesbian / mother community. They feel the stresses of motherhood are universal.

> I don't feel that I've missed out on anything by not knowing other gay parents. I feel that with my partner, we discuss it [parenting]. She complements me – makes me stop and think about it. That's where I need the support. It doesn't involve my lifestyle.

Telling the Children

There are informal rules about how and when to tell your children they are adopted. Unfortunately, we have no such guidelines about how or when to tell our children that we are lesbian. Some of us remain unsure about whether to tell them at all, or delay the communication indefinitely because we cannot decide how to approach the issue.

> Friends tell me I should "say something" to my daughter, who just started school this year, about my being a lesbian. I can't imagine what to say. "By the way dear, this loving relationship between your two mothers ... well, it's not socially acceptable." Or maybe, "You know how some people think boys are better than girls, and some people think white people are better than black people? Well, some people think straight people are better than gay people, and that only men and women can love each other in this way." Or, perhaps I should simply say, "Don't tell anyone we sleep in the same bed – it's none of their business." How do I tell my five-year-old child – a staunch defender of oppressed minorities – that pretty soon she will have to start defending herself because of her own minority status?

Some lesbians feel unable to tell their children at all because of an uncertain relationship with the father, or because they fear, especially if the children are older, that the possibility of rejection is not worth the risk. They feel that raising their children to be open and tolerant of individual differences is more important than disclosure of personal sexuality.

> My children know I won't tolerate prejudices. They are very open. They don't think of homosexuality as sick, just different. If I were to be defensive about it, when the issue came up ... well, it hasn't occurred to my daughter that there's anything to defend. With my son, I have to make more effort in listening to what he's saying. I'm very concerned that they don't grow up judging people.

Many lesbians find that making concessions in their relationships with lovers, for the sake of "keeping up appearances" in front of their children, becomes second nature.

Of course we are discreet. As two women we can do quite a lot [together without being obvious]. I can look at her and she knows what I would like to do, so it's okay. We do have a lot of time together – my kids are older; we have the house to ourselves a lot. It's a fortunate sense of timing.

While children do occasionally react with hostility or anger to the information that "mom is a lesbian," many children not only actively accept the situation, but, in many cases, are also proud of their mother for living what she believes despite social pressures to conform. Many mothers feel that it is better to tell the children, and less of a risk in the long run, than if the children found out "on the street."

When we tell our children we are lesbian, sons and daughters are forced to recognize that *they* have a choice about their own sexual orientation. At the very least, they will know that a minimum of two ways of being exist. This is more than most of us had – as teenagers, most of us thought there was nothing except compulsory heterosexuality. Many of us who are now mothers attempted to deny our sexuality, or were unable to recognize our feelings for women, simply because we had no idea such a choice existed.

I want them to learn from our relationship that two women can be close and loving, caring and sensitive to each other's needs, can try to work through the difficulties of being lesbian mothers. Can love in spite of the social pressures and can grow in spite of the non-support. I would like for them to be able to choose their sexual partners, would like for me to be able to accept their choices. Would like for them to look back on our relationship as a good one in which we tried to understand and learn from each other. To say that we were happy even though it was difficult.

Our Daily Lives
A mother is a mother. Some things are no different, lesbian or otherwise. You still need to feed your kids.

While I have emphasized the ways we are different from our heterosexual counterparts, there are also similarities in our everyday lives. We get up in the morning, get ourselves and the kids' breakfast, go to work or go to the grocery store, do the laundry, pay the bills, or forget to pay the bills, or have nothing to pay the bills with. We yell, love, cry, and fall into bed at night, exhausted. In our heads we do not always label ourselves as lesbian / mother. We do not always feel so very different from other mothers, other women, other parents who learn from our children a new way of being and becoming.

In everyday ways I accept the children as ours – they are a part of our lives. In general, I welcome their presence. Other times I resent it, would prefer to be alone with my lover, to go wherever we wanted to go, be spontaneous without having to figure out either what to do with the kids, or how to take them and still make the excursion enjoyable. They are interesting small people, they present a view of the world which I have lost. Their dependency and stubbornness I wish I could exhibit so freely, their lack of cynicism also. They still believe the world is fundamentally a good place: that bad people can simply be shown where they went wrong and then all would be well; that hungry people should just get more food; poor people more money; sad people more love. The irony, of course, is that they are generally correct. These things could be done if we would view the world as children do.

Notes

1. This article is written from a lived-by-member perspective. It is based on personal experience, interviews, and workshops with other lesbian mothers.

2. This voice and other voices throughout this article are extracted from interviews conducted in 1987 in Nova Scotia. I would like to thank those who shared with me, often anonymously, their experiences as lesbian / mother.

3. In Nova Scotia's one infertility clinic, it is all but impossible for a woman to get artificially inseminated unless she is white, middle class, and married.

3

Man Royals and Sodomites

Some Thoughts on the Invisibility
of Afro-Caribbean Lesbians

Makeda Silvera

I WILL BEGIN with some personal images and voices about woman-loving. These have provided a ground for my search for cultural reflections of my identity as a Black woman artist within the Afro-Caribbean community of Toronto. Although I focus here on my own experience (specifically, Jamaican), I am aware of similarities with the experience of other Third World women of colour whose history and culture has been subjected to colonization and imperialism.

I spent the first thirteen years of my life in Jamaica among strong women. My great-grandmother, my grandmother and grand-aunts were major influences in my life. There are also men whom I remember with fondness – my grandmother's "man friend" G., my Uncle Bertie, his friend Paul, Mr. Minott, Uncle B., and Uncle Freddy. And there were men like Mr. Eden, who terrified me because of stories about his "walking" fingers and his liking for girls under age fourteen.

I lived in a four-bedroom house with my grandmother, Uncle Bertie, and two female tenants. On the same piece of land, my grandmother had other tenants, mostly women and lots and lots of children. The big verandah of our house played a vital role in the social life of this community. It was on that verandah that I received my first education on "Black women's strength" – not only from their strength, but also from the daily humiliations they bore at work and in relationships. European experience coined the term "feminism," but the term "Black women's strength" reaches beyond Eurocentric definitions to describe what is the cultural continuity of my own struggles.

The verandah. My grandmother sat on the verandah in the evenings after all the chores were done to read the newspaper. People – mostly women – gathered there to discuss "life." Life covered every conceivable topic – economic, local, political, social, and sexual: the high price of salt-fish, the scarcity of flour, the nice piece of yellow yam bought at Coronation market, Mr. Lam, the shopkeeper who was taking "liberty" with Miss Inez, the fights women had with their menfolk, work, suspicions of Miss Iris and Punsie carrying on something between them, the cost of school books....

My grandmother usually had lots of advice to pass on to the women on the verandah, all grounded in the Bible. Granny believed in Jesus, in good and evil and in repentance. She was also a practical and sociable woman. Her faith didn't interfere with her perception of what it meant to be a poor Black woman; neither did it interfere with our Friday night visits to my Aunt Marie's bar. I remember sitting outside on the piazza with my grandmother, two grand-aunts and three or four of their women friends. I liked their flashy smiles and I was fascinated by their independence, ease, and their laughter. I loved their names – Cherry Rose, Blossom, Jonesie, Poinsietta, Ivory, Pearl, Iris, Bloom, Dahlia, Babes. Whenever the conversation came around to some "big 'oman talk" – who was sleeping with whom or whose daughter just got "fallen," I was sent off to get a glass of water for an adult, or a bottle of Kola champagne. Every Friday night I drank as much as half a dozen bottles of Kola champagne, but I still managed to hear snippets of words, tail ends of conversations about women together.

In Jamaica, the words used to describe many of these women would be "Man Royal" and / or "Sodomite." Dread words. So dread that women dare not use these words to name themselves. They were names given to women by men to describe aspects of our lives that men neither understood nor approved.

I heard "sodomite" whispered a lot during my primary school years, and tales of women secretly having sex, joining at the genitals, and being taken to the hospital to be "cut" apart were told in the schoolyard. Invariably, one of the women would die. Every five to ten years the same story would surface. At times, it would even be published in the newspapers. Such stories always generated much talking and speculation from "Bwoy dem kinda gal naasti sah!" to some wise old woman saying, "But dis caan happen, after two shut-pan caan join" – meaning identical objects cannot go into the other. The act of loving someone of the same sex was sinful, abnormal – something to hide. Even today, it isn't unusual or uncommon to be asked, "So how do two 'omen do it? ... what unoo use for a penis? ... who is the man and who is the 'oman?" It's inconceivable that women can have intimate relationships that are whole, that are not lacking because of the absence of a man. It's assumed that women in such relationships must be imitating men.

The word "sodomite" derives from the Old Testament. Its common use to describe lesbians (or any strong independent woman) is peculiar to Jamaica – a culture historically and strongly grounded in the Bible. Although Christian values have dominated the world, their effect in slave colonies is particular. Our foreparents gained access to literacy through the Bible when they were being indoctrinated by missionaries. It provided powerful and ancient stories of strength, endurance, and hope which reflected their own fight against oppression. This book has been so powerful that it continues to bind our lives with its racism and misogyny. Thus, the importance the Bible plays in Afro-Caribbean culture must be recognized in order to understand the historical and political context for the invisibility of lesbians. The wrath of God "rained down burning sulphur on Sodom and Gomorrah" (Genesis 19:23). How could a Caribbean woman claim the name?

When, thousands of miles away and fifteen years after my school days, my grandmother was confronted with my love for a woman, her reaction was determined by her Christian faith and by this dread word sodomite – its meaning, its implication, its history.

And when, Bible in hand, my grandmother responded to my love by sitting me down, at the age of twenty-seven, to quote Genesis, it was within the context of this tradition, this politic. When she pointed out that "this was a white people ting," or "a ting only people with mixed blood was involved in" (to explain or include my love with a woman of mixed blood), it was a strong denial of many ordinary Black working-class women she knew.

It was finally through my conversations with my grandmother, my mother, and my mother's friend five years later that I began to realize the scope of this denial which was intended to dissuade and protect me. She knew too well that any woman who took a woman lover was attempting to walk on fire – entering a "no man's land." I began to see how commonplace the act of loving women really was, particularly in working-class communities. I realized, too, just how heavily shame and silence weighed down this act.

A conversation with a friend of my mother:

> Well, when I was growing up we didn't hear much 'bout woman and woman. They weren't "suspect." There was much more talk about "batty man businesses" when I was a teenager in the 1950s.
>
> I remember one story about a man who was "suspect" and that every night when he was coming home, a group of guys use to lay wait him and stone him so viciously that he had to run for his life. Dem time, he was safe only in the day.
>
> Now with women, nobody really suspected. I grew up in the country and I grew up seeing women holding hands, hugging-up, sleeping together in one bed and there was no question. Some of this was based purely on emotional friendship, but I also knew of cases where the women were dealing but no one really suspected. Close people around knew, but not everyone. It wasn't a thing that you would go out and broadcast. It would be something just between the two people.
>
> Also one important thing is that the women who were involved carried on with life just the same, no big political statements were made. These women still went to church, still got baptised, still went on pilgrimage, and I am thinking about one particular woman name Aunt Vie, a very strong woman, strong-willed and everything, they use to call her "man-royal" behind her back, but no one ever dare to meddle with her.
>
> Things are different now in Jamaica. Now all you have to do is not respond to a man's call to you and dem call you sodomite or lesbian. I guess it was different back then forty years ago because it was harder for anybody to really conceive of two women sleeping and being sexual. But I do remember when you were "suspect," people would talk about you. You were definitely classed as "different," "not normal," a bit of a "crazy." But women never really got stoned like the men.
>
> What I remember is that if you were a single woman alone or

two single women living together and a few people suspected this ... and when I say a few people I mean like a few guys, sometimes other crimes were committed against the women. Some very violent, some very subtle. Battery was common, especially in Kingston. A group of men would suspect a woman or have it out for her because she was a "sodomite" or because she act "man-royal" and so the men would organize and gang rape whichever woman was "suspect." Sometimes it was reported in the newspapers, other times it wasn't – but when you live in a little community, you don't need a newspaper to tell what's going on. You know by word of mouth and those stories were frequent. Sometimes you also knew the men who did the battery.

Other subtle forms of this was "scorning" the women. Meaning that you didn't eat anything from them, especially a cooked meal. It was almost as if those accused of being "man-royal" or "sodomite" could contaminate.

A conversation with my grandmother:

I am only telling you this so that you can understand that this is not a profession to be proud of and to get involved in. Everybody should be curious and I know you born with that, ever since you growing up as a child and I can't fight against that, because that is how everybody get to know what's in the world. I am only telling you this because when you were a teenager, you always say you want to experience everything and make up your mind on your own. You didn't like people telling you what was wrong and right. That always use to scare me.

Experience is good, yes. But it have to be balanced, you have to know when you have too much experience in one area. I am telling you this because I think you have enough experience in this to decide now to go back to the normal way. You have two children. Do you want them to grow up knowing this is the life you have taken? But this is for you to decide....

Yes, there was a lot of women involved with women in Jamaica. I knew a lot of them when I was growing up in the country in the 1920s. I didn't really associate with them. Mind you, I was not rude to them. My mother wouldn't stand for any rudeness from any of her children to adults.

I remember a woman we use to call Miss Bibi. She lived next to us – her husband was a fisherman, I think he drowned before I was born. She had a little wooden house that back onto the sea, the same as our house. She was quiet, always reading. That I remember about her because she use to go to the little public library at least four days out of the week. And she could talk. Anything you want to know, just ask Miss Bibi and she could tell you. She was mulatto woman, but poor. Anytime I had any school work that I didn't understand, I use to ask her. The one thing I remember though, we wasn't allowed in her house by my mother, so I use to talk to her outside, but she didn't seem to mind that. Some people use to think she was mad because she spent so much time alone. But I didn't think that because anything she help me with, I got a good mark on it in school.

She was colourful in her own way, but quiet, always alone, except when her friend come and visit her once a year for two weeks. Them times I didn't see Miss Bibi much because my mother told me I couldn't go and visit her. Sometimes I would see her in the market exchanging and bartering fresh fish for vegetables and fruits. I use to see her friend too. She was a jet Black woman, always had her hair tied in bright coloured cloth and she always had on big gold earrings. People use to say she lived on the other side of the island with her husband and children and she came to Port Maria once a year to visit Miss Bibi.

My mother and father were great storytellers and I learnt that from them, but is from Miss Bibi that I think I learnt to love reading so much as a child. It wasn't until I move to Kingston that I notice other women like Miss Bibi....

Let me tell you about Jones. Do you remember her? Well she was the woman who lived the next yard over from us. She is the one who really turn me against people like that and why I fear so much for you to be involved in this ting. She was very loud. Very show-off. Always dressed in pants and man-shirt that she borrowed from her husband. Sometimes she use to invite me over to her house, but I didn't go. She always had her hair in a bob cut, always barefoot and tending to her garden and her fruit trees. She tried to get me involved in that kind of life, but I said no. At the time I remember I needed some money to borrow and she lent me, later she told me I didn't have to pay her back, but to come over to her house and see the thing she had that was sweeter than what any man could offer me. I told her no and eventually paid her back the money.

We still continued to talk. It was hard not to like Jonesie – that's what everybody called her. She was open and easy to talk to. But still there was a fear in me about her. To me it seem like she was in a dead end with nowhere to go. I don't want that for you.

I left my grandmother's house that day feeling anger and sadness for Miss Jones – maybe for myself, who knows. I was feeling boxed in. I had said nothing. I'd only listened quietly.

In bed that night, I thought about Miss Jones. I cried for her (for me) silently. I remembered her, a mannish looking Indian woman, with flashy gold teeth, a Craven A cigarette always between them. She was always nice to me as a child. She had the sweetest, juiciest Julie, Bombay, and East Indian mangoes on the street. She always gave me mangoes over the fence. I remember the dogs in her yard and the sign on her gate. "Beware of bad dogs." I never went into her house, though I was always curious.

I vaguely remember her pants and shirts, though I never thought anything of them until my grandmother pointed them out. Neither did I recall that dreaded word being used to describe her, although everyone on the street knew about her.

A conversation with my mother:

Yes, I remember Miss Jones. She smoke a lot, drank a lot. In fact, she was an alcoholic. When I was in my teens she use to come over to our house – always on the verandah. I can't remember her sitting down – seems she was always standing up, smoking, drinking and reminiscing. She constantly talked about the past, about her life. And it was always women: young women she knew when she was a young woman, the fun they had together and how good she could make love to a woman. She would say to whoever was listening on the verandah, "Dem girls I use to have sex with was shapely. You shoulda know me when I was younger, pretty and shapely just like the 'oman dem I use to have as my 'oman."

People use to tease her on the street, but not about being a lesbian or calling her sodomite. People use to tease her when she was drunk, because she would leave the rumshop and stagger down the avenue to her house.

I remember the women she use to carry home, usually in the daytime. A lot of women from downtown, higglers and fishwomen. She use to boast about knowing all kinds of women from Coronation market and her familiarity with them. She had a husband who lived with her and that served her as her greatest protection against other men taking steps with her. Not that anybody could easily take advantage of Miss Jones, she could stand up for herself. But having a husband did help. He was a very quiet, insular man. He didn't talk to anyone in the street. He had no friends so it wasn't easy for anyone to come up to him and gossip about his wife.

No one could go to her house without being invited, but I wouldn't say she was a private person. She was a loner. She went to the rumshops alone, she drank alone, she staggered home alone. The only times I ever saw her with somebody were the times when she went off to the Coronation market or some other place downtown to find a woman and bring her home. The only times I remember her engaging in conversation with anybody was when she came over on the verandah to talk about her women and what they did in bed. That was all she let out about herself. There was nothing about how she was feeling, whether she was sad or depressed, lonely, happy. Nothing. She seemed to cover up all of that with her loudness and her vulgarness and her constant threat – which was all it was – to beat up anybody who troubled her or teased her when she was coming home from the rumshop.

Now Cherry Rose – do you remember her? She was a good friend of Aunt Marie and of Mama's. She was also a sodomite. She was loud too, but different from Miss Jones. She was much more outgoing. She was a barmaid and had lots of friends – both men and women. She also had the kind of personality that attracted people – very vivacious, always laughing, talking and touching. She didn't have any children, but Gem did.

Do you remember Miss Gem? Well she had children and she was also a barmaid. She also had lots of friends. She also had a man friend name Mickey, but that didn't matter because some women had their men and still had women they carried on with. The men usually didn't know what was going on, and seeing as these men just come and go and usually on their own time, they weren't around every day and night.

Miss Pearl was another one that was in that kind of thing. She was a dressmaker, she use to sew really good. Where Gem was light complexion, she was a very black Black woman with deep dimples. Where Gem was a bit plump, Pearl was slim, but with big breasts and a big bottom. They were both pretty women.

I don't remember hearing that word sodomite a lot about them. It was whispered sometimes behind their backs, but never in front of them. And they were so alive and talkative that people were always around them.

The one woman I almost forgot was Miss Opal, a very quiet woman. She use to be friends with Miss Olive and was always out of her bar sitting down. I can't remember much about her except she didn't drink like Miss Jones and she wasn't vulgar. She was soft spoken, a half-Chinese woman. Her mother was born in Hong Kong and her father was a Black man. She could really bake. She use to supply shops with cakes and other pastries.

So there were many of those kind of women around. But it wasn't broadcast.

I remembered them. Not as lesbians or sodomites or man royals, but as women that I liked. Women whom I admired. Strong women, some colourful, some quiet.

I loved Cherry Rose's style. I loved her loudness, the way she challenged men in arguments, the bold way she laughed in their faces, the jingle of her gold bracelets. Her colourful and stylish way of dressing. She was full of wit; words came alive in her mouth.

Miss Gem: I remember her big double iron bed. That was where Paula and Lorraine (her daughters, my own age) and I spent a whole week together when we had chicken pox. My grandmother took me there to stay for the company. It was fun. Miss Gem lived right above her bar and so at any time we could look through the window and onto the piazza and street which was bursting with energy and life. She was a very warm woman, patient and caring. Every day she would make soup for us and tell us stories. Later on in the evening she would bring us Kola champagne.

Miss Pearl sewed dresses for me. She hardly ever used her tape measure – she could just take one look at you and make you a dress fit for a queen. What is she doing now, I asked myself? And Miss Opal, with her calm and quiet, where is she – still baking?

What stories could these lesbians have told us? I, an Afro-Caribbean woman living in Canada, come with this baggage – their silenced stories. My grandmother and mother know the truth, but silence still surrounds us. The truth remains a secret to the rest of the family and friends, and I must decide whether to continue to sew this cloth of denial or break free, creating and becoming the artist that I am, bringing alive the voices and images of Cherry Rose, Miss Gem, Miss Jones, Opal, Pearl, and others....

There is more at risk for us than for white women. Through three hundred years of history we have carried memories and the scars of racism and violence with us. We are the sisters, daughters, mothers of a people enslaved by colonialists and imperialists.

Under slavery, production and reproduction were inextricably linked. Reproduction served not only to increase the labour force of slave owners but also, by "domesticating" the enslaved, facilitated the process of social control. Simultaneously, the enslaved responded to dehumanizing conditions by focusing on those aspects of life in which they could express their own desires. Sex was an area in which to articulate one's humanity but, because it was tied to attempts "to define oneself as human," gender roles, as well as the act of sex, became badges of status. To be male was to be the stud, the procreator; to be female was to be fecund, and one's femininity was measured by the ability to attract and hold a man, and to bear children. In this way, slavery and the post-emancipated colonial order defined the structures of patriarchy and heterosexuality as necessary for social mobility and acceptance.

Socio-economic conditions and the quest for a better life have seen steady migration from Jamaica and the rest of the Caribbean to the United States, Britain, and Canada. Upon my arrival, I became part of the so-called "visible minorities" encompassing Blacks, Asians, and Native North Americans in Canada. I live with a legacy of continued racism and prejudice. We confront this daily, both as individuals and as organized political groups. Yet for those of us who are lesbians, there is another struggle: the struggle for acceptance and positive self-definition within our own communities. Too often, we have had to sacrifice our love for women in political meetings that have been dominated by the "we are the world" attitude of heterosexual ideology. We have had to hide too often that part of our identity which contributes profoundly to make up the whole.

Many lesbians have worked, like me, in the struggles of Black people since the 1960s. We have been on marches every time one of us gets murdered by the police. We have been at sit-ins and vigils. We have flyered, postered, we have cooked and baked for the struggle. We have tended to the youths. And we have all at one time or another given support to men in our community, all the time painfully holding onto, obscuring, our secret lives. When we do walk out of the closet (or are thrown out), the "ideologues" of the Black communities say "Yes, she was a radical sistren but, I don't know what happen, she just went the wrong way." What is implicit in this is that one cannot be a lesbian and continue to do political work and, not surprisingly, it follows that a Black lesbian / artist cannot create using the art forms of our culture. For example, when a heterosexual male friend came to my house, I put on a dub poetry tape. He asked, "Are you sure that sistren is a lesbian?"

"Why?" I ask.

"Because this poem sound wicked; it have lots of rhythm; it sounds cultural."

Another time, another man commented on my work, "That book you wrote on domestic workers is really a fine piece of work. I didn't know you were that informed about the economic politics of the Caribbean and Canada." What are we to assume from this? That Afro-Caribbean lesbians have no Caribbean culture? That they lose their community politics when they sleep with women? Or that Afro-Caribbean culture is a heterosexual commodity?

The presence of an "out" Afro-Caribbean lesbian in our community is dealt with by suspicion and fear from both men and our heterosexual Black sisters. It brings into question the assumption of heterosexuality as the only "normal" way. It forces them to acknowledge something that has always been covered up. It forces them to look at women differently and brings into question the traditional Black female role. Negative response from our heterosexual Black sisters, though more painful, is, to a certain extent, understandable because we have no race privilege and very, very few of us have class privilege. The one privilege within our group is heterosexual. We have all suffered at the hands of this racist system at one

time or another and to many heterosexual Black women it is inconceivable, almost frightening, that one could turn her back on credibility in our community and the society at large by being lesbian.
These women are also afraid that they will be labelled "lesbian" by
association. It is that fear, that homophobia, which keeps Black
women isolated.

The Toronto Black community has not dealt with sexism. It has
not been pushed to do so. Neither has it given a thought to its
heterosexism. In 1988, my grandmother's fear is very real, very alive.
One takes a chance when one writes about being an Afro-Caribbean
lesbian. There is the fear that one might not live to write more.
There is the danger of being physically "disciplined" for speaking as
a woman-identified woman.

And what of our white lesbian sisters and their community? They
have learnt well from the civil rights movement about organizing,
and with race and some class privilege, they have built a predomi-
nantly white lesbian (and gay) movement — a precondition for a
significant body of work by a writer or artist. They have demanded
and received recognition from politicians (no matter how little). But
this recognition has not been extended to Third World lesbians of
colour — neither from politicians nor from white lesbian (and gay)
organizations. The white lesbian organizations / groups have barely
(some not at all) begun to deal with or acknowledge their own racism, prejudice, and biases — all learned from a system that feeds on
their ignorance and grows stronger from its institutionalized racism.
Too often white women focus only on their oppression as lesbians,
ignoring the more complex oppression of non-white women who are
also lesbians. We remain outsiders in these groups, without images
or political voices that echo our own. We know too clearly that, as
non-white lesbians in this country, we are politically and socially at
the very bottom of the heap. Denial of such differences robs us of
true visibility. We must identify and define these differences, and
challenge the movements and groups that are not accessible to non-
whites — challenge groups that are not accountable.

But where does this leave us as Afro-Caribbean lesbians, as part of
this "visible minority" community? As Afro-Caribbean women we
are still at the stage where we have to imagine and discover our existence, past and present. As lesbians, we are even more marginalized,
less visible. The absence of a national Black lesbian and gay movement through which to begin to name ourselves is disheartening. We

have no political organization to support us and through which we could demand respect from our communities. We need such an organization to represent our interests, both in coalition-building with other lesbian / gay organizations, and in the struggles that shape our future – through which we hope to transform the social, political, and economic systems of oppression as they affect all peoples.

Though not yet on a large scale, lesbians and gays of Caribbean descent are beginning to seek each other out – are slowly organizing. Younger lesbians and gays of colour are beginning to challenge and force their parents and the Black community to deal with their sexuality. They have formed groups, "Zami for Black and Caribbean gays and lesbians" and "Lesbians of Colour," to name two.

The need to make connections with other Caribbean and Third World people of colour who are lesbian and gay is urgent. This is where we can begin to build that other half of our community, to create wholeness through our art. This is where we will find the support and strength to struggle, to share our histories and to record these histories in books, documentaries, film, sound, and art. We will create a rhythm that is uniquely ours – proud, powerful, and gay. Being invisible is no longer. Naming ourselves and taking our space within the larger history of Afro-Caribbean peoples is a dream to be realized, a dream to act upon.

4

Redefining Difference

Disabled Lesbians Resist

Joanne Doucette

> I ask my friends: "Do you know there is a disabled lesbian cau-
> cus?" The reaction is: "Oh! My Goodness! How can they?
> What do they do? How can they have sex?"

SEXUAL DIFFERENCE, ESPECIALLY lesbianism, contradicts stereotypes of disabled women. Disabled women are thought to be
childlike and passive, asexual and conforming. Lesbians, sexual by
definition, confound this narrow image. The general public, disabled
people, and even non-disabled lesbians assume that disabled lesbians do not exist, rendering us effectively invisible. This invisibility protects us and, at the same time, isolates us. Some disabled lesbians directly challenge myths about disabled women by coming
out, but this exposes them to the rage and anxiety of others – including too often other disabled women and other lesbians. We are seen,
and see ourselves, as different, as outsiders – outside the mainstream, rejected by the disabled community, excluded by the lesbian
world. We have no community of our own. We are different.

We face at least triple oppression – as disabled people, as women,
and as lesbians. It is hard for disabled lesbians to separate the different types of oppression they experience. Instead, oppression is experienced as a whole, a pervasive system:

> I feel oppressed as a lesbian, but I can't say it's separate from
> being Native or disabled. It all runs together ... I find the whole
> system sucks.[1]

Public Attitudes and Common Stereotypes

Common assumptions about disabled lesbians are that we are defective, inferior, and morally and physically flawed on the basis of our gender, our disability, our sexual orientation, and perhaps also on the basis of race, social class, ethnic origin, or age. Disabled lesbians are also the target of common stereotypes about disabled people.

Public attitudes towards disability isolate us from non-disabled society. Lack of accessibility is a major problem for all disabled people. For example, there are too few ramps, wheelchair accessible places, sign language interpreters, FM systems, or books on Braille or tape. The world is designed as if disabled people did not exist or had no right to exist. Our every attempt to manoeuvre in a public situation is a forceful reminder of our outsider status:

> People have assumed that because we have a hearing impairment we are also stupid in some way, that we can't think. We've been called "slow" and the usual stereotype of "retarded" as well.

Disabled women are commonly infantilized. A disabled lesbian mother gave an excellent example:

> I was taking my kids to the Exhibition when they were smaller. My daughter would be about eight or nine. She'd be standing on one side of the wheelchair with the counter on the other side in the Food Building. I would be waiting to be served and they would talk to HER: "Now, what would you like?" And I'd have to pipe up and say, "Well, now, I would like such and such."

Additionally, it is commonly assumed that disabled women are asexual; hence cannot be mothers or lovers:

> Some people think there's no such thing as disabled lesbian mothers. It's not true. I'm the proof of that.

Disabled lesbians face a high degree of abuse, both verbal and physical, as adults and children:

> Teased? I had bad experiences in public school because I was given the job of answering the phone in the office next door and I couldn't hear the phone ring. I was the scapegoat of the whole

class for that whole year. They'd make up jokes behind my back and then they'd say, "Oh, she CAN hear." Just the usual shit that people say about the hearing impaired.

Her sister, also a hearing impaired lesbian, said:

In high school, we'd look around and everybody at the back of the class would just be laughing and we knew we were the focus of it. Or they'd pick our desks up and put them at the front of the room. Or try and kick us down the stairs from behind.

Stereotypes about disability affect disabled lesbians on the job as well as in social and personal lives. Jane Smith, a hearing impaired lighting designer, said:

Professionally ... from the beginning I was just excluded from participating in sound designing and learning more about sound because it was assumed "what was the point" because I was hearing impaired. And as lighting designer now, who does a lot of music, I've been discouraged at a number of points along the path.

Unemployment is extremely high among disabled women in general. For some disabled lesbians, the closet is the cost of the job. As one said, "At work, I'm straight. After that, I'm gay." Narrow stereotyping and blatant lesbophobia abounds:

They seem to parallel lesbianism with alcoholism and drug addiction and being completely and totally psychologically fucked up!

Disabled lesbians who are employed feel sexism keenly. Its presence on the job was mentioned more than in disabled lesbians' personal lives, perhaps because, for most disabled lesbians, relationships with men are minimal in their personal lives but inescapable at work. One commented:

Well, I asked my boss once if I could maybe do large appliances. "No," he says, "I wouldn't mind, but they are heavy and even if a dyke came in here, I'd still turn her down."

Others report being slotted into narrow job ghettos:

> Back when I was finishing high school, I was steered towards secretarial school. You know, I was totally discouraged from wanting anything else besides being a secretary.

Violence is a reality for disabled women: "I feel very oppressed as a woman – going out and getting hassled all the time." Disabled lesbians are harassed because we are women, because we are disabled, and because we are lesbian. For example, I appear "dykey." I have short hair, wear "men's clothes," and walk with a certain body posture many identify as lesbian. I am commonly verbally abused on public transit and have been spat upon. I was visibly disabled. At the time of that incident I was using a cane.

Racism is alive and well in the Canadian mainstream, as Native disabled lesbians testify:

> It's hard to get social assistance because people have a stereotypical view of Native People. And housing, people will just say, "Oh, well, it's already taken." They realize that you're Native so they won't give you the housing.

Racism is also found among oppressed minorities, and disabled people are no exception. Another described her experience:

> Disabled women have stereotyped attitudes, like on my articulation. They can't believe that a Native person could be so articulate. They say, "If I was blind, I wouldn't know you were a Native woman!"

Racism is also a reality among lesbians:

> I have been in situations where there is an attitude of racism. White women have the attitude that they have the answer for everything. They have to have everything down pat ... And Native lesbians or women of colour get the subtle message that we are too radical or too hostile for white women.

Disabled lesbians, excluded in many ways from the workforce, are further isolated by poverty. In an economy based upon consumption, those who cannot buy have no power, and are assigned to further rolelessness. One disabled lesbian stated:

> I feel the shit I have to deal with because I am poor and on social assistance is the worst. But, of course, I would not be poor and on social assistance if I were not disabled and a woman.

Another remarked on her experience living in a large public-housing project:

> I can't get credit at Simpsons. You can't get credit at the banks.... Public housing is seen as the bottom of the ladder – the slums. They get an overall picture. They think it's the slums – poor and run-down. They think that anyone who lives here doesn't care. People here care ...

Disabled lesbians are also isolated from other disabled people by lesbophobia. Most of those interviewed had never discussed lesbianism with heterosexual disabled women, or heard them talk about it. As one disabled lesbian declared: "Lesbianism is not talked about ... disabled women don't talk about sexuality that much." When it does come up, the disabled heterosexual's response is far from tolerant. Another disabled lesbian said:

> The attitude is, "How can that be?" They are so afraid of their own sexuality. They just can't deal with their own sexuality so they can't deal with lesbianism. They think I can't find a man.

Additionally, disabled lesbians are seen as man-hating, hypersexual, aggressive women who want to destroy the family:

> They were afraid, one woman in particular, that it [lesbianism] was going to be contagious. She was afraid that if she hung around with me, she was going to go down the tubes.

Many disabled women attempt to prove their human status and worth by clinging very closely to stereotypical definitions of women. To be married or have a man is seen as the ultimate success, especially if he is non-disabled and can provide a reasonable income.

Women without men, not just disabled women, but women in general, have traditionally been seen as failures and burdens on society. Women who cling to the Harlequin Romance ideal are deeply threatened by disabled lesbians because we provide an alternative to a vision that creates an identity for them, that promises some meaning and status. A disabled lesbian who occasionally acts as an attendant to heterosexual disabled women remarked:

> They think that we want to be like men, that we wouldn't make good attendants ... that we might find it a turn-on or something, that there is something deficient or wrong with disabled lesbians. Many disabled women are isolated from the world and the TV sets the norms for them so they see lesbianism as so sick.

Another commented on the disability rights movement in general:

> I have heard some pretty homophobic personal remarks by disability rights leaders, remarks which were not challenged. I do not particularly want to get involved with such groups, not because I am a separatist, but because I feel wounded by such comments. Some disabled women at a DAWN [DisAbled Women's Network] conference strongly objected to a minority rights clause in our constitution which enshrined lesbian rights. An Open Letter DAWN did to the disability rights movement on homophobia and mailed to dozens of disability rights organizations received absolutely no response – nothing. It was like dropping a pebble into a dark well and hearing nothing, not even a splash. I know some people discourage family members from attending DAWN because there are lesbians here. The homophobia is very real. How are you supposed to feel when the very thing that keeps you going, your love, is scorned, denied and mocked or rejected as sick or sinful? Sometimes, I just hate the people who do this to us; other times I am more willing to educate them, assuming that they are just ignorant, not wilfully malicious.

Internalized Oppression and Difference
The disabled lesbians I spoke to grew up with a strong sense of difference. As one related, "I felt like an outsider. Games are so important to kids. I never belonged to any of them." Another recalled:

I knew I was different. I was cursed. Everything. When I got polio, I was shot right down.... Kids were very cruel. Teasing. They beat me up quite a few times. I learned to be able to hop on one foot, with the left leg in the brace up in the air and hop around in a circle. My boot and the brace ... as my weapon to keep them at a distance.

A sense of difference is exacerbated by racism:

Just being Native was different because I stuck out like a sore thumb in school.... It started with, as early as I remember, watching cartoons and that and watching the way Indians were portrayed. And I knew that I was Native and ... I felt badly.... I remember having to play cowboys and Indians and the Indians always lost!

Many hide their disability from other lesbians and their lesbianism from heterosexuals. One learning disabled lesbian said of her lesbian friends, "They don't know I have a disability. It's hidden. I don't write when I talk with them." Such silence buys the appearance of belonging, but at the price of subterfuge. This is psychologically damaging and socially isolating.

Some disabled lesbians have great difficulty admitting their disability even to themselves. Being disabled is not an identity that people are taught to take pride in. Most disabled people do not have access to an alternative culture offering another vision of what it means to be disabled. Very few have contact with the disabled rights movement and many do not know it exists. One disabled lesbian stated, "I don't take pride in being disabled."

We learn simply and effectively to hate ourselves. Jane Smith remarked on the isolation she experiences as a hearing impaired lesbian:

You feel like an asshole, you feel like an idiot and it's very humiliating and you start to devalue yourself and it's a very dangerous situation to get into.

A Native lesbian who uses a wheelchair said, "I go inside myself. I used to ask myself what is wrong with me."

Many disabled lesbians are active in lesbian circles, politically, culturally, socially, and sexually. Disabled lesbians I interviewed played baseball, went to bars, shot pool, played hockey, and dated. They read lesbian literature, saw lesbian films and plays, and supported lesbian culture. Some were part of lesbian discussion groups and self-help groups. Some volunteered in women's services that had a strong lesbian component. Yet they usually report a sense of isolation from other lesbians.

On the attitudes of other lesbians, one said:

> I do not think that lesbian feminists have quite the fixed stereotypes that the general public has, perhaps because there is a higher level of awareness of us within this segment of the population. I do find, however, that, like the general public, they often do not see accessibility as a human right, but as a privilege and so they can get affronted when we are not grateful for something they have done. They then see us as demanding.... Most lesbians are just as uneducated and prejudiced ... as the rest of the population.

Another said:

> Some lesbians are really afraid of women who look different and get hamstrung because they want to do the right thing, but do not want to get close. Maybe they are afraid it [disability] is catching.

A mobility impaired lesbian said:

> Well, they sit back and they watch. They distance themselves. They are afraid of how to handle the situation. They are afraid of offending. It's fear – that's the thing that stands out.

Another commented:

> They're just ignorant, that's all. They don't acknowledge the issues. They think disabled women are poor and helpless, that they can't look after themselves and that's some of the stereotyping.

Non-disabled lesbians can be patronizing and have "the 'oh, how brave of you to attend our event' attitude which treats us as hero-martyrs." A hearing impaired lesbian said:

> When we're socializing, if we start to dance, people's jaws drop because we're not supposed to dance. That happens practically all the time. It's really amazing. That's from other lesbians! Like you're asexual, assuming that you just don't have a sexual life. You know the kind of attitude, well you're just a nice little girl – pat, pat, pat. A lot of the time, it's really unconscious on the part of the person. You get so quick on picking it up. It can be a subtle modulation in the tone of voice. When they find out you're hearing impaired, they change. Sometimes they shout, other times they get this tone in their voice as if they're talking to a child.

Paradoxically, the burden of change or action is placed on the disabled lesbians:

> The general response is, "It's your problem. Tough luck. You're going to have to do something about it. Because you're the one who is different. So you are going to have to FIT IN and pull your socks up and do so." This ignores the reality of disability and denies accountability.

Resistance
Coming out can be an act of resistance, as one mobility impaired lesbian described:

> About six or seven years ago, I realized, "That's enough! I am suppressing part of myself." ... I am proud [now]. I feel I'm more complete. I'm not hiding a part of myself. When you suppress one part, before you know it, you suppress all of yourself.

Yet coming out is a two-edged sword. It can result in more isolation, public violence, rejection by friends and families, loss of jobs, ejection from nursing homes and other institutions, and denial of services.

Most of the disabled lesbians I spoke with, while affirming the necessity of political action, public education, and speaking out, were ambivalent about speaking out themselves, given their experiences with trying to break stereotyping. Disabled lesbians often feel that talking back singles them out without changing the situation. One commented:

> I do have a visual impairment and a back and leg problem. I get the message that I'm a complainer. People don't want to hear about pain. They invalidate it with comments like, "Everybody has pain. You're nothing special." Or they come up with quick fixes, like, "Try this, try that." I get the message: "Shut up, and quit being disabled."

Those I talked to work very hard to build a strong sense of self-worth and pride. Some reported therapy and support groups help them to find a sense of self-respect:

> To just hear other people talk so that I don't think that I'm crazy, to have real vocal, active Native people who are disabled to talk of their experience.

We want our experiences validated. We call for solidarity among disabled lesbians, with others who are oppressed by racism, sexism, homophobia, and capitalism. Some call for specific strategies. For example, a lesbian with low vision said:

> Any activity which claims to be for all women should be pressured, heavily and relentlessly, about accessibility and outreach to disabled women. We should encourage women's organizations having any kind of women's event to have disabled women on the planning committee. This should be the norm or policy for every feminist organization.

For disabled lesbians, resistance involves recreating a positive sense of difference through contact and mutual support, wherever possible and wherever found. It implies hope in the possibility of survival, and beyond that, change.

There seems to be a concensus among those I interviewed, one that confirms my sense of what most disabled lesbians I know feel about the future. Disabled lesbians have a strong sense of being different, and are different. We have suffered for our difference, not been accepted by non-disabled lesbians or by heterosexual disabled people, as well as been kept down by sexism, racism, attitudes towards poor people, and ageism. The experience of oppression is total. Disabled lesbians reject the idea that one form of oppression could be or should be separated from the rest.

We call for a new way of thinking about difference, of welcoming it and celebrating it. In our criticisms of the society we live in, there is a vision of how life could be, one that everyone I interviewed works towards, implicitly or explicitly, collectively or individually.

Recognizing the reality of the oppression she experiences as a mobility impaired lesbian mother, a lesbian advised other disabled lesbians: "There's a whole life there to grab. Don't be afraid." Another called for change: "Quit just acknowledging my disability and give me support. Show your support through action. That's what I'd like to see."

Disabled lesbians are re-evaluating some of the assumptions society holds about who we are. From our position as ultimate outsiders, we have the potential for startling new visions of how the world could be – if anyone will let us in long enough to listen to us.

Notes

1. Information about the lives of disabled lesbians is hard to obtain. We are invisible even to other lesbians. I am a disabled lesbian and an organizer and activist with DAWN [DisAbled Women's Network], a national organization of disabled women which is primarily heterosexual in membership. In 1987-88 I interviewed eleven disabled lesbians, whom I had either met in DAWN or found through word of mouth.

Those interviewed were from twenty-two to forty-four years old. Occupations vary, including student, mother, cashier, lighting technician, and free-lance artist. Others receive disability pensions or welfare. Six are Anglo-Saxon, one is half Ukrainian, two are Native Canadians, and two are Metis. Eight define themselves as working class; one as lower middle class; one as upper middle class; and one as "regular class like everyone else." Incomes ranged from $4,000 to $18,000 a year.

One has learning disabilities; three are mobility impaired (use of canes, crutches, or wheelchairs); one is mobility impaired with an invisible disability (partial paralysis); one is invisibly disabled with Chronic

Epstein-Barr virus syndrome; one has Epstein-Barr and is hearing impaired. Three others are also hearing impaired. One has low vision and back problems.

In this article I discuss the oppression of disabled lesbians and strategies of resistance from the perspective of disabled lesbians, ourselves. This work does not represent the opinions of all disabled lesbians. Rather, it is an attempt to distil the experiences of the disabled lesbians I spoke to in order to reflect on how we resist our oppression.

5

Working Dynamics
in the Social Services

The Relevance of Sexual Orientation
to Social Service Work

Janice Ristock

SINCE 1983 I HAVE worked in a variety of feminist collectives providing shelter and support to women who are transient, psychiatrized, and / or leaving abusive situations. All of these collectives see themselves as offering an alternative service. Within them I have generally found that we can be open with each other about our feminist politics and our lesbianism. But in my experience, this openness does not generally extend to the women who are the recipients of our service. We do not share our experiences as lesbians even though we know the intimate details of their lives.

This strikes me as being a paradox, for on one hand we see ourselves as providing an alternative feminist service, while on the other hand we perpetuate a public / private dichotomy, and we rationalize that we need to maintain "professional distance." Thus we operate on the assumption that our lesbianism does not have a place in our work. This is not to say that these feminist collectives are opposed to lesbians coming out to the women seeking shelter. Rather, they leave disclosure up to individual discretion. In my view, this reflects an embeddedness in liberal ideology. Leaving the choice of disclosure up to the lesbian worker perpetuates individualism and the standard of heterosexuality and denies that our experiences as lesbians are relevant to our profession.

As lesbians in the social services, we are often in the contradictory position of providing a needed service to marginalized people — many of whom are lesbian or gay and struggling with their sexual orientation – yet we feel we are unable to disclose our sexual orientation because of the potential discrimination we may encounter; because of our own internalized homophobia; and because of the powerful ideology of compulsory heterosexuality.

An example of this form of discrimination was evident at the Drina Joubert inquest held in Toronto in the early 1980s. Drina was a transient woman who froze to death on the streets of Toronto, which led to an inquest that included women giving testimonies of their lives on the street and in shelters. The media reported that many women said the shelters were full of and run by lesbians and that they therefore preferred to stay on the streets, and these testimonies supposedly indicated the unsuitable conditions in the shelters. I found this report to be both interesting and alarming, because the fact is that most of the shelters indeed are probably "full of and run by lesbians." But because we have not acknowledged our lesbianism as an orientation relevant to our work, we are left to defend ourselves as individuals. We are therefore more vulnerable to attack and accusation. I am not suggesting that we all must be "out" in our work, but I am suggesting that we need to analyze our complex position within the social services.

To explore this question, in 1987 I interviewed six lesbian social service workers at the Toronto Counselling Centre for Lesbians and Gays (TCCLG) who together represent a broad range of social service work.[1] Their positions include: a front-line worker for the Children's Aid Society, a relief worker at a feminist collective, a second-year social work student, a social worker at a traditional psychiatric institute, a community college instructor for a child care program, and a director for a youth counselling program. Even though their work is varied, they share many common experiences.

When asked why they work in the social services, all of the women reported their desire to work with people and said they found the work personally gratifying. Many of them also identified the theme of growth and change as a positive aspect of social service work, as the following four comments show:

I believe that people can grow and learn and I want to be part of that process.

I find the role of assisting / facilitating change very challenging.

I get a lot out of working with people at deeper levels – personal change accompanies social change.

It's an opportunity to put my feminist politics into action.

The comments suggest that these social service workers adhere to the feminist adage "the personal is political." That is, their work with individual women involved consciousness raising and the facilitation of personal change. In this way, their social service work also contributes to the larger feminist goal of social change. Yet there is an inherent tension between our personal lives and our political convictions. This tension became apparent when I asked about their openness at work regarding sexual orientation.

Five of the six women reported being "out" to some people at work. That is, they are selective about whom they disclose their sexual orientation to. They spoke of feeling protected yet constrained by this selective openness:

The only possible benefit at this point in time is that colleagues look at what I do rather than get hung up on what I am ... there are many difficulties ... I encounter ignorance and prejudice on an almost daily basis.

It's provided me with some temporary security. This year I have been pursuing registration as a psychologist and landed immigrant status in Canada. I felt vulnerable.

I protect myself from homophobic students and administrators. But I don't feel as free as I would if I were totally out.

The other woman reported being "out" to everyone. She said, "I am outspoken on many issues." Even she, however, experiences difficulties:

I often find myself taking up issues with people concerning homophobia, compulsory heterosexuality and feminism ... and being expected to do so.

Tension exists, then, both between their personal and public lives and between the personal and the political. These women have expressed a commitment to facilitating personal and political change, yet given the reality of our homophobic society they are forced to cautiously gauge the risks involved in making the political statement of declaring themselves lesbians. There are both benefits and difficulties in "coming out" and in not "coming out." In addition, the contradictions between our personal and political struggles are not obliterated by adherence to a rationale that states the necessity of maintaining a private / public dichotomy in social service work. Our political and personal struggles are not confined to the private sphere.

An even greater area of contradiction became evident as the women recounted their experiences as service providers interacting with service recipients. They spoke openly of their pain in feeling they could not give their best service because they are in an ambiguous and vulnerable position.

> With some gay and lesbian clients it might have been a benefit to them if I were out. With others who were struggling with identity issues it might have been better not to know my orientation. Of course, they likely assumed I was straight, so ...

> Benefit? I have a greater sensitivity to privacy and boundaries. Difficulty? I can't engage at certain levels. That is, clients often want to know if I'm married or have children in order to better understand them.

> They finally know that they know a lesbian ... but they don't know many people who are out and therefore associate me as representing a stereotype.

> Although I'm regarded as an "expert" on gay and lesbian in-patients, they suffer by knowing I can't be out. It reinforces their own oppression.

> I feel torn – sometimes my silence ends up supporting heterosexism.

Once again the contradictory nature of our work is evident. As lesbian feminists we believe in working towards social change and ending oppression based on class, gender, race, and sexual orientation.

The reality of our work environments, however, makes our political convictions difficult to achieve. We are often placed in the role of being social control agents in our social service work, while at the same time we are controlled by the heterosexist social service system. The women I interviewed feel the constraint in their social service role and acknowledge its limiting effect on their interaction with service recipients.

In fact, they all feel that their discreetness regarding their sexual orientation is beneficial only from the agencies' perspective. As one woman commented, "My agency probably prefers that I'm not out so their position is not at all controversial." Yet these three women further recognize that their organizations should be struggling with the issues that confront lesbians and gays:

> [My] agency is missing the boat as far as relating to a very sizable gay and lesbian community.

> They would have to struggle with a massive issue if they were to become openly accepting of gays, which I doubt they are prepared to do.

> We should discuss more what our silence does to the residents. It's like we support the myth that lesbianism is bad.

These women indicated through their responses the complex and contradictory nature of being a lesbian social service provider. A homophobic social service system prevails regardless of the type of social service agency. We all need job security, so we are placed in a position of feeling compromised. One woman commented, "I have to present a façade and I'm not able to relax about who I am." Even the woman who risks being open to everyone about her lesbianism has to struggle and defend her position. She becomes the stereotype, the representative, a token – and larger issues such as compulsory heterosexuality remain difficult to address. These comments generally suggest that our lesbian identity does have an impact on our work and that this role of lesbian social service worker becomes filled with tension.

To bridge this feeling of contradiction in their work, the women I interviewed choose to volunteer at TCCLG where, as a centre for lesbians and gays run by lesbians and gays, their sexual orientation is clearly not an issue. When asked about their reasons for volunteering, they described their desire to support the community:

> I want to contribute to the gay and lesbian community. The service is badly needed.

> I particularly wanted to feel part of the gay and lesbian community.

> It's a way of putting something back into the community. I can be out and professional. At the same time, it has an integrating function for me.

Other reasons include the chance to develop and gain new skills, and the opportunity to work with other lesbian and gay professionals. In this way, they are able to be open about their sexual orientation while providing a needed service to other lesbians and gays.

Their comments also reflect the creation of a dichotomy between the heterosexual community and the lesbian and gay community. On one hand, this distinction is understandable given the homophobic work environments they describe. On the other hand, our understanding of the concept of "community" needs to be challenged because it implies that there is a strong feeling of homogeneity amongst lesbians and gays. The distinctions we make between "their community" and "our community" often deny the difficulties that we as lesbian feminists experience within the lesbian and gay population.

I explored this further by asking women about their experiences at TCCLG. One woman commented, "It is so traditional as an agency and male oriented." Another woman expected the Centre to be a community and political group but found instead new areas of tension. These women came to the Centre in search of a positive environment to work in but were confronted with a new set of difficulties. The tension was best described by one woman as, "The difference between feminism and gay liberation politics." That is, feminism is a movement oriented towards social change, which seeks to end the oppression of women by challenging the male supremacy that underlies our culture; while much of the gay liberation movement focuses on the desire to have gay men freed from their intolerable "deviant" positions and accepted within the existing (dominant) political and social structure. Thus, the values and goals of each movement are often very different.

The women at the Centre recently formed a lesbian caucus in an attempt to have lesbian issues addressed. In this work setting, they can be open about their lesbianism in their social service work, but still feel constrained by the predominance of gay liberation politics, which often contradicts their feminist politics.

In summary, the themes of contradiction and struggle emerge when lesbian social service workers talk about their work, whether in a conventional setting or in an alternative setting. In a conventional setting, we experience contradiction because of the complex and sometimes subtle predominance of homophobia. We are forced to make compromises for ourselves, our clients, and our agencies. We must continue to explore the theme of contradiction so that we can better understand our roles as service providers and the impact our sexual orientation has on our work. Perhaps then we can make better decisions about how to support each other, when and how to disclose our lesbianism, and how to educate others about lesbian and gay issues.

The women I spoke with do social service work as volunteers in a lesbian and gay organization because they have acknowledged their need to be "out" in their work. They also believe that the lesbian and gay community needs their skills. But once again, we must be aware of the differences and tension evident within the lesbian and gay community. By acknowledging the contradictions and differences between feminism and gay liberation politics, we can provide services that are good for both the service recipients and the service providers.

As lesbian social service providers, we must view our work with an understanding of the contradictory relationships that exist between our personal realities and our public realities, between the personal and the political, between the heterosexual community and the lesbian and gay community, between the politics of gay liberation and the politics of feminism, and between the relationship of service provider and service recipient. These areas merit further investigation.

In her book *The Politics of Reality* Marilyn Frye points to the importance of understanding how our lesbianism affects our work:

> If the lesbian sees the women, the woman may see the lesbian seeing her. With this, there is a flowering of possibilities. The woman, feeling herself seen, may learn that she *can be* seen; she may also be able to know that a woman can see, that is, can author perception.[2]

Notes

1. I administered open-ended questionnaires and conducted follow-up interviews with six lesbian feminist social service workers in 1987. My sample is made up of six of the nine lesbians who were volunteering at the Toronto Counselling Centre for Lesbians and Gays, and whose full-time employment or training was also in the social services.

2. Marilyn Frye, *The Politics of Reality* (Trumansburg, New York: The Crossing Press, 1983), p. 172.

6

Lesbian Teachers

Coping at School

Didi Khayatt

IN THIS ERA of resurging conservatism, despite Bill 7 (which includes sexual orientation protection in the Ontario Human Rights Code), it is not particularly safe for a lesbian teacher to come out if she intends to stay in teaching. Most remain hidden. Some actively conceal their preference, others find ways not to call attention to themselves.[1] The need to not draw attention to their sexuality, to not provoke questions, suspicions, or harassment because of their sexual preference, leads many lesbian teachers to take precautions to ensure that their private lives do not become public.

A teacher's authority depends on a combination of self-confidence, professional respect and / or reputation, and credibility. Self-confidence comes from teaching experience, while professional respect or reputation is part of a process: how a teacher is treated by colleagues, students, or administration, depending on how she is perceived by them. How she is perceived by them depends on facts such as her gender, her age, her ethnic, religious or social background, her ability, her qualifications, and her character. Her credibility is built on a combination of self-confidence and her professional respect and reputation. Credibility includes her "right" to speak as an "expert"; in other words, her authority to speak from her knowledge and her position in the classroom and school.

Teachers, as official representatives of the state, are commonly assumed to embody dominant social values. Historically, female teachers were hired not only on the basis of their "natural" ability to nurture and their proper place as child rearers, but also because they could be paid less than men. Teaching was seen as practical training for young women whose "real" vocation was believed to be marriage and motherhood.

The notion of lesbian teachers contradicts mainstream assumptions about the female teacher. It is a notion that profoundly and fundamentally conflicts with and deviates from accepted traditional standards of "virtue" and "decency" for women in general and female teachers in particular. The very word "lesbian" implies sexual activity and stands in direct contradiction to the characteristic image of the passionless woman and sexless teacher so prevalent since the nineteenth century. Lesbians are (wrongly) viewed as "anti-family." They are financially and sexually independent from men, conditions that are seen as undermining the very fabric of society as organized by men. However, the most crucial consideration is that, as teachers, lesbians are in charge of children, youngsters who are "innocent," "malleable," and "vulnerable," and for whom a teacher is a model to emulate and respect.

A teacher's private life is ostensibly invisible in the classroom, yet heterosexual teachers generally find it easy to include personal details in a class discussion; they can talk about their mates and / or children. Lesbian teachers frequently find this less possible. With heterosexuality considered normal and heterosexuals assuming that theirs is the "natural conception of the world," most lesbian teachers are aware that if their lesbianism were made public there would be negative consequences – such as loss of respect and authority. This reality leads many lesbian teachers to be particularly conscious of their behaviour and how they are perceived. One teacher explained:

> I was nervous as could be if I went on any demonstrations, whereas before [as a heterosexual] I had no problems. I did gay demonstrations. That did not bother me because I wasn't gay, so if anybody challenged me, it was easy to say "I'm not gay, it doesn't bother me." But once I was [lesbian], it made me very nervous.

The Significance of Sexual Orientation Protection

Teachers I interviewed felt that even if boards of education officially condemned discrimination against lesbians and gay men, coming out would still complicate their professional lives. For example, they could still lose their "authority" in the classroom, their credibility with peers, and their "appropriateness" with parents. According to one young teacher:

> The thing is that when you teach elementary school the parents feel really close to you if you are the kind of person they can talk to. Especially the mothers, they come in and they can talk about their kids. It's really nice for them to have someone to talk to. And I would think about how those women would open up to me. And I would think "if they only knew that I'm a lesbian and that their child – a six-year-old little thing – is with me." They would just be shocked. They would be pulling their kids out. And yet here they are saying that "that's the best thing that's ever happened to Suzie, and it's really great, and I'm so glad I could talk to you, you really understand ..."

Questioned about how a sexual-orientation protection clause might affect her life, another teacher said:

> I would be protected from firing. I would not be protected from ostracism, or harassment, or from students, or from colleagues.

Several teachers, however, felt that legal protection is not enough:

> I think I could survive my job [with a protection clause], because I think it would be very difficult to prove that anything that I had ever done was in any way harmful to students that I have taught. On the other hand, I think the feeling of distrust or feeling someone was always there waiting for me to make some kind of move which would validate their concerns might be a little bit too much for me. I don't know. It is difficult to tell when one gets one's back up how much one is willing to put up with. I'm not sure that I'd want to work in an environment like that. But on the other hand I might get my back up enough to say: tough! I'm doing my job!

One teacher known as a feminist at her school was opposed to the idea of coming out publicly, even with legal protection:

> I knew that what little legitimacy I had as a feminist, what little clout I had, would be completely gone if I was known as a lesbian. "What would you expect from a dyke!" *That's* the sort

of thing I'd hear. I had worked up a fair bit of credibility in the administration and with certain members of the staff [she was on the Affirmative Action Committee], and I just knew in some respect that that would be gone. That there was no way that anything that I said from then on about feminism would be given any credence – because, "why would you want to deal with a lesbian?" – and that bothered me. Also, the possible reaction of the students. I see as important that a radical feminist influence be there, and be more or less taken seriously. And they do. At least the younger kids take it seriously enough to want to know more, and the older kids take it seriously enough to be heartily offended. So I do have some influence. That would be gone. Like, I remember when Billie Jean King – as someone put it recently – "was yanked out of her bisexual closet," one of the girls in my home class came to me the next day and said, "Did you read the news about Billie Jean King?" I said "Yes." And she said, "She used to be my favourite tennis player but not any more!" I thought, well, that would be the reaction of a lot of people: I really liked her before but now she's gross.

One young teacher felt that her lesbianism did not really interfere with her career, but qualified the statement with, "Since I'm not an ambitious person and since I'm not looking beyond my own classroom ..." This teacher was convinced that the mere suspicion of her sexual preference could potentially ruin her chances for promotion.

Another teacher who had just recently come out had been a politically active feminist for many years, in both community and school. She had made a point of including lesbian writers (in addition to Black and working-class women writers) on her reading list for senior students. She talked about how her new sexual identity affected her attitude in the classroom. Previously, she had frequently spoken out in favour of lesbians, confident and secure in her heterosexuality. "Now," she said, "if we are doing a book that is written by a lesbian, I probably say statements that separate me from the book." As a heterosexual feminist, she had encountered endless harassment based on her beliefs and activities. She chose to teach courses related to women and was outspoken regarding sexism and other issues. "What people thought was that if I'm saying all this about women, then I must obviously hate men; I must be a lesbian."

But since she was not, at the time, she continued her struggle undeterred. Later, as a lesbian, she toned down her forcefulness. She wondered at her previous innocence:

> I think I was naive. I did not understand the extent of being called lesbian. Because I knew I was straight, I knew that I could always argue anyway, that even if people did go and say I was a lesbian to whoever, that I knew I could prove that I was straight. I felt that that offered me some safety. I think that was a bit naive. I don't know how I could have proved it. But I felt that. And I felt that it was important for me to stand up and support lesbians.

Coping in a Potentially Hostile Environment

Choosing not to reveal one's sexual identity can take different forms. You can adjust your bearing and way of dressing to fit a particular self concept; you can neglect to conform to traditional gender-specific dress and behaviour codes on the basis of "dressing for comfort"; or you can simply choose to emphasize adherence to a non-conforming political group that may seem to provide a "safer cover" for your sexual preference.

Some of the women I interviewed preferred to be perceived as heterosexual, although they may not have actively attempted to portray themselves as such. Others did not care what people thought as long as there were no confrontational remarks about their looks. Given that in this culture, as in most, heterosexuality is closely linked with gender identification, it stands to reason that men would want to be recognized as men and women as women. The easiest way to do so is to emphasize gender-specific dress and behaviour. As Marilyn Frye suggests, "Queerly enough, one appears heterosexual by informing people of one's sex very emphatically and very unambiguously, and one does this by heaping into one's behavior and upon one's body ever more and more conclusive sex-indicators."[2]

For lesbian teachers who do not want to broadcast their sexual preference, it is important that they not appear masculine. They may choose to avoid traditional "feminine" attire, but they cannot afford to act like, dress like, or behave like men. Conventional wisdom, based on the turn of the century sexologists' notion of "sexual inversion,"[3] says that women who look like men are undoubtedly lesbian. It is the image that often comes to mind when an individual is not familiar with lesbians – an image promoted by fiction writers, movie directors, medical doctors, sociological and psychological theses, by those who benefit from women's conformity to a pre-scribed gender model of inferiority and dependency. Even as we acknowledge that the "masculine" lesbian is more of a stereotype than a reality, it is a prescriptive image that is frequently heeded by many lesbians who find themselves in situations where they cannot afford to come out. Whether they see themselves as "passing as heterosexual" or merely "dressing for comfort," most (if not all) the teachers I interviewed were careful not to be seen as "mannish." More importantly, they were also careful not to be mistaken as actively interested in appealing to men.

The words of the teachers I interviewed suggest that lesbians are usually conscious of how they are perceived and often of how they want or expect to be seen. As well, most of the teachers had some notion of mainstream stereotypes, of what is considered "feminine," and of what they could do to conform. Whether they chose to ignore or take into account these images, each teacher voiced concerns about how others saw her – and what, if anything, she did to avoid confrontation regarding her sexual preference. One older teacher summarized her feelings:

> I struggled the first half of my life to be a woman. I used to try to get my hair done and dress properly. By the time I was in my late thirties I gave it up ... since then, I dress the way I please.... I was scared, but I took precautions.

Another teacher told the following story:

> I was brought into the office by the principal and we talked about the way I dressed. Now, the way I dressed at the time – I wore, like cords and, usually a shirt and a vest and jacket. Gen-erally, I wore Wallabies [sport shoes with laces]. Well, they give you courses on how to get hired and how to dress, and that sort of thing, and he didn't think I was dressing particularly appro-priately. So I gave him a very good argument about how my dress was appropriate and he was convinced. At least he said, "Well, you sound as if you've thought about it." Which is just a nice way of saying, "Alright, you can do what you want." As the year wore on, I discarded the jacket, and in the summer, of

course, I don't wear a woollen vest. Last year, I began to discard the Wallabies and turn up in Nikes [running shoes]. Last year, what you see me in now, cords, vest, shirt, and sneakers is how I taught. The kids kind of liked it. The staff tolerated it. And the principal didn't say anything.

Most of the teachers I interviewed mentioned the topic of dress and appearance even when, in some cases, I did not question them on the subject, revealing a concern for appearance extending beyond the limits of mere variety. Many voiced an interest in not being noticed and some stated that they did not care. One young teacher explained:

> I am not a person who devotes a great deal of time, energy, or money to dress. I find myself going through periods where I tended to dress more casually and would wear plaid skirts quite comfortably, but I find now that there's been a shift from that and a tendency to dress in what is for me comfortable but, at the same time, somewhere acknowledges current style. I'm definitely more comfortable in trousers. I've not worn a skirt for years. I wear high heels quite comfortably, but they're definitely shoes that I feel comfortable with as opposed to what happens to be the current rage. I dress simply and without any deliberate attempt to present a "feminine" image.

This teacher was well liked and respected. She went on to say that she found it curious that she received the most comments when she deviated from her usual style of dress. When she wore more formal attire for graduation or other social occasions, she said, "I find myself amused at the response that I get. There's a definite surprise that I should dress that way."

How one dresses can depend on age and current mainstream fashions. It is easier to wear trousers when pant suits are popular than to stand out as the only woman not in a skirt or dress. Age itself can afford an excuse for "comfortable clothes," because our culture is ageist as well as patriarchal. "Older" women are assumed to be "past their prime," meaning unappealing to men. Given presumed male disinterest, women "of a certain age" are perceived as "too old to care," "too prim / prude to wear ..." or "too late to dare." Indeed, age itself may provide a means of "passing."

One very young teacher found herself changing her style when she began teaching: "I never wear high heels and never make-up, but that summer [her first teaching job] I wore skirts and looked feminine – well, to a certain degree." An older, more experienced teacher, however, dressed to suit herself: "I think that I dress in a style which is more indicative of my personality rather than to hide or display something. It's just part of me." She added, however, "I am sometimes conscious of an appearance that is butchy, and I would go out of my way to avoid that."

Most of the teachers I interviewed claimed that they did little to appear heterosexual or more conventionally "feminine." Yet at one point or another during an interview a woman would disclose how she concealed her sexual preference. For instance, from a middle-aged teacher:

> I never went about trying to portray something that would make me appear to be a normal heterosexual-type person. I didn't worry too much about my feminine appearance. Again, in the Phys. Ed. field, I was usually in the tunic or sweatsuit – much more comfortable in slacks or jeans than in a skirt or dress. That, to me, was a pattern in my life and I didn't change that pattern in any way. I was perhaps a bit uncomfortable when people would discuss the topic of homosexuality in any form, and I didn't join in the conversation because of my own feelings of, perhaps, discomfort, but I certainly didn't go about portraying a pattern or a behaviour that would make people think I was heterosexual.

At a different point in the interview, this same teacher also said:

> I told the woman that I met in 1968, we will be living together, I am the stereotype, I am butch, etc. For the safety of our profession I expect you to socialize with men and basically not give people an opportunity to talk about us.

Another teacher, slightly younger, recognized her own process clearly:

> The hiding comes to me in areas where I want to be more open, to be more open with my family, I want to be more open with my friends. I don't care one iota whether people where I work collectively understand my lifestyle. It is [not] important to me

because these people are not important to me. Individually, there might be a few, but if they're important, then I would inform them – and if they don't understand, then that's their hangup. But then, maybe I'm more concerned than I'm conscious of.

One teacher went to great lengths to describe how little she cared about what people thought of her, saying that she dressed, looked, and conducted her life exactly as she pleased, even though she taught in a small community where she was known to most parents. Yet, later in the interview, she admitted:

I had a relationship with a woman [who] was such a blatant lesbian, she used to frighten me because she walked down the middle of the street and declared what she was. And yes, it annoyed me that she would play this kind of game with my livelihood. It didn't matter to her, but it did to me.

Again, another teacher spent most of the interview time asserting her non-conforming lifestyle, insisting that she always presented herself exactly as she is both at school and in the community. Yet when she began to account for the reasons why she enjoyed the company of other lesbians, she said, "Because I can relax more." When questioned further, she conceded that with lesbians she was more at ease, "not necessarily having to guard every word, every gesture on every occasion."

Some teachers were anxious that their living arrangements might reveal their sexuality. For instance, one teacher who lived in a small one-bedroom apartment with her lover said she hesitated to invite any of her colleagues over for fear of probable questions. Another teacher said that the one time in her life when she actively conveyed a picture different from the actual situation was when she and her lover bought a two-bedroom house:

Maybe that's hiding. We have two bedrooms and I call one mine and one my lover's.... I wouldn't have somebody from work and have one bedroom.

Another teacher in more or less the same situation dubbed the extra bedroom "the BB – the Bogus Bedroom."

Essentially, for many of the teachers I spoke to, concealing their lesbian identity involved less of an active production of a certain image and more of an avoidance of any overt or blatant statements. One young teacher who was a single mother was sure she did not "look like a lesbian," but also realized that motherhood provided her with some protection. She commented:

> That's both good and frustrating at the same time. Certainly people assumed that if I have a kid that I couldn't be a lesbian. When I was pregnant, if my lover and I walked arm in arm on the street, it was very confusing to people.

Another teacher felt that because she had a husband and children, suspicion would be minimal. Even though she did not live with her husband, she understood "the fact that he came to visit every once in a while would be a form of protection." This teacher admitted that despite her almost perfect cover, she "played the game in most towns I worked in." She added, "I went out of these towns for my recreation as much as possible."

Having a man in her life is obviously the best way a lesbian teacher can deflect suspicion. Several remembered using this tactic at some point in their lives. Said one: "I probably did at one stage drop the name of the man I'd been seeing or had done something with. I think I am less likely to do that now." Moreover, a teacher I interviewed had more than her job to lose if her lesbianism became public. She was recently separated and feared she might lose her children if her husband discovered her sexual preference. At the time of the interview, she had been seeing a man regularly and, simultaneously, was involved with a woman. She observed:

> It's occurred to me, I'm in a relationship with this man for a year and a half. He's a very easygoing person and he's intelligent and he's fun to be with. He's not someone I'd like to spend my life with.... I've been questioning why I'm in this relationship because if I were looking for something permanent with a man, I would probably be out looking, or ending this relationship because it isn't going in the kind of way that one might hope for – isn't as intense, and I don't see it long range. And yet it is comfortable. I wonder if I'm using it in a kind of way so that – well, there's a couple of ways that I feel that I might be using it: one is that I have a relationship and so I'm not alone,

and since I don't see myself or I don't know how to see myself in a primary relationship with a woman – at least now, possibly always – it's an unlikely thing to happen. The other thing is that it validates my heterosexuality to the outside.

Each of the teachers I interviewed found her own specific way to not draw attention to her private life. Whether she dressed to conform or dressed for comfort, whether she chose to shield her sexuality behind the screen of a "safer" political label, or whether her lesbianism was made invisible because the circumstances in her life necessitated a more conforming image, each struggled to retain a certain honesty, an integrity balanced with a commonsense, practical need to protect her career and her lifestyle. In the end many found that the easiest way to conceal their lesbianism in the workplace was, as one teacher concluded:

I suppose the most obvious way: I don't brag about the situation. I don't admit it. I don't broadcast it. I just carry on being – well, maybe my defence is being surface friendly and basically more or less uninvolved with my colleagues, my students, etc., so there never comes a need or a time in which any kind of personal – and I consider this capital P, personal – discussion becomes relevant. I don't keep it in an area in which I am open in any way to personal attack – as far as I can help it.

Another teacher concurred:

In an attempt to keep one's life a secret, I think one way would be that you don't tell people what you're doing, where you're going, the people that you're seeing.

One teacher said she really never had to lie outright about her sexuality:

You don't have to lie about it. It just doesn't come up. People do not question you. I mean, what are they going to say to you? "Are you a lesbian?"

It may be true that few, if any, people confront a lesbian teacher with their suspicions or conclusions. However, malicious gossip does not need final proof. For this reason, most of the teachers I interviewed spoke of ways they actively took measures to avoid provocation. One of the teachers said:

There is a certain circumspect behaviour that you have to follow. For instance, the fact that I have been living with my lover – openly, in a sense for over ten years, same house, same everything – people always say "how's ——, where's ——," and so on. And in the last five or so years I have stopped trying to cover up her existence in my life. I used to never mention her name, right? And grabbing at any male name I could think of – brothers-in-law – you name it, and throwing them into the conversation and stuff like that – as ways of covering and showing there were men and women in my life. It didn't matter if it was the garbage man. But then, about five years or so ago I thought: this is so stupid. I mean, this isn't the way it is and I am not going to try to manufacture a life that is a blatant lie. I am simply going to live it here. But the circumspect behaviour is: you can do *that* much, don't take it any further. Within the context of the straight school society you don't talk your lesbian position, you just talk about your friend. If people would put that together correctly – good. More is the better inasmuch as the available men on staff don't bug you, so you don't have to go through all that. In a sense, your life becomes honest without coming out in a direct "I am" declarative way.

Notes
1. This article is modified from my Ph.D. dissertation, which was a larger study of lesbian teachers for which I interviewed eighteen lesbian teachers (whether or not they use that particular term) between 1982 and 1986. The women I interviewed varied in age from twenty-four to sixty-five, with most between thirty-five and forty-five. They varied in their ethnic and racial backgrounds as well as in their religious convictions. Although their profession makes them middle class, they include women from both the working class and upper class.

It was difficult to find lesbian teachers. I found them mostly by word of mouth. As a lesbian teacher myself, I picked up on many clues and was generally able to guess. However, I really could not go up to a woman who had taken pains to conceal her sexual preference and ask: "Are you a lesbian?" First, she might not like it, and second, I, too, would be coming out to her. I began by interviewing lesbian teachers to whom I was already "out" and who, I knew, would talk to me. Beyond that, other people suggested possibilities to me. Not all of the people I contacted consented to be interviewed. For every four potential respondents, only one came through.

The teachers interviewed taught in Ontario public (tax-supported) schools at both the elementary and secondary levels. When I was writing my thesis, the Ontario tax system did not fund the Catholic separate school boards beyond grade 10. Since Bill 30 was passed by the Liberal provincial government of Premier David Peterson in June 1986, Ontario residents have a choice of which system to support. Despite Bill 30, I decided to exclude the Catholic system in my study because I believe that religion, as an added factor, both limits and obscures an analysis of the state in public education.

2. Marilyn Frye, *The Politics of Reality: Essays in Feminist Theory* (Trumansburg, New York: The Crossing Press, 1983), p. 24.

3. See, for example, work by Edmund Bergler, *Counterfeit-Sex: Homosexuality, Impotence, Frigidity* (2nd Edition, New York: Grane and Stratton, 1958); or, Frank S. Caprio, *Female Homosexuality: A Psychoanalytic Study of Lesbianism* (London: Icon, 1955), as examples of work based on nineteenth century sexologists such as Krafft-Ebing and Ellis. The concept of "sexual inversion" imbued literature from the late nineteenth century well into the 1950s. For Krafft-Ebing and George Beard, as well as Havelock Ellis and Sigmund Freud, homosexual object choice implied an inversion of sexual character. In other words, the concept of "inversion" refers to those people whose behaviour, thought, and character do not correspond with what is expected from their own gender, but rather are congruent with the manners and behaviours of the opposite sex. Thus, homosexuality was not only a deviation of sexual practice but a complete inversion of character.

7

Lesbian Life in a Small Centre

The Case of St. John's

Sharon Dale Stone

and The Women's Survey Group

LESBIAN CULTURE IS alive and well in Newfoundland. For the most part, St. John's, the province's capital and largest city, is the place to find signs of lesbian life, but this is not to say that all of Newfoundland's lesbians live there. As in the rest of Canada, lesbians both hidden and "out" live all over the province, in cities and towns and outports.

Often, lesbians originally from small towns in Newfoundland end up moving to St. John's to attend Memorial University or to find work. Most lesbians in St. John's are "bay dykes" (they are from Newfoundland, but not from St. John's), and a small number are "come from aways" (not from Newfoundland). Lesbians rarely move to St. John's just to meet and be with other lesbians. Those who leave home to be part of a large lesbian community traditionally move to big cities on the mainland, especially Toronto.

There are approximately two or three hundred lesbians who are active in "the lesbian community" in St. John's, within a total population of the city and surrounding area of about 200,000. St. John's may be small compared to Toronto, but is large compared to many other Canadian cities. The majority of people have an Irish Catholic background. There are few Native Peoples and people of colour – nor are there many people who are not Christian. The predominance of the Catholic and British Protestant churches contributes to a conservative and sexually repressive situation.

Most lesbians are reluctant to come out of the closet because of widespread homophobia and discrimination. The Provincial Human Rights Code has no provision for non-discrimination on the grounds of sexual orientation. Moreover, the government is either directly or indirectly the largest employer in the province. Local school boards, all of them parochial, have moral codes prohibiting the employment of homosexual teachers and staff. Local hospitals and most public service agencies will not hire homosexuals. Since much of the known lesbian population is employed in one of these areas, it is dangerous for lesbians to make themselves visible.

Until 1973, when the Community Homophile Association of Newfoundland (CHAN) was established in St. John's, there were no specifically lesbian or gay organizations in Newfoundland. CHAN provided lesbians and gays an opportunity to meet and socialize but took on very little political action and kept a low profile, with meetings and socials held mostly in members' homes. CHAN eventually dissolved as members began to frequent a local dance bar.

By the late 1980s, there were two main organizations for lesbians and gay men. The oldest, the Gay Association In Newfoundland (GAIN), was started in the late 1970s by a small group of lesbians interested in a social and political alternative to the local bar scene. Both lesbians and gay men are involved with GAIN, although gay men predominate. In 1986, another organization, the Memorial University of Newfoundland Gay and Lesbian Association (MUNGALA), was formed to provide a political and social outreach group. Members include students, faculty, and staff. GAIN and MUNGALA often work co-operatively on social events and political action. They lobby for amendments to the Human Rights Code, fundraise for the local AIDS Education Committee, and have loose associations with the local Status of Women Council. Both sometimes use the Women's Centre for contacts and meetings.

Groups for lesbians tend not to be political in nature. They form and break up quickly, as interest develops and wanes. In 1980, for example, some women formed a lesbian reading group (colloquially called "Dyke Lit"), with meetings rotating among members' homes. Each meeting included discussion on a lesbian book – usually a novel, but also plays and lesbian poetry – and a social, providing an enjoyable way for lesbians to get to know each other in a non-threatening environment. The group was not long-lived, however, as meetings did not continue past 1981.

Another group with a short existence was the Lesbian Discussion

Group, formed in the 1980s as a parallel and adjunct to a Women's Studies Discussion Group, which focused on topics such as theories on the psychology of lesbianism. A lesbian support group was also formed, and under the auspices of the Women's Centre a lesbian mothers' group was started. By 1988, however, none of these lesbian-only groups were still meeting.[1]

Lesbians in St. John's who want to be part of a group are more inclined to go to a feminist organization, such as the St. John's Women's Centre. Even those who attend meetings of lesbian and gay organizations tend to be cautious about having their interest known. At MUNGALA, for instance, attempts to create a membership list have failed because few want their name on such a list. Indeed, aside from gay bars (there are no women-only bars), the Women's Centre is one of the few places where lesbians new to the city can go to contact other lesbians.

Most lesbians in St. John's do not get involved with either feminist or gay organizations. On the whole, sports such as basketball, ball hockey, softball, squash, and pool are much more popular than either discussion or political groups. A lot of lesbians belong to sports groups, which allows them to both play sports and get to know other lesbians. Few lesbians are interested in politics — not because they fear visibility, but because they would rather do other things in their free time.

When a group of lesbians in St. John's decided to conduct a survey to see what they could learn about local lesbians, the smallness of the city and the insularity of the community meant that very few lesbians were willing to answer even an anonymous questionnaire. Of a hundred questionnaires distributed, thirteen were returned.[2] Fear possibly had something to do with the low number of responses – not knowing who would see the information or whether it might get into the "wrong" hands. Also, because the known lesbian population in St. John's is so small and close-knit, many may have been afraid that any information they gave about themselves would make them identifiable.

The fear of being publicly identified as a lesbian is not peculiar to small centres. Certainly, there are many lesbians in big cities who are afraid of anyone knowing about their lifestyle. The fear can be greater in a small town or city, because there are fewer opportunities for employment and fewer resources. In a large city, if a lesbian loses her job because of her lesbianism, chances are that she can find another one without relocating. In a small city, however, if she loses her job, chances are good that her situation will become well known throughout the city, and she will not be able to find other work. There are also not that many employment opportunities in a place the size of St. John's, which, like the rest of Newfoundland, suffers from chronic economic depression.

The St. John's Questionnaire

The questionnaire, based on only thirteen responses, was not representative of all lesbians in St. John's. Yet the answers given were thoughtful and diverse enough to begin to paint a picture of what life there can be like.

The ages of the respondents, who were all white, varied between twenty-four and forty-one. All but two were born in Newfoundland. While all of them had friends who knew about their sexuality, less than half had told their parents. One, who had been "out" for fifteen years, commented that she thought her parents probably knew about her sexual preference, but it was never discussed. Thus, she was in the situation of many lesbians vis-à-vis their parents: the parents had probably guessed the truth, but by refusing to ask questions or otherwise talk about it, they could ignore what was going on.

The Women's Survey Group taped one of their discussions of the survey results, and a number of points were made which shed further light on social conditions. On the desire to remain in the closet, one member said:

> Essentially, I don't have to worry about my family, 'cause they already know. But I would worry about repercussions to my family. People who know them and know me. That's happened to me. My sister had a friend when she was much younger, who wasn't allowed to play with her any more because of me. That's the sort of thing that keeps me from being really political and really public.
>
> Unfortunately, that's a kind of vicious circle. The more we're invisible, the more important those things become. And the more we're invisible, the more that kind of intolerance just stays where it is. And it's hard to know how to get out. Because it then encourages all the myths that we must be monsters, that we're peculiar.

Another added:

> I had no problems at all with my family, but one friend, a real
> buddy, now she's scared of me. She won't talk to me. She's
> totally scared of me.

A third contributed:

> I just bought a new house. And next door, they have a little girl
> and a boy. And if they knew that I'm gay, they'd be sure to keep
> their kids away, right? It's just so ridiculous.... It's a Catch 22.
> So what do you do?

The survey found that ten of the thirteen respondents knew of lesbian and / or gay relatives, while one suspected her cousins, but did
not know for sure. For the most part, they had cousins who were
homosexual; two had sisters who were lesbian, and two had mothers
who were lesbian. This finding may give the reader pause, but the
sample is too small to draw any conclusions. What seems likely is
that, since the respondents' families live in the same area, and since
St. John's is a small community, the respondents are in a position to
know whether other family members are also homosexual. Many
lesbians who live in large cities may also have homosexual relatives
but are not as likely to run into a relative in a social situation. Large
cities offer a choice of bars to go to and a wide variety of activities, so
not everyone goes to the same place when they want to go out. In St.
John's, on the other hand, lesbians frequently run into the same
people, because there are few public places where they can feel at
ease in their lesbian identity. As well, many lesbians in large cities
come from smaller places, and are not necessarily in close contact
with relatives.

The respondents were not asked how they felt about having a
homosexual relative, but one whose mother was also lesbian commented on how proud she felt to have a lesbian mother. It seems
likely that other respondents also felt pleased that other family
members were homosexual. At the least it meant that they were not
in the situation of being "the only one" in the family – a situation
that can create a profound sense of alienation for lesbians.

Knowing about a homosexual relative can sometimes make the
coming out process easier for lesbians. It is often the case that

lesbians have a difficult time accepting a lesbian identity, or feeling positive about it, because they have heard only negative stories about lesbianism. Knowing a lesbian or gay man personally, however, helps greatly to dispel myths that homosexuals are different from everyone else and doomed to a life of misery.

On the other hand, when asked about what had influenced their ideas about lesbian sexuality, no one specifically indicated that relatives had any influence. Almost all said that other women had influenced their ideas, while six also mentioned the influence of books. One commented that nothing in particular had really influenced her, and added, "It would be misleading to say that I have a specific 'idea' that I'm aware of."

All respondents had access to books about lesbians, and some said they had access to lesbian art and films. One named the films she had seen: *Desert Hearts*, *Personal Best*, and *Lianna*. A few commented on a lack of sufficient access to lesbian literature and said they ordered their books from outside Newfoundland. One ordered books from as far away as the Women's Bookstore in Toronto.[3]

It is doubtful that all lesbians in St. John's are as well-read as these respondents appear to be. Nevertheless, the responses do indicate that, even in small communities, lesbians are not necessarily isolated from what is going on elsewhere. Indeed, there are numerous bookstores across Canada that sell lesbian books by mail, and there are many lesbian and / or feminist periodicals. The periodicals especially allow readers to keep abreast of current issues and debates, and encourage readers to contribute to debates via letters or by writing articles themselves.

Respondents were offered a choice of labels and asked which they used to describe themselves. Nine accepted the label "feminist." In other words, only four did not consider themselves feminists. The predominance of feminists among the respondents almost certainly makes them unrepresentative of the lesbian population. Although many lesbian-feminists see their lesbianism and feminism as inseparable, general observations suggest that most lesbians do not identify with feminism; perhaps lesbians are often assumed to be feminist because lesbian-feminists *tend* to be more outspoken on lesbian rights than others. Members of the Women's Survey Group, in fact, have commented that most lesbians in St. John's are apolitical.

Eight respondents were involved with feminist organizations, including the Women's Centre and the St. John's NDP Women's Caucus. Opinions varied on how they thought lesbians were viewed by feminists. One said that "heterosexual feminists may be threatened by and wary of lesbians." Two used the word "intimidated." Another gave the opinion that, since "lesbians in this city are the backbone of the feminist community," feminism was not a divisive issue. Most, including those who did not identify as feminist, thought that lesbians were fully accepted by feminists. These views are encouraging because they indicate that lesbians feel they can find at least some understanding and support outside a lesbian-only context.[4]

Only four were active in lesbian and gay organizations that engaged in political action. Two said they supported such organizations by attending some of their social events, especially dances. In this sense, the respondents seem to be representative of lesbians in St. John's. This finding highlights the general lack of interest among lesbians in involvement in lesbian and gay organizations.

Responses were mixed on whether or not lesbian and gay organizations served a useful purpose. Most thought that they met social and support needs. Respondents usually said this regardless of whether they were personally involved. Only one wholeheartedly felt that such organizations met political needs, while another pointed out that there was no political (gay) community in St. John's because it was "too small a city to be very out." On public education concerning homosexuality, four thought the organizations were doing a good job, one thought there was not enough of this activity, and one answered that though the organizations tried hard, they received little response or support in turn.

One of the more intriguing results of the questionnaire had to do with the issue of bisexuality: three respondents identified themselves as bisexual. Given that the cover page of the questionnaire was clearly marked, "Survey of *Lesbians* in Newfoundland" (emphasis added), this response is indeed significant. It provides strong evidence that many bisexual women identify, at least to a certain extent, with lesbians.

The bisexual women did have a sense of belonging to a "gay community." One noted, for example, that even though she was equally attracted to both sexes, she felt "most comfortable in the gay community." None sensed, however, that bisexuality was viewed positively by lesbians in St. John's. One commented that for this reason,

"I generally keep quiet about it." Another felt that bisexuality was viewed "VERY poorly," underlining "very" three times. She added:

> There is as much prejudice against bisexuals in the lesbian community as there is against gays in the straight world.... As a bisexual, I feel very uncomfortable in some lesbian groups. For example, I was involved in this lesbian discussion group and the first question that an individual in the group put forward was whether they should admit bisexuals or not. This made me very embarrassed. Does an individual have to sign some contract that says they will only screw women? I do not view sexuality as a stagnant thing and people should not be obligated to be gay or straight. They should do what pleases them and not have to be made to feel humiliated or ashamed of what they do or who they choose to have a relationship with.

Bisexual women who "keep quiet" about their sexuality when among lesbians have good reason for their silence. One lesbian who commented on bisexual women said:

> I think bisexual women are unfairly getting the best of both worlds – making it with women and at the same time getting heterosexual privileges.
> I don't need men for anything and I can do without the kind of "protection" that stems from penises and the power associated with them.

Another lesbian offered a similar view on bisexual women:

> I've always felt that the word "bi-sexual" was a way out for the homo / gay person to protect their "norms" of society. Sort of the transition, before the final decision, which usually ends up being only gay. I was bisexual at some point.
> My opinion is that human sexuality has no grey areas, and "bi-sexual" is a grey area. To me it's either gay or straight. In other words, some people can deal with being called "half-norm" but not "ab-norm."

Certainly, many lesbians go through a period of calling themselves bisexual when they are first coming out. Like the lesbian who believes there are no grey areas, many say in retrospect that their bisexuality was a way of hanging on to a degree of respectability – unlike lesbians, bisexuals are not commonly perceived as having renounced all relations with men. The bisexual women in this survey, however, were not just coming out. All three of them had their first sexual experience with a woman more than fifteen years earlier, all of them had had at least three relationships with women, and one said she was currently in what she considered to be a permanent and monogamous relationship with a woman. In other words, it would be difficult to argue that bisexuality was just a "phase" for them.

It is a popular perception among lesbians that bisexual women are "really" lesbians but afraid to label themselves as such. Few lesbians seem willing to think of sexuality as flexible or as having "grey areas."[5] In this regard, the lesbian respondents are typical of lesbians in other regions.

The last question on the survey – "How would you like things to be different for gays in Newfoundland?" – elicited a variety of responses. A common observation was that things were not very open due to widespread homophobia: there was very little understanding or acceptance among heterosexuals. One noted that homophobia "tends to make lesbian functions, etc. very subversive and therefore short-lived." Another, who was not born in Newfoundland, said that she had "experienced much more acceptance of my being lesbian outside of Newfoundland."

Only one respondent explicitly argued that more political action was needed. As she put it:

> [We need a] well organized politically active gay community ... Some people still will not sign petitions on sexual orientation for "personal reasons." I believe that for personal reasons we all should be more active politically. There are many gays who are not active politically even to a minimal degree.

Several others commented that what was needed was more public education about homosexuality. According to one, the people of Newfoundland needed to be informed and helped to understand that "gays are not perverts."

Two answered the last question by talking about the problems of living in a small community. Whereas one saw the problem as being not enough places to go and not enough organized activities, the other raised a different issue:

It appears because of the small "out" population of gays, that forming long-term relationships is difficult. Lack of people to choose dates from sometimes puts me in a position of choosing the wrong individual, someone who I know is not necessarily good for me, as in compatibility, etc.

Only one respondent to the survey brought up the difficulty of finding a suitable lover given the smallness of the lesbian population in St. John's — an issue discussed at length by the Women's Survey Group. Lesbians in the group said:

A lot of people in this community don't get involved with other people because they know so much about them. If you lived in Toronto or somewhere, you would meet someone you may never have seen before, or whom you might have seen from a distance, but you wouldn't know anything about them. And you would accept what they presented to you as being themselves. But here, you think, somebody told me this and somebody told me that. I know that she did this with somebody or other.

Here, if you meet someone, you know six different people who [will tell you about her past relationships]. If it's not so condensed, there's more of a possibility that you will meet someone and you can accept them at face value. I think that's a deficit in this community, that we don't have that opportunity.

I remember once about four or five years ago sitting down at a dinner table where my lover and myself were living, and the people at the table — there was my ex-lover and my ex-ex-lover, my lover's ex-lover, and I was living with a lover of my ex-lover. It [the smallness of the community] hit me really strongly then.

Finding a Space in a Small Centre

Life for lesbians in St. John's is not all that different from life in a large metropolis, but the problems lesbians face living in a large centre can be compounded in a smaller centre. There is not as much room for diversity. It is not so easy to keep one's life private, without being the subject of gossip. As one lesbian pointed out, there is gossip in the big city, "but it's not the same."

On the other hand, living in a small community offers the advantage of being able to get to know everyone. There are, for example, numerous private gatherings. Friendship networks are usually wide ranging. Unlike in a large city, where it is often difficult for newcomers to break into established networks, lesbians in St. John's seem more willing to welcome newcomers and help them become integrated. This is probably because there are relatively few lesbians to begin with, so they have a heightened appreciation of the importance of "sticking together."[6]

St. John's is not a lesbian paradise. Like any other place, there are a variety of problems. Lesbians in St. John's are not, on the whole, very visible. They have too much to lose, including their standing in the larger community and their jobs. Fear of becoming too visible keeps many of them out of organizations that focus explicitly on lesbian and gay issues. Instead of working on something like public education about homosexuality, the few lesbians who are interested in politics would rather put their energy into feminist organizations.

None of these problems, however, are peculiar to St. John's. In the end there are lesbians who are happy to call St. John's home. Newfoundlanders may not be very interested in acknowledging lesbianism as a positive lifestyle, but it is difficult to see the local climate as being any more hostile than anywhere else (except in terms of the weather). Lesbians, it seems, are able to carve out a space for themselves and thrive, even in small cities.

Notes

1. Interestingly, the Women's Survey Group, which was formed to gather information for this article, is probably the longest-standing lesbian group ever in St. John's.
2. The questionnaire was distributed haphazardly at various gatherings. As surveys go, this is not an unusually low response. In her book *Minority Stress and Lesbian Women* (Lexington, Mass.: Lexington Books, 1981), Virginia Brooks discusses rates of return for various questionnaire surveys of lesbians, noting the "considerable variation" (pp. 189-90).
3. Although there is no women's bookstore in St. John's, lesbian literature is available at the Women's Centre as well as at several retail outlets, including one of the main bookstores and a local health food store.
4. It must be stressed that these opinions reflect the perceptions of respondents, and are not necessarily an accurate representation of relations between lesbians and heterosexual feminists. Members of the Women's Survey Group have pointed out that acceptance is often little more than

paying lip-service to the prevailing norm of appearing tolerant. For a discussion of liberal tolerance, see Jeri Dawn Wine's contribution in this book.

5. This has been found in surveys that ask lesbians what they think about bisexual women. See, for example, Rebecca Shuster, "Sexuality as a Continuum: The Bisexual Identity," in Boston Lesbian Psychologies Collective (eds.), *Lesbian Psychologies: Explorations and Challenges* (Urbana and Chicago: University of Illinois Press, 1987).

6. Most lesbians in St. John's also maintain friendships with gay men, whom they view as allies. On the whole, gay men are popular with lesbians and well-liked. Interestingly, gay men frequently offer to act as dates for lesbians at heterosexual functions, and lesbians frequently do the same for gay men. This practice is so prevalent that at busy times of the year, such as Christmas, someone could have as many as two or three requests for this service in the same evening.

Part II
Problems and Possibilities
in a Lesbophobic Society

8

Lesbians and the Law

Mary Eaton

THE LEGAL STATUS of lesbians has been largely ignored in legal circles.[1] Jurists critical of traditional legal doctrine dealing with the institution of heterosexuality and the law focus almost exclusively on the claims of gay men, subsuming lesbian existence into their analyses.[2] Similarly, feminist legal theorists often concentrate on the law's treatment of female sexuality while ignoring the challenge that lesbian sexuality offers to such a critique.[3] Caught in this way between the counterpull of two strains of critical legal thinking, the unique position of lesbians has been largely left unrecognized and unexamined.[4]

Lesbians have not, however, been completely ignored, legally speaking. Judges in Canadian courts have certainly had to confront lesbians and / or the fact of lesbian existence in a variety of contexts involving various legal issues. There are at least two points of departure for study of the legal status of lesbians and lesbian existence. The first is to explore case and statute law in which lesbians and / or lesbianism played a part, to determine how lesbians are treated by the legal regime. The second point of departure is to examine the various equality guarantees at both the legislative and constitutional level, to indicate the possibility of achieving better relations with the justice system and its agents.

THE LEGAL STATUS OF LESBIANS

The Law of Spouses

Many economic and social benefits, sanctioned by law, accrue to life partners who are categorized as "spouses." While many legislative provisions are vague on this matter, most statutes define spouses as people of the opposite sex who are legally married to one another, or who are living in a common-law relationship of some duration. The status of being a person's spouse allows these people, among other things, to make income-tax deductions, to be entitled to many employment related benefits such as medical and dental care, to receive compensation for criminal injuries or work-related accidents, to be economically provided for in the case of intestacy, and to be economically provided for in the case of dissolution of a love relationship of some permanence. In Ontario alone, seventy-nine statutes govern to varying degrees the economic and social relationships between people involved in life-partner arrangements.[5]

Several cases in Canada have dealt, directly or indirectly, with the issue of whether partners in a same-sex familial relationship are "spouses." In Re North et al. and Matheson, two gay men went through a form of marriage ceremony and applied to the Registrar to have the marriage registered.[6] When the Registrar refused to do so, the couple applied to the court for an order compelling the registration. Philp, Co. Ct. J., did not allow the application, holding that no marriage existed. The legislation in question did not explicitly limit legal marriages to those between persons of the opposite sex; however, the judge relied on common law and dictionary definitions to conclude that marriages could only take place between men and women.[7]

In Anderson v. Luoma, two women had lived together for a number of years, had children together, and shared their assets.[8] When they dissolved their relationship, one applied to the court for maintenance for herself, support for the children, and for an order for equal division of the assets of the union. Dohm, J., held that the plaintiff could not rely on the Family Relations Act to support her position, for the Act did not "purport to affect the legal responsibilities which homosexuals may have to each other or to children born to one of them as a result of artificial insemination. The Act's application is, in general, directed to the spousal and parental relations of men and women in their role of husband, wife and parent."[9] There have been other cases, with similar effect.[10]

Perhaps the most disheartening case was *Re Carleton University and C.U.P.E., Local 2424.*[11] In that case a gay man, a member of a bargaining unit covered by a collective agreement, sought to obtain some of the spousal benefits available under that agreement for his male dependent partner. The contract contained a non-discrimination clause prohibiting discrimination on the basis of sexual orientation. But some of the articles of the contract dealing with employment benefits expressly provided for those benefits to accrue to the "spouses" of members of the bargaining unit, and further defined spouses as partners of the opposite sex. In essence, the Board of Arbitration found that no conflict existed between these provisions. It held that the language of the agreement was clear, and that if spouse was to include same-sex partners, or if the parties had intended the non-discrimination clause to override the accepted definition of spouse, the parties could have said so in the contract. Moreover, the board found that neither its decision nor the collective agreement was inconsistent with the Ontario Human Rights Code, which defined spouse in precisely the same way and also provided for non-discrimination on the basis of sexual orientation.

Lesbians also suffer legal liability in ways not attributable to spousal status, though prima facie to a lesser extent. Examples include: credibility issues in court; the lack of protection that the criminal law provides for manifestations of lesbian-hating including physical attack and pornographic assault; and criminal sanctions against lesbian sexuality. In fact, the scope of hetero-patriarchal legalism is broad, with the result that in no sphere of its reach is the lesbianism of a participant irrelevant.

Lesbians and the Criminal Law

Lesbians can come into contact with the criminal justice system in a number of ways. As offenders, and only with respect to sexual offences, lesbians can be charged with crimes of two types: first, crimes of sexual aggression, determined by a lack of consent on the part of the victim; and second, breaches of sexual taboo, where the consent of the participants is largely irrelevant.[12]

An assault of a sexual nature committed by a lesbian against another woman falls into the first category. Before amendments were made to the Code in 1983, such behaviour was prohibited by section 149(1) (indecent assault on a woman), or theoretically by s.143 (rape). With the creation of the new crime of sexual assault, the Code continues to prohibit aggressive lesbian sexuality.[13]

Indeed, there is one reported Canadian case of a sexual assault committed by a lesbian against a heterosexual woman. In *R*. v. *Vogel*, a woman was charged and convicted of sexual assault.[14] It was alleged that she was a guest at the home of a couple on Christmas eve in 1985 and that after the couple had retired she had entered their bedroom and joined them in bed. The court did not recount what exactly transpired at that point.

It is difficult to take issue with the prohibition of such acts since, by their nature, they violate the principle of sexual autonomy for women. On the other hand, different standards are clearly being applied in the application of these types of provisions. The above case is illustrative. One problem is that the court did not fully lay out the facts of the case, so we are left to ponder exactly how the event transpired. It is a matter of some curiosity that both the woman and her husband were in bed at the time the offence occurred. Several scenarios, which need not be repeated here, come readily to mind. Courts may indeed be more willing to find that an offence has been established on the evidence merely because the accused is a lesbian, especially where the victim is heterosexual. In any event, it appears that this type of behaviour on the part of lesbians is relatively rare.

More problematic is the prohibition of consensual lesbian sexual activity. Section 157 of the Criminal Code formerly provided that: "Every one who commits an act of gross indecency with another person is guilty of an indictable offence and is liable to imprisonment for five years."[15] During the Trudeau years, the Code was amended to provide that the section creating the offence of gross indecency did not apply to any act engaged in, in private, between any two persons over the age of twenty-one, both of whom consented to the act. This is the so-called "age of consent" law. In 1987 the age of consent was lowered to eighteen years of age.[16]

A review of the caselaw reveals only one reported instance where a lesbian was charged with an act of gross indecency under s.157. In *R*. v. *C*., the accused met D.T., a seventeen-year-old woman.[17] D.T. initiated a sexual relationship with C. and eventually moved in with her. When D.T. informed her mother about the relationship, the mother sent her daughter an airline ticket to get D.T. out of the province and away from C. After D.T. did not use the ticket, the mother sent D.T.'s older brother to go and fetch her. The brother spotted the two women on the street and tried to force D.T. into his car. When she refused to go with him, the brother went to the police, who got a search warrant, entered C.'s home, and found the two women in bed. C. was then arrested.

At the trial, McCarthy, D.C.J., found that an act of gross indecency had taken place between the two women. A substantial part of the evidence, and of the judge's reasoning, consisted of a description of what exactly the two women were doing together, or what lesbian love-making was all about.

The accused appealed her conviction to the Newfoundland Court of Appeal. Morgan, J.A., writing for the court, held that the evidence did not establish gross indecency. The court offered no explanation whatsoever for this finding, and so the issue of the legal status of lesbian sexuality remains an open one.

In 1987 s.157 was repealed and replaced with s.159(1) which makes "anal intercourse" an indictable offence, punishable by a maximum of ten years' imprisonment. The new section does not define anal intercourse, leaving the scope of this section also open to the further pronouncement of the courts.

Lesbians may also come into contact with the criminal justice system as direct or indirect victims. The obscenity provisions of the Criminal Code as applied to material containing the depiction of "lesbianism" serve as an example of indirect victimization.[18] Conversely, lesbians may be attacked simply because of their status as lesbians and in this sense become direct victims of criminal behaviour.

Perhaps the most explicit example of the court's awareness (and acceptance) of the male response towards lesbians can be seen in *R. v. Richard*.[19] In this case the accused returned home one day to find his wife and another woman wrestling on the floor. He suspected that the two women were having an affair, and his suspicions were confirmed when he asked them about it. Thereupon he asked them for a "threesome," but his request was refused. His response was to savagely beat the two women for over an hour and a half, permanently scarring the face and neck of the woman who was not his wife. On an appeal for his conviction of attempted murder, the Court of Appeal held that the discovery of his wife having a lesbian affair would have been a mitigating circumstance but "*unfortunately*, at least *some* of the strength of the plea in mitigation was lost" when the accused asked for a threesome. The court's reluctance to allow the accused to rely on his mitigation plea is patent. The court could not, in good conscience, endorse the accused's anger and at the same time endorse his pleasure.

Lesbians and Family Law: Divorce Law

It is around family law issues, and particularly issues of custody, that courts deal most often with lesbians. Two issues especially come into play: lesbianism and divorce; and lesbian custody.

Before the proclamation of the Divorce Act of 1968, adultery provided the only basis for divorce. Beginning in the 1950s, most common-law jurisdictions extended the fault grounds for divorce. In Canada, this extension was reflected in s.3(b) of the Divorce Act of 1968, which provided that a wife or husband could petition for divorce on the grounds that their spouse had been guilty of rape, sodomy, bestiality, or had committed a homosexual act. The enactment of s.3(b) seemed to allow for a certain amount of judicial voyeurism in respect of lesbian sexual activity, an interpretation borne out by a review of the caselaw.[20]

The first case decided under s.3(b) was *Morrison* v. *Morrison*.[21] In that case two married women had met each other, left their respective husbands, and moved to Hamilton to live together. After his wife left, Mr. Morrison petitioned for divorce on the grounds that Mrs. Morrison had committed a homosexual act. Mr. Morrison offered as evidence of his wife's transgressions: his description of life in the household and his conversations with his wife; a love letter that had passed between the two women; and the former lover's description of what the two women did in bed together.

Nicholson, J., began by determining the proper judicial approach to be taken to s.3(b). He noted that "homosexual act" was not defined in the legislation, but that it had to be taken as something different from sodomy and bestiality because of the inclusion of all three terms in the same section. The court professed to be uncomfortable with the definitional exercise.[22]

Nicholson, J., found that the two women were engaged in an "unnatural relationship." He stated, in regard to the love letter, "It need hardly be said that this is a most unusual letter to pass between two married women and in my opinion bears out the petitioner's evidence that these two women engaged in a most unusual relationship." Finally, in dealing with the *viva voce* evidence the court concluded at page 483:

In the case at bar the evidence is that the respondent engaged in mutual fondling of the naked body of Mrs. G. and that Mrs. G. did engage in the same conduct with the respondent to such an extent that each woman would reach a sexual climax or orgasm. This being so I find that from my understanding of the conduct of homosexuals that the respondent has engaged in a homosexual act.

The judgment betrays the existence of some prurient interest on the part of the court. It seemed unnecessary for the court to enter into an inquiry, to the extent that it did, about exactly what the women did together, much less whether they reached orgasm. On one hand it was apparently the position of the court that it did not know what a homosexual act was, and that it did not really want to find out. This professed ignorance allowed it to assert its right to know exactly what the two women were doing together. On the other hand, however, the court never did offer a definition of "homosexual act." Moreover, the conclusion of Nicholson, J., contained the assertion that he already had an understanding of what the conduct of homosexuals involved. In consequence, it appears that the judge was able to envision lesbian sex, and that sex sans penis was not a physiological or psychological impossibility in his mind; rather, lesbian sex was something about which he was aware and which he desired to have described to him.[23]

Another item to be reckoned with from this line of authority is the equation of homosexuality and fault. How is it that rapists and "homosexuals" are placed on the same footing? It has been held that the collection of offences in s.3(b) comes about by virtue of their sharing "deviate" status.[24] In a great many ways, however, sexual offences and consensual sexual activity ought not to be treated in similar fashion. Since the repeal of s.3(b) in 1986, leaving cruelty as the only remaining fault ground for divorce under the Divorce Act, only one decision to date has refused to permit evidence of homosexuality to support a granting of a petition for divorce on the basis of fault.[25]

Lesbians and Family Law: Custody Issues

One of the most effective mechanisms for keeping lesbians quiet and closeted has been the possibility of losing their children in custody disputes. Until the last two decades, the law books were devoid of any lesbian custody cases, most likely because many women were reticent about even trying to win a legal battle given the probable outcome and the costs involved. Recently, more and more lesbians have begun to challenge prevailing norms about "the good mother," and have been asserting their rights as mothers in the courts.

But the courts continue to erect hurdles that lesbian mothers must leap over to retain or obtain custody of their children. In child custody law, legislatures have generally laid down the imprecise test of "the best interests of the child" as a guide to judicial decision-making in this area. Sometimes, as in Ontario, factors may be enumerated in the legislation to assist judges in their determinations;[26] however, such lists are not exhaustive, and the discretion and power remains with the judiciary to determine what those "best interests" are in any given case. Naturally, with such wide powers, there is both the potential for abuse and the scope to inject personal prejudices, majoritarian impulses, popular morality, and preconceptions of appropriate gender-specific behaviour.

With respect to the issue of lesbianism, judges have brought into play several presumptions (and hence barriers) about lesbian parenting: most often, presumptions about lesbianism and parenting abilities, and about lesbians and parental conduct.

With respect to parenting ability it has been repeatedly stated by the courts that while "homosexuality" is not a bar to custody, it is a factor to be considered.[27] Precisely what is meant by the courts when they say this is manifestly unclear. In some cases, according to the courts, being a "homosexual" does not make a person an unfit parent insofar as parenting ability is concerned. One could surmise that this means that "homosexuals" are as able to feed and clothe their children as heterosexuals, a proposition so self-evident it need hardly be stated.

In caselaw, confusion is sure to abound because the concerns of the court often centre around issues that appear unrelated to the conduct of a lesbian parent, but are intricately tied to the status of lesbianism itself. In this sense, "homosexuality" may indeed operate as a bar. All judges are doing is identifying the disadvantages that flow from having a lesbian parent, disadvantages that flow from occupying the social position of a lesbian in the world, and denying custody on that basis.

For example, the supposed danger of a child growing up to be lesbian or gay when reared by a homosexual parent remains a presumption on the part of the court. That so-called danger would appear to exist outside the scope of parental control if it is really lesbianism itself which is its cause. Similarly, judges have expressed some consternation over the social stigma that children of homosexual parents may experience. With regard to this matter as well, it is not so much within the sphere of parental capability to control the bigotry of others. It could be said, then, that what the members of the judiciary are doing is merely disclaiming their own prejudices, and pinning it on the body social.

Social stigma and the fear of too many queers are just two of the ways the courts have manipulated the conduct-orientation distinction to deny lesbian mothers the right to rear their children. But there are other ways as well. *Case* v. *Case*, the first reported Canadian decision dealing with this issue, concerned the custody rights of a lesbian who was active in the lesbian community and politically involved. The court began its decision by stating that homosexuality, while not a bar, was a factor to be taken into consideration by the court. In denying custody to the lesbian mother, the court concluded that the children would "be too much in contact with people of abnormal tastes and proclivities."[28] While some commentators appear to be of the view that the ratio of the decision rested upon the woman's political activism, other commentators and courts as well consider *Case* to be a decision on the basis of homosexual orientation.[29] In any event, what *Case* demonstrates is the difficulty of drawing, in practice, the distinction between the status of being a lesbian and how one behaves as a lesbian. Moreover, the distinction is flexible enough to be manipulated and used against lesbian interests.[30]

In *Elliott* v. *Elliott*, MacKinnon, J., of the British Columbia Supreme Court decided the custody issue before the court in a manner similar to the judge in *Case*.[31] In *Elliott*, the mother provided the court with the evidence of two family court counsellors as well as a psychiatrist. All three testified that there was no indication that this mother's lesbianism would be harmful to the child in any way. Moreover, the psychiatrist officially filed materials showing that lesbianism in the parent has no effect on the psycho-sexual development of the child. The judge, nevertheless, held that there was no evidence before him to assist him in determining whether having a mother in a homosexual relationship would harm or disturb the children emotionally.

The absence of evidence on that issue was held against the mother in that the *potential* of emotional harm or disturbance was a factor militating against granting the mother custody. The effect of *Elliott* is to place the burden of proof on lesbian litigants to prove lack of harm flowing from the status of being lesbian. In the absence of such costly proof, lesbianism does indeed operate as a bar to custody, because courts seem prepared to give effect to stereotype. Indeed, in almost every reported case dealing with the issue of custody, lesbian mothers have tendered expert evidence to rebut stereotypical presumptions held by the courts, presumptions relied upon by opposing litigants. It seems that all an opposing party need do is to raise "concerns" about the children living with and being brought up by a homosexual for the burden to be triggered. Nowhere does one find courts placing any obligation on those who express such "concerns" to substantiate them in any way.

Apart from the mere status of being lesbian, a lesbian mother's conduct will be intensely scrutinized by the courts in custody determinations. While courts may sometimes accept that there is nothing inherently harmful in being a lesbian, vis-à-vis parenting abilities, the conduct of a particular lesbian may render her an unfit parent in the eyes of the court. Apart from the mere status of being a lesbian, a lesbian mother's level of "discreetness," her level of "militancy," her degree of commitment to lesbianism as opposed to heterosexuality, and her attitudes about her children's sexuality all operate as factors that can serve to deny her custody.

While scrutinization of parental conduct takes place for any party in any custody litigation, the particular form it takes for lesbian mothers is fundamentally different. Essentially, the bad lesbian mother is a woman who is certain that she is a lesbian, is not ashamed of being a lesbian, and who is committed to changing the social status of lesbians. The good lesbian mother will be completely and utterly secretive. The good lesbian mother is a woman who teaches her child that she is a freak, that there is absolutely nothing positive about what she is in terms of her lesbianism, that she is something to be ashamed of.

In many cases courts particularly concern themselves with the nature and extent of lesbian sexual activity in the home. Courts are very sensitive about the display of lesbian sexuality in front of children. To a limited extent, that concern may be valid: unbridled seuxal activity of any sort, without regard to children's needs to be reassured and educated about the existence and pleasure of positive forms of human sexuality, can be harmful to their healthy sexual development. The fallacious underpinnings of the concern are revealed, however, when one views the extent of control the courts exercise on lesbian mothers in this regard. At times it seems that the courts' real mission is not to protect children, but to directly thwart lesbian sexuality.

In one case, that of Gayle Bezaire, the judge at first instance granted custody to Bezaire on the condition that she not live with *anyone* without prior approval by the court. In imposing this condition the trial judge said:

> I realize that out of economic necessity it might become. necessary that Mrs. Bezaire reside with someone else, but I have indicated that I am attempting to improve the situation and that includes negativing any open, declared and avowed lesbian or homosexual relationship.[32]

Through the imposition of that condition, the trial judge attempted to ensure that Gayle Bezaire's children would not be exposed to lesbian sexuality in any way.[33] The decision was not merely an effort to keep the mother in the closet, but to directly control her sexuality.

In *Bernhardt* v. *Bernhardt* the husband, on a motion to vary a previous order granting custody to the lesbian mother, called his former wife's landlord as a witness to testify that she heard kissing sounds emanating from the apartment of the two women.[34] The suggestion apparently was that even having two women kissing in front of the children would be detrimental to them. The trial judge found that the behaviour of the two women, including their somewhat open sexual life, was worse than that of the father, who had been accused of incestuous behaviour with his daughter, and who had failed to even bring his lover to court. Similarly, in *K* v. *K* a psychiatrist testifed that separate accommodations for the two women lovers would be a preferable living arrangement – or at least separate bedrooms.[35]

LEGAL PROTECTIONS FOR LESBIANS

Lesbianism and Human Rights

Human Rights legislation has been enacted across Canada to redress discrimination in certain spheres of decision-making.[36] These statutes generally provide relief against the effects of discrimination in areas such as employment, housing, and in the provision of goods and services customarily available to the public. While initially this sort of legislation only prohibited discrimination on the grounds of race, over time other protected grounds were added. Yet it has only been recently that sexual orientation has been added as a prohibited basis of discrimination.

Quebec, in 1977, became the first jurisdiction to provide protection against discrimination on the basis of sexual orientation.[37] Ontario followed in 1986, passing its Equality Rights Statute Law Amendment Act. S.10 of that Act prohibited discrimination on the basis of sexual orientation under sections 1 through 5 of the Code.[38] But discrimination on this ground in Ontario is not prohibited in all circumstances. Apparently, one may still legally discriminate against lesbians and gays in many respects because the amendments do not apply to all sections of the Code.

Two other jurisdictions have also since added sexual orientation as an explicit prohibited ground of discrimination: Manitoba and the Yukon Territory, both in 1987.[39]

It may nonetheless be possible for lesbians to successfully claim human rights protection, even in the absence of explicit guarantees of the prohibition of discrimination on the basis of sexual orientation. There are three ways in which such protection may be accomplished: (1) under guarantees that prohibit discrimination generally, but do not list the grounds upon which the discrimination may not be based; (2) under guarantees that prohibit discrimination against family status; or (3) under guarantees of sex equality.

(1) NON-ENUMERATED GROUNDS: On October 23, 1974, an organization called The Gay Alliance Toward Equality (GATE) attempted to place an advertisement in the *Vancouver Sun* advertising *Gay Tide*, a gay liberation paper published by the organization. The newspaper refused to accept the ad, primarily based on its view that homosexuality was offensive to public decency and that the ad would offend some of its subscribers. GATE complained to the British Columbia Human Rights Commission and was successful in the first instance. The case eventually made its way to the Supreme Court of Canada.[40] What remained accepted, at all levels of the dispute, was that the section of the Code then applicable was broad enough to extend protection on the basis of sexual orientation. Hence similarly worded sections in other jurisdictions may provide the same support. This type of broad provision, which is not dependent upon the listing of enumerated grounds of discrimination, may provide human rights protection even where sexual orientation is not explicitly mentioned as a grounds worthy of such protection.[41]

(2) FAMILY STATUS: In a recent decision by the Canadian Human Rights Tribunal, a gay man was successful in his claim that his employer and his union discriminated against him on the basis of "family status."[42] Mossop, a translator for the Department of the Secretary of State, had been living with another man in a familial relationship for ten years. His lover's father passed away, and Mr. Mossop requested a day of bereavement leave, pursuant to the collective agreement. This request was denied by the employer on the basis that the relevant section of the collective agreement only applied to persons of the opposite sex.

The Tribunal held that the term "family status" was ambiguous in meaning. In applying a purposive approach to ascertain a meaning of that term, the Tribunal concluded at page sixty that, "Prima facie, homosexuals in a relationship are not excluded from relying on that prohibited ground of discrimination."

The Mossop case represents a great leap forward in human rights jurisprudence regarding "homosexuals." Other human rights bodies have rejected the claims of lesbians and gays based on grounds other than sexual orientation. From one perspective, the result in *Mossop* was made possible because of recent pronouncements from the Supreme Court of Canada regarding the proper interpretive approach to be taken in construing this special type of legislation, as *quasi*-constitutional.[43] While the argument has not yet been made elsewhere, the possibility exists that other human rights statutes containing expressions similar to "family status" may be amenable to the same approach to interpretation of their meaning as was applied in *Mossop*.

(3) SEX: There are profound political implications in the subsuming of lesbian rights under protections based on "sexual orientation."[44] The question then arises as to whether there is any legal possibility of staking a legal claim for equality on the basis of sex discrimination. There is judicial authority for the view that discrimination against lesbians and gays cannot amount to sex discrimination.

In *Board of Governors of the University of Saskatchewan* v. *Saskatchewan Human Rights Commission*, an out gay man, Douglas Wilson, was a graduate student at the university and also employed as a sessional lecturer.[45] In attempting to establish an academic gay association, Wilson placed an advertisement in a campus newspaper. After the advertisement appeared, Wilson was informed by the head of the department that he would no longer be permitted to enter the public schools to supervise practice teaching carried out by students of the College of Education. That decision was confirmed and supported by the dean of the department and the president of the university.

Wilson complained to the Human Rights Commission that he had been discriminated against because of his sex. After his complaint was filed, the university applied to the court for an order of prohibition, which if granted, would preclude the university board from considering the matter further.

Johnson, J., who granted the application, held that the board would be without jurisdiction to hear Mr. Wilson's complaint. He held that the meaning of the word "sex" as it appeared in the section of the Act could not be construed to include the circumstances then before the court.

Johnson, J., considered that the plain and ordinary meaning of the phrase discrimination on the basis of sex

> would generally be considered to be on the basis of whether or not that person was a man or woman, not on his sexual orientation, his sexual proclivity or sexual activity. In other words, sex as used in s.3 would generally and popularly be regarded as referring to the gender of the employee or prospective employee and not to the sexual activities or propensities of that person.[46]

The jurisprudential record thus far indicates that the chances of success on this ground are limited. But the decisions in the Saskatchewan case were rendered well before the Supreme Court of Canada set down interpretive guidelines for the construction of human rights legislation. We have seen, for instance, the effect of these decisions on the final outcome of the Mossop case. There is cause for hope, in other words, that the restrictive interpretations of the meaning of sex equality will not rule the day when future lesbian claims are made.[47]

The Canadian Charter of Rights and Freedoms

With the entrenchment of the guarantee of equality in the Canadian Charter of Rights and Freedoms on April 15, 1985, lesbians gained new possibilities for obtaining legal parity.[48] Section 15 reads:

Every individual is equal before and under the law and has the right to equal protection and equal benefit of the law without discrimination, and, in particular, without discrimination based on race, national or ethnic origin, colour, religion, sex, age, or mental or physical disability.

"Sexual orientation" was not included in the list of prohibited grounds of discrimination.[49] Nonetheless, it has been accepted, or at least argued, and is now clear law that the enumerated grounds of s.15 are not exhaustive.[50] Other groups not explicitly listed within the framework of the section can still claim and possibly receive constitutional protection against discriminatory laws. The main question in light of these recent developments is whether or not s.15 covers sexual orientation.

Thus far, three lower court decisions have dealt with the issue of whether discrimination on the basis of sexual orientation is prohibited by s.15 of the Charter. While these cases were decided before the Supreme Court's decision in *Andrews* v. *Law Society of British Columbia*, the reasoning in these cases is not inconsistent with what the Supreme Court has said, and thus these judgments may still stand and be applied in subsequent cases.

In *Andrews* v. *Ontario (Minister of Health)*, the most articulate Charter case to date dealing with the rights of lesbians and gay men, a challenge was launched against Ontario's state-supported hospital insurance scheme.[51] In that case, Karen Andrews wished to have her life partner treated as a dependent under the Health Insurance Act. Under the regulations issued pursuant to that Act, dependents were defined, inter alia, as spouses.

Mr. Justice McRae of the Ontario Supreme Court expressed profound doubt that Andrews could claim the protections of s.15 in the circumstances before him. Relying on appellate determinations of the proper approach to take in determining whether a violation of s.15 existed, the learned justice found that homosexuals were not "similarly situated" to heterosexuals for the purposes of the law:

Heterosexual couples can procreate and raise children. They marry or are potential marriage partners and most importantly they have legal obligations to support their children whether born in wedlock or out and for their spouses.... A same-sex partner does not and cannot have these obligations.[52]

In the alternative, MacRae, J., found that even if homosexuals were similarly situated to heterosexuals, and a violation of the equality guarantee could be made out, the law could nonetheless be salvaged under s.1 of the Charter. He found that whatever discrimination existed, it was reasonable and demonstrably justifiable because of the state's interest in supporting *traditional* families.[53]

Andrews, Anderson and *Stiles* were decided prior to the Supreme Court of Canada's decision in *Andrews* v. *Law Society of British Columbia. Andrews* (s.c.c.) is the first decision coming out of Canada's highest court that deals with the construction of the equality provision in the Charter. In *Andrews* the court took a much different approach to the construction of s.15 than did the courts in other jurisdictions and Canadian appellate courts. For this reason, an analysis of Canadian equality law generally and with respect to lesbians in particular must consider the Supreme Court of Canada's decision in *Andrews.*

That case involved a challenge to a provision in British Columbia's Barristers and Solicitors Act, which made Canadian citizenship a requirement for admission to the bar and hence for practising law in that province. Under Canadian immigration law a person had to be a permanent resident for three years before she or he could become eligible for citizenship, so the Act imposed a burden of a three-year wait for applicants who had otherwise acquired all the necessary qualifications to be called to the bar. The question before the court was whether this three-year burden amounted to a violation of s.15(1) equality rights, and if so, whether this violation was reasonable and demonstrably justified pursuant to s.1.

Mr. Justice McIntyre, who wrote the majority judgment on the matter of the interpretation of s.15, held that equality is a comparative concept. Legal inequality exists where laws impact adversely on some groups but not on others, and where these differences in impact are the result of, by design or otherwise, the giving of effect to irrelevant personal differences between the groups under consideration. Mere difference, nor indeed identity in treatment, will necessarily trigger a violation of s.15. What is to be determined in every case is whether the distinction fosters prejudice or disadvantage.[54]

What we are left with, then, is the constitutional guarantee of equality for those groups who have traditionally been the victims of prejudice, where the distinguishing features of that group are irrelevant to the purposes of the law in question. In all probability, the courts will look upon lesbians as the kind of "discrete and insular minority" that has suffered prejudice in the social, political, and legal contexts and that, therefore, will pass the threshold test for gaining s.15 protection.[55] Arguably, the locus of the legal battles to come will be over whether the things that make lesbians different – the distinguishing features of our lives and our communities – will be treated as irrelevant. How is this issue to be determined?

In the past, courts have utilized the "similarly situated" test to assist them in making this determination, as in the Karen Andrews case. The court criticized this test but did not wholly reject it.[56] And the application of this similarly situated test, after all, led to the dismissal of Karen Andrews' action. While it is too early in the development of our constitutional jurisprudence on equality to make unequivocal statements, the litigation of lesbian difference will no doubt be a long hard struggle.*

*Editor's note: In late 1989 Federal Court Justice Dubé ruled in a case involving a federal prison inmate that Section 15 of the Charter covers sexual orientation, even though it does not list sexual orientation as a prohibited ground of discrimination. According to The Gazette (Montreal), this "is the first time a Canadian court has found sexual orientation to be protected under the charter's powerful equality section." (Nov. 7, 1989, p. B1.)

Notes

1. I use the woman-specific term "lesbian" here, as opposed to the gender-neutral and inclusive term "homosexual," to emphasize the gendered nature of lesbian existence and oppression. Where I do use the term "homosexual," it appears in quotes.

2. Sometimes this is accomplished through the use of gender neutral language, that is, by subsuming lesbians and gay men into the all embracing class "homosexuals," and then proceeding to analyze legal doctrine as if it did not differentiate between gay men and women. At other times legal discourse on "homosexuals" achieves gender blindness through analyses of particular bodies of law that in effect only extend to gay males, but that are conducted as if they do apply to both lesbians and gays.

3. See, for example, Sheila Noonan and Christine Boyle, "Prostitution and Pornography: Beyond Formal Equality," Dalhousie Law Journal, Vol. 10, p. 225 (1986).

4. I cannot initiate a theoretical analysis of the relationship between lesbians and the legal structure here. All that I will attempt is a preliminary discussion of where lesbians appear in the legal world, and what legal potential exists for challenging the ways in which we do appear. Admittedly, none of this tells us why things are the way they are under the regime of law.

5. Per McRae, J., in *Andrews* v. *Ontario (Minister of Health)* (1988), 64 O.R. (2d) 258 (H.C.J.), p. 261.

6. *Re North et al. and Matheson* (1974), 52 D.L.R. (3d) 280 (Man. Co. Ct.).

7. The legislation in question was section 2 of the Vital Statistics Act, R.S.M. 1970, c. V60, which provided that a duly authorized person could solemnize the ceremony of marriage "between any two persons."

8. *Anderson* v. *Luoma* (1986), 50 R.F.L. (2d) 126 (B.C.S.C.).

9. *Anderson* v. *Luoma* 140, quoting the words of Wallace, J., dismissing an application by the same woman for interim relief [reported at (1984), 42 R.F.L. (2d) 444 (B.C.S.C.).]. It is also noteworthy that Dohm, J., also dismissed the plaintiff's claims for maintenance and support under the common law, quite apart from the legislation. The learned justice did, however, allow a division of some of the assets under the doctrine of constructive trust, which was developed by the Supreme Court of Canada in *Pettkus* v. *Becker* [1980], 2 S.C.R. 834.

10. In *Andrews* v. *Ontario (Minister of Health)*, McRae, J., said (p. 261): "The recently enacted *Equality Rights Statute Law Amendment Act, 1986*, S.O. 1986, s.64, defines spouse in some 33 acts and although it does not define spouse for the purpose of the [Act before me] it consistently defines a spouse as someone of the opposite sex. I have been referred to a number of dictionaries.... All define spouse as an opposite sex partner." See also *Vogel* v. *The Government of Manitoba* (1983), 4 C.H.R.R. D / 1654 (Board of Adjudication).

11. *Re Carleton University and C.U.P.E., Local 2424* (1988), 35 L.A.C. (3d) 96 (Wright).

12. Glanville Williams, *Textbook of Criminal Law* (London: Stevens & Sons, 1979), p. 186.

13. R.S.C. 1985, c. C-46, s.271; In the United Kingdom, where indecent assault by a woman on a woman remains an offence [*Sexual Offences Act, 1956*, s.14], there is an average of less than ten prosecutions per year: Paul Crane, *Gays and the Law* (London: Pluto Press, 1982), p. 10.

14. *R.* v. *Vogel* (unreported) January 13, 1988 (Alta. Q.B.).

15. This section, which is derived from the Offences Against the Person Act,

1861 (U.K.), originally prohibited such activity solely between males. The original form of the section has remained virtually unchanged in the United Kingdom; that is, it still does not apply to acts of gross indecency between women, or between women and men: Sexual Offences Act, 1956, s.13. In Canada, however, this offence was made gender inclusive in the revised Code of 1955 (at that time it was s.149). The reason for this change remains obscure. It is indeed curious that Canada chose to follow a different legislative direction than the United Kingdom. In that jurisdiction, the original reason for not including prohibitions against lesbian sexual activity was that criminalization would bring such activity "to the notice of women who have never heard of it, never thought of it, never dreamed of it": statement of a member of the House of Lords, quoted in Jeffrey Weeks, *Coming Out: Homosexual Politics in Britain from the Nineteenth Century to the Present* (London: Quartet Books, 1977), pp. 106-107.

16. R.S.C. 1985, C. C-46, S.159(2).
17. *R. v. C.* (1981), 30 Nfld. & P.E.I.R. 451 (Nfld. Dis. Ct.).
18. Although I have not seen actual materials that have been the subject of obscenity charges, I believe it is fair to say that often they would be viewed as pornographic from a feminist perspective. Indeed, such materials are, more times than not, magazines or films directed to a male audience for male reader's sexual satisfaction. This being so, I am not suggesting that male pornography depicting "lesbianism" has anything to do with lesbianism as lesbians perceive themselves. What is crucial about this area of the law, however, is that the courts fail to make any distinction between this pornography and lesbian lives.

Until recently, in virtually every reported obscenity case in which "lesbianism" formed part of the materials, judges have found the materials to be obscene: *R. v. Before and After (1982) Ltd.* (1982), 39 Nfld. & P.E.I.R. 17 (Nfld. District Ct.); *R. v. Cinema International Canada Ltd.* (1982), 13 Man. R. (2d) 335 (Man. C.A.); *R. v. Tremblett* (1975), 8 Nfld. & P.E.I.R. 482 (Nfld. Mag. Ct.); *R. v. Saint John News Co. Ltd.* (1982), 47 N.B.R. (2d) 91 (N.B.Q.B.); *R. v. Penthouse International Ltd. et al.* (1979), 96 D.L.R. (3d) 735 (Ont. C.A.). Indeed, materials have been adjudged to be obscene by virtue of the inclusion of "lesbianism" alone. There are at least two possible ramifications of the court's treatment of "lesbianism" in the obscenity law context: first, there are obvious implications for the lesbian press in terms of what we are able to communicate to each other; second, there are implications for feminist constructions of female sexuality and the law, because it is apparent on the face of it that heterosexual obscenities and "lesbian" obscenities are not similarly treated by the courts.

19. *R.* v. *Richard* (1982), 16 Man. R. (2d) 355 (Man. C.A.).

20. Katherine Arnup has suggested that this judicial titillation is apparent from the lesbian caselaw in this area, a suspicion I share [see her " 'Mothers Just Like Others': Lesbians, Divorce, and Child Custody in Canada," *Canadian Journal of Women and the Law*, Vol. 3, p. 18 (1987)]. Arnup's proposed reading of the lesbian divorce caselaw is also supported by a comparison of gay and lesbian cases, which yields a striking lack of judicial interest in the details of gay male lovemaking. This absence of interest suggests a different relationship of sexuality and the legal regime for lesbians and gay men.

21. *Morrison* v. *Morrison* (1972), 2 Nfld. & P.E.I.R. 465 (P.E.I.S.C.).

22. Ibid., p. 479.

23. In a similar vein, see: *Gaveronski* v. *Gaveronski* [1974] 4 W.W.R. 106 (Sask. Q.B.); and *Guy* v. *Guy* (1982), 35 O.R. (2d) 584 (Ont. S.C.).

24. See *Guy* v. *Guy*. See also Arnup, " 'Mothers Just Like Others.' "

25. See "Divorce bid refused as judge rules homosexuality not 'cruelty,' " *The Globe and Mail*, April 26, 1989, p. A5.

26. *Children's Law Reform Act*, R.S.O. 1980, c. 68, s.24.

27. See for example, *Bezaire* v. *Bezaire* (1980), 20 R.F.L. (2d) 358 (Ont. C.A.).

28. *Case* v. *Case* (1974), 18 R.F.L. 138 (Sask. Q.B.). A similar betrayal of judicial attitude was evidenced in *Elliott* v. *Elliott* (unreported) January 15, 1987 (B.C.S.C.) where MacKinnon, J., said: "Whatever one might accept or privately practice, I cannot conclude that indulging in homosexuality is something for the edification of young children."

29. Harvey Brownstone, "The Homosexual Parent in Custody Disputes," *Queen's Law Journal*, Vol. 5, p. 199 (1980); Margaret Leopold and Wendy King, "Compulsory Heterosexuality, Lesbians and the Law: The Case For Constitutional Protection," *Canadian Journal of Women and the Law*, Vol. 1, p. 163 (1985); and *Re Barkley and Barkley* (1980), 28 O.R. (2d) 136 (Ont. Prov. Ct.).

30. The selective use of legal dichotomies against women is not new and lesbians, as women, should not be surprised to find that the same process is used against them. See, for example, Katherine O'Donovan, *Sexual Divisions in Law* (London: Weidenfeld and Nicolson, 1985).

31. *Elliott* v. *Elliott* (unreported) January 15, 1987 (B.C.S.C.).

32. Quoted by the Court of Appeal, *Bezaire* v. *Bezaire*, p. 361.

33. Though not in the form of an explicit condition, a similar obligation to not live with a lesbian lover was placed on a lesbian mother in the *Elliott* case. There, the mother lost custody of her children and later applied for an order to vary the custody order on the grounds that she was no longer living with her lover. She was successful that time, but lost custody again when she later moved in with the woman she loved.

34. *Bernhardt* v. *Bernhardt* (1979), 10 R.F.L. (2d) 32 (Man. Q.B.).

35. *K* v. *K* [1976] 2 W.W.R. 462 (Alta. Prov. Ct.). In *Re Barkley and Barkley* (1980), 28 O.R. (2d) 136 (Ont. Prov. Ct.), probably the most liberal decision on this issue in Canada to date, Nasmith, Prov. Ct. J., found that the relationship between the two women in the case was hidden except insofar as they shared the same bed. Here again is an example of the court presuming rampant sexuality in a lesbian home and finding that only the most restrictive lifestyle will assuage its fears in this regard.

36. Generally speaking, legislation of this kind applies to private action, while constitutional protections apply to public or state action. Anti-discrimination law under the Charter of Rights and Freedoms is discussed in the following section.

37. *Quebec Charter of Human Rights and Freedoms*, R.S.Q. 1977, C. C-12, S.10.

38. By mid-1989 there had been no decisions on this ground: telephone conversation with the Ontario Human Rights Commission, June 1, 1989.

39. *The Human Rights Code*, S.M. 1987, C. 44, S.9(2)(h); S.Y.T. C. 3, S.6(g). By mid-1989 there had also been no decisions under these sections: conversations with the Manitoba and Yukon human rights commissions, June 1, 1989.

40. The issue was whether forcing the paper to accept the ad would offend its right to freedom of speech and the press. The majority of the Supreme Court held that the paper had a right to control the content of the advertising it published, and so GATE was ultimately unsuccessful. In fact, most human rights legislation across the country contains "free speech" exceptions in one form or another. Depending, therefore, on the construction of these sections, anti-discrimination guarantees on the basis of sexual orientation could be severely circumscribed in some instances.

41. Only Alberta and Nova Scotia appear to have included this type of provision. Section 3 of the Individual's Rights Protection Act of Alberta provides for non-discrimination in public accommodation. Section 4 provides for non-discrimination regarding tenancy. Both sections contain the phrase "or of any other person or class of persons," after having listed several specific grounds upon which such discrimination is prohibited.

Similarly, the Nova Scotia Human Rights Act, by s.12, prohibits discriminatory publications or advertisements against "any person or class of persons" without specifying any particular grounds whatsoever.

42. *Mossop* v. *CUPTE and the Secretary of State* (unreported) April 13, 1989 (Canadian Human Rights Tribunal).

43. Based on the ratio of the court in those cases, the Tribunal noted (on page 61) that "Value judgments should play no part in this process [of interpretation] because they may operate to favour a view of the world as it might be preferred over the world as it is."

44. The reasons for this are complex, but a useful starting point for this discussion is Marilyn Frye's "Lesbian Feminism and The Gay Rights Movement: Another View of Male Supremacy," in Marilyn Frye, *The Politics of Reality: Essays in Feminist Theory* (Freedom, California: The Crossing Press, 1983), p. 128.

45. *Board of Governors of the University of Saskatchewan* v. *Saskatchewan Human Rights Commission* [1976] 3 W.W.R. 385 (Sask. Q.B.).

46. Ibid., p. 389.

47. In fact, there is a hint in the *Mossop* case that a claim on the basis of sex discrimination may indeed have been possible. On page 68, in relation to the articles of the collective agreement, the Tribunal stated: "It will be noted that it excludes a person of the same sex who, *but for gender*, would otherwise be included as a common law spouse" (emphasis added).

48. Although I am addressing, in a preliminary fashion, only the equality guarantee embodied in s.15 of the Charter, other fundamental rights and freedoms may be implicated in litigation over the differential treatment of lesbians and gay men. Indeed, this process has already begun. See: *R.* v. *Sylvestre* (1986), 23 C.R.R. 313 (F.C.A.) (s.7 challenge); *R.* v. *Lebeau*; *R.* v. *Lofthouse* (1988), 41 C.C.C. (3d) 163 (Ont. C.A.) (s.2, s.7, and s.8 challenge); and *Andrews* v. *Ontario (Minister of Health)* (s.2 and s.7 challenge).

49. For an excellent discussion and review of the legislative history in this regard, see Arnold Bruner, "Sexual Orientation and Equality Rights" in Anne F. Bayefsky and Mary Eberts (eds.) *Equality Rights and the Canadian Charter of Rights and Freedoms* (Toronto: Carswell, 1985), p. 457.

50. *Equality for All: Report of the Parliamentary Committee on Equality Rights* (Ottawa, 1985), p. 29; Margaret Leopold and Wendy King, "Compulsory Heterosexuality, Lesbians and the Law: The Case for Constitutional Protection," *Canadian Journal of Women and the Law*, Vol. 1, p. 163 (1985). In the United States, it has sometimes been accepted that homosexuals are a protected group under the Fourteenth Amendment

to the Bill of Rights, guaranteeing the "equal protection of the laws." Argument in the United States has centred around the *degree* of protection homosexuals are entitled to. See: Harris M. Miller, "An Argument for the Application of the Equal Protection Heightened Scrutiny to Classifications Based on Homosexuality," *Southern California Law Review*, Vol. 57, p. 797 (1984). Similar questions surrounding the degree of protection to be afforded non-enumerated as opposed to enumerated grounds under s.15 may arise in Canada. Thus far, our courts have not yet addressed this particular problem. As to "clear law," in *Andrews* v. *Law Society of British Columbia* (unreported), February 2, 1989, the Supreme Court of Canada held that s.15 applies to discrimination on the basis of citizenship, a non-enumerated ground.

51. *Andrews* v. *Ontario (Minister of Health)*. In *Anderson* v. *Luoma*, the court summarily dismissed even the idea that provisions of the Family Relations Act of British Columbia that conferred benefits to heterosexual spouses discriminated against same-sex spouses. The woman who had applied to the court to get support, maintenance, and an order for division of the assets of the union argued that if the legislation restricted its provisions to opposite-sex couples, it infringed her right to equality. In response to this argument, Mr. Justice Dohm simply said (on page 142), "The answer is found in s.1 of the Charter" – a brand of judicial dismissiveness that is both infuriating and manifestly unhelpful. Whatever one may think of Dohm's obvious lack of respect for the import and seriousness of the argument, his attitude is by no means unique. In the federal all-party report *Equality for All*, the Boyer Commission, in discussing whether sexual orientation ought to be covered by s.15, concluded that it should be, but at the same time, in another portion of the report, recommended that a uniform definition of "spouse" under federal law should be restricted to people of the opposite sex.

In a third case, a RCMP officer said he was discriminated against when he was forced to resign after admitting to homosexual experiences. The Attorney General brought a motion to have the plaintiff's statement of claim struck out on the basis that it disclosed no reasonable cause of action. Dube, J., dismissed the motion, stating that the plaintiff "may have a good cause of action under s.15 of the Charter": *Stiles* v. *Canada (Attorney General)* (1986), 3 F.T.R. 234 (F.C.C.), p. 236.

52. *Andrews* v. *Ontario (Minister of Health)*, p. 263. Before *Andrews* the test to determine a violation of s.15, as laid down by the Ontario Court of Appeal, was threefold: (1) Is the individual a member of a distinct class?

(2) Is that class similarly situated to the class not adversely affected by the law? and (3) Is that class discriminated against pursuant to the law?

53. *Andrews* v. *Ontario (Minster of Health)*, p. 265. The province never even argued that the state's interest lay in maintaining traditional families (conversation with A.M. Delorey, who, as a student-at-law, worked on the case).

54. What the court meant in constructing the approach to be taken towards s.15 claims was somewhat clarified in *R.* v. *Turpin* (unreported) May 4, 1989, where Wilson, J., noted that a search for the indicia of discrimination includes stereotyping, historical disadvantage, and vulnerability to political and social prejudice.

55. *United States* v. *Carolene Products Co.*, 304 U.S. 144 (1938), quoted by Wilson, J., p. 3.

56. *Andrews* v. *Ontario (Minister of Health)*, p. 12.

9

Sexual Dis / Orientation or Playing House

To Be or Not To Be Coded Human

Becki Ross

EARLY IN 1985 Evelyn Gigantes, the New Democratic Party Member of Provincial Parliament (Ottawa Centre), proposed a private member's bill to amend the Ontario Rights Code and prohibit discrimination against lesbians and gay men. The amendment remained before the legislature for a full year before it was adopted by the standing committee on the administration of justice and then finally on May 6, 1986, became part of the omnibus Bill 7 (Section 18). Late in November 1986 the highly controversial amendment came before the Ontario Legislature and the minority Liberal government called for a free vote.[1]

Though one could conclude otherwise, the amendment itself did not magically appear on the parliamentary agenda: its actual existence was firmly rooted in, and served as a clear testament to, the historic efforts of countless lesbian and gay community activists. In 1975, members of the Coalition for Gay Rights in Ontario (CGRO) began work aimed at legal equality for lesbians and gay men.[2] Later the Right to Privacy Committee in Toronto (RTPC) joined the campaign for legal change. The efforts of these lesbian and gay lobbyists to achieve parliamentary endorsement for sexual orientation protection became more organized and concerted as the days scheduled for House debate approached.[3] In an October 1986 brief to the Ontario Legislature, "Discrimination against Lesbians and Gay Men: The

133

Ontario Human Rights Omission," CGRO members described their position:

> Unjustifiable prejudice against lesbians and gay men is expressed in harassment, hate propaganda and even murder. Public policy in Ontario reflects and reinforces homophobic prejudice, particularly in such areas as education, family law, police / community relations and the administration of health (a matter of increasing concern in light of the AIDS crisis). Governmental complicity in anti-gay discrimination contributes to discrimination in the private sector.... If Ontario is in fact a leader in human rights legislation, it must amend its Human Rights Code to include sexual orientation.[4]

I followed the Bill 7 debate as a spectator in the legislature gallery, both during the long days of discussion and on the day of the bill's eventual passage. For me the affair came to signify a crystallized moment of confrontation with one mechanism of the Canadian state: the manufacture of laws. Only later did I sense the full and direct implications of this amendment for my own lesbian self, and the magnitude of what was at stake. At the time, I recall, I was in no way prepared for the experience as it actually unfolded.

An Outsider Inside "The House": A Lesbian Chronicle
When I arrived at the Legislative Assembly of Ontario on the afternoon of December 2nd, 1986, numerous security guards directed me to the appropriate reception area, where I found it was necessary to complete a "request for visitors" pass. While I was awaiting my official gallery document, I was handed a plastic card and instructed to visit the coat-check, where I was required to give up my coat, jacket, bag, and umbrella. I returned to collect my Christmas card-like pass. Stuffing it in my hand, I took the elevator, accompanied by yet another security guard, to the fourth floor, where I was met by several more uniformed guards. It was then necessary for me to walk underneath the arched security device twice, much to one guard's consternation, as my metal jewellery repeatedly set off the alarm. Once seated in the "public" gallery, I, an officially approved observer, familiarized myself with the Thirty-Third Parliament-1986 floor-plan and the list of the House rules of order and conduct I was commanded to uphold as a "privileged" onlooker.

The architectural design of the legislature gallery was such that it was virtually impossible to learn who else was present without craning one's neck and twisting one's body into a variety of positions. In effect, the body / bawdy of lesbians and gay men seated in the House during the Bill 7 debate was a physically divided body.

It quickly became clear to me that I had no place in this arena; I did not belong, except as one pair of unblinking eyeballs. I was not permitted to engage in the unfolding debate – either by recording my thoughts or the official voices, or by standing up to remedy my obscured vision, or by vocally or bodily registering my dis / pleasure at the content of the endless speeches. Without doubt, these restrictions work in the best interests of the House. Certainly, the enshrined sanctity of the House proceedings is concretely preserved and displayed through the regulation of any gallery-originated disturbance or interruption. Onlookers are continually reminded of this (accomplished) sanctity, and by virtue of my obedience, I participated in / actively in its accomplishment.

Sitting quietly, painfully silent, I sensed I was part of an assembly of warm bodies. I was caught up in one arm of masculinist state formation – the formation of state policy. But caught up differently than the elected play-actors below me. I became mesmerized by the state rituals, symbols, language, suit / able codes of dress. There was a surreal character about it all – it seemed spectacle-like. And yet I remember myself waging a constant struggle *not* to believe that what went forward was all perfectly normal, legitimate, or that I was in any way *represented* on that floor. To be or not to be "tolerated."

Hour upon hour, I felt like a piece of stiffened cardboard. At certain moments I noticed my tight and rigid body, a body coiled and wrapped around itself. I remember my breathing was laboured. Sharp and shortened intakes. Days later, I carried the ache around with me.

Peering over the railing I watched and listened, intently. One morally conservative parliamentarian after another – lobbied heavily by members of the Coalition for Family Values, National Citizens Coalition, Ontario Conference of Catholic Bishops, Pentacostal Assemblies of Canada, Canadian Baptist Federation, Canadian Organization of Small Businesses, REAL Women of Canada, and others – claimed passionately that "homosexuals" were demanding "special rights." That homosexuals were insisting on "preferential treatment." That homosexuals were "child molesters" and "pedophiles."

That the passing of the sexual orientation amendment in Quebec had led to a stark reduction in the province's birth rate.[5] That the fundamental social unit – THE (patriarchal, heterosexual, nuclear) FAMILY was severely endangered. That "society" has every right to prefer heterosexual behaviour as a matter of social policy.

George McCague, Dufferin-Simcoe (PC):

I have laid out a scenario that suggests that the Bill 7 amendment is the first step on the long road to recognizing homosexual marriage, along with the adoption of children. No one should take pride in immoral behaviour, but is it not worse to encourage another to take pride in behaviour that is destroying him or her?... Homosexual marriage would be harmful to family life and would be socially undesirable. The family remains the essential building block of society, and its continued resilience in the face of impossible economic and social tensions is a hallmark of its preservation.... Homosexuality, on the contrary, is essentially anti-family. The law has every right to discourage people from entering into paths that are demonstrably destructive, physically, and psychologically, first to the homosexual and then to society.

Nicolas G. Leluk, York West (PC):

Sexual orientation refers to a sexual preference which includes homosexuality, lesbianism and could include paedophilia and necrophilia ... this is an inappropriate addition to the Human Rights Code.... the Ontario government is attempting to ram through a totally disgusting piece of legislation.

Cam Jackson, Burlington South (PC):

The government could well require that sexual orientation be taught as an approved alternative lifestyle and mandatory curriculum guidelines reflecting this logic would be an actual extension. I believe that this would be inappropriate for our elementary schools and for their students who are in their most sensitive development years and may be struggling with their personal identity. I believe this bill to be vrong.

Jack Pierce, Rainy River (PC):

It is a pleasure for me to stand up to speak in opposition to the inclusion of the amendment in Bill 7 (my emphasis).

Honourable David Peterson, London Centre (L):

But then I say to myself, supposing that when one of my children was 16 or 18 he came to me and said, "Dad, I am a homosexual," what would you do then? Obviously you would be concerned. Obviously, there would be repercussions. Obviously, you would look at yourself and ask, "What did I do wrong?"[6]

Predictably, there was no discussion on the floor of the taken-for-granted ways in which people's lives are ideologically and materially organized as heterosexual.[7] Indeed, none of the legislators felt compelled to "come out" as heterosexual. There was no mention of how heterosexism and homophobia contribute to the restabilizing of capitalist, patriarchal social order. And only one statement, made by a woman, unmasking heterosexual men as child abusers, to counter the dominant reactionary descriptions of a child-targeted lesbian and gay menace.[8] The reality that men who murder women are, in almost three of four instances, the women's (heterosexual) husbands or lovers was a topic not introduced.[9]

I was troubled, though not surprised, that the several male members of parliament I knew to be gay elected to hide behind the respectability accorded them as state agents and to pass as heterosexual. Did they believe that coming out in the House would damage their reputation, their credibility? How did each reconcile the hypocrisy of his own negation? Did their ears burn from the charges of "paedophile" or "pervert" or "molester"? Did they wriggle uncomfortably in their seats, or want to scream to deafen their "morally principled" colleagues? In their privileged, authorized capacity, were they impervious to the general climate of man-made contempt? Or, to the contrary, would such a declaration of difference be absolutely irrelevant given the reign of masculine homosociality? As Luce Irigaray notes, "Heterosexuality has been up to now just an alibi for the smooth workings of man's relations with himself, of relations among men."[10]

As I sat there, on one level I wondered whether these state agents in Harry Rosen suits and Ralph Lauren ties, largely manning their way through this charged debate, could or would ever know that it was *my* lesbian life and the lives of all lesbians and gay men that they were ripping out of context, throwing like footballs, bouncing like basketballs, around the floor of the House. Curiously, I, Becki Ross — white, middle-class lesbian feminist — was nowhere to be seen, or heard. My life was rendered an abstraction. I could not locate my self inside the repeatedly stated category, "homosexual." Typically, homosexuality is perceived through a male lens as gay male experience, and it was no different inside the legislature. I squirmed in my seat, itching to decry the designations "homosexual" and "gay." I forced myself to swallow the all-consuming urge to reiterate Annabel Faraday's contention: "Men, whether straight or gay, share a similar position because of their gender in patriarchal societies, in general, and in western capitalist cultures in particular."[11] I yearned to describe out loud (and *be heard*) the gross economic and cultural differences between most lesbians and gay men. At the same time, and especially, I, with others, needed to articulate the ways in which lesbians (and gay men) are divided within ourselves along lines of class, race / ethnicity, ability, age, sexual practice, feminist politics, and more.[12]

In the House I felt battered and stretched apart, tossed about on a stormy sea, a vessel rubbed raw. I felt angry, hated, and ridiculed. JUDGMENT DAY. It was obvious that my loving women was dangerous, and that this loving was clearly under attack (though the attack was not unfamiliar to me). That I live, with my family, differently, at the margins, without social approval, with fear, without safeness, was not to be found on the state agenda. That I REFUSE to service man/men sexually, physically, emotionally, did not matter.

LESBIANS DIE   IMMORAL CONSPIRACY
KILL HOMOSEXUALS   STOP HOMOSEXUAL UNITY
THEY DON'T PRODUCE: THEY SEDUCE[13]

Below me, I could see / feel that the "state" was neither a neutral nor an abstract entity. "It" was not a mechanical apparatus separate from and outside of me. Here, I learned that the state was not a mysterious lurking monster, though most of the 125 embodied and articulating properties of this particular element of state organization appeared grotesquely monstrous to me. More gradually, I realized that each member present was infused with the power necessary to accomplish pieces of the organization of my own everyday, ordinary life. In effect, my lesbian life was being managed, administered, and ruled, largely by "the sons of educated men" right before my horrified eyes.[14]

I wonder now whether the members assembled for the Bill 7 debate were not stupefied by the ordinariness of the lesbians and gay men present, perched as we were in the galleries – by the ways we sat, composed, clothed, heterogeneous in composition. I sensed that every time one such politician unofficially stole a glance towards the galleries, he (or she) expected to view a full-blown orgy: lesbians and gay men fucking each other indiscriminately, without pause. Sweaters and skirts, pussy juices / semen and high-pitched obscenities flying. AIDS-in-the-making. Lesbians and gay men "flaunting it." Each unapologetically, unreservedly coming on to her / his neighbour. Gay men fucking the animals (pigs? dogs? goats?) or children they cleverly managed to sneak in. Someone passing around a "homosexual" sign up / on / in sheet; someone else still, discreetly selling buttons: THE FUTURE IS FEMALE; TALL, DYKE AND HANDSOME; FUCK VANILLA – S / M IS WHERE IT'S AT.

How neatly the parliamentarians danced over and made invisible the labour, the energy, the anguish of committed lesbian and gay activists. How utterly simple to fully erase the identities of those who not only have fought and still fight within the context of a lesbian and gay liberation movement to have visions, but also wrestle with how to make these "do-able."

In all likelihood, the assembled legislators would not care to know that I am enabled (though only just) by my receipt of state-supplied funds to invent lesbian erotica within the confines of a state-funded educational institution and, deeper still, while nourished by those in my lesbian studies support group. Or that I am a collective member of *Rites*, a magazine for lesbian and gay liberation; or even that I continue to lobby against the Customs Canada seizure of lesbian- and gay-produced visual / textual matters.[15]

Certainly, my uncle, a Liberal cabinet minister and nine-year member of the provincial legislature, had no idea that for me his vote carried implications that stretched far beyond the hallowed chambers of Queen's Park. Not out to Uncle as a lesbian, I grappled for weeks before the debate with my desire to register with him my carefully forged arguments in support of the amendment. Of course, I had little knowledge of the extent to which my articulated position might influence my uncle. Still, I had something to say. Something important. And yet, I wavered.

Simply stated, I could have put forward liberal notions of "equality," "individual rights," "tolerance" and / or "justice." I could have said that I do and have done waged and non-waged work with lesbians and gay men. I could have said that I live under the same roof as four lesbians, in separate apartments. I could have said that a gay man runs a flower shop and a lesbian sells fruit at the end of my street. I may have been able to say that I have *one* gay friend. However, in the final instance, the announcement – I AM LESBIAN – made without hedging, was not one I was prepared to utter on the telephone, in a letter, or in a meeting with my uncle. And I decided that there was no way I could argue for the amendment with integrity, with passion, without making my lesbian self known. Or without describing in detail the limitations of this particular piece of legislation, firstly in relation to my everyday lived reality, and then more generally in relation to the lives of many lesbians and gay men. Fearful and anxious, I knew I needed to define more fully the conditions under which I explicated my lived difference/s. In the hands of others, on occasion, this information has been used against me. I knew I needed to have more control over what went forward.

So I did not contact my uncle before the vote. Once again, embattled, I felt compelled to practise silence. For those of us-lesbians who were in the galleries on the days of the debate, and at the Lesbian and Gay Rights Rally in Toronto on the eve of November 20, 1986, and for those who struggle visibly and relentlessly for lesbian and gay liberation, I know there are countless dykes (and fags) who made and will continue to make the decision to practise silence.

A Necessary But Not Sufficient Victory
The amendment "prohibiting discrimination against homosexuals" did pass in the House (64-45) on the evening of December 2, 1986.[16] At the sweet historic moment – when the verdict was handed down / up – those persons relegated to the "public" galleries spontaneously combusted: I and other lesbians and gay men alike exploded out of our seats and engaged in sustained, illegal, and very animated applause: hooting and hollering and hugging and some weeping. Making our appearance, our political force, our difference / s known, we stood up to be counted, to insist that we matter. And then, we

left, we filed out one by one and proceeded to pick up the momentarily suspended struggle called our lives.

Much attention in mainstream media was paid to the "courage" demonstrated by the legislators in voting for the sexual orientation amendment.[17] As models of social justice, they were seen to possess the ability to hear the voice of the people, and to vote with their consciences, their hearts. I've asked myself since: "Did these official House representatives genuinely, honestly, believe that one single, social action, one single moment, one amendment to an amendment, would make it 'all right' and would somehow not only legislate liberty, but also ensure its realization?" Of course, they could not possibly be this naive.

Teetering on the edge of my seat in the House, my heart stopped for the briefest instant before my uncle voted in favour of the amendment. Despite knowing this tiny kernel of information, my knowing he mouthed "aye," I knew it would not make the prospect of coming out to my biological family members any less troublesome. In the least.

Undeniably, the passing of Bill 7, Section 18, marks a tiny step forward. My body still trembles violently when I contemplate the depth and magnitude of our lesbian and gay fury had this Bill *not* passed. In theory, it protects lesbians and gay men in areas of wage employment, housing, and public services, though each group may experience this protection differently. With respect to paid employment gay men have much more to gain than lesbians: they are more likely to be employed in positions with benefits such as health and dental insurance and drug plans, which can then be extended to partners. In general, gay men are more likely to purchase "family" memberships at clubs and community centres. They are more likely to buy life insurance (though AIDS testing may increasingly discourage this) and to take advantage of tax benefits, inheritance rights, and pension plans for surviving partners. Moreover, the organization and launching of court cases will more likely be pursued by gay men.[18] In sum, gay men will continue to be more economically advantaged than lesbians, who for the most part will continue to have more to lose. And not to forget, after all is said and done, there are endless ways that those wielding power (employers, property owners, social service providers, judges, police officers, army personnel, and so on) can and will circumvent this piece of protective legislation, on the basis of other grounds.

On another level, the Bill could catalyse the intensification of homophobic suspicion and more concerted physical and psychological harassment of lesbians and gay men on the streets, in the workplace, in the media, and elsewhere.[19] More visible, vocal, organized, and defiant lesbian and gay resistance may also mean more easily targeted homophobic and heterosexist attacks. A much less publicized decision was made by these championed lawmakers *not* to include sexual orientation in the harassment sections of the Ontario Human Rights Code. And, clearly, increased incidents of brutal lesbian / gay bashing and the mushrooming of a highly organized conservative backlash will not likely be stamped out or even curtailed by the adoption of this anti-discrimination Bill.[20]

Indeed, in relation to dominant state formation, this contradictory piece of state action does not carry the power to effect radical social change despite its apparently revolutionary character; and as such, does not in any significant way challenge entrenched liberal-democratic state authority. As an expression of state-interested accommodation, legal reform does not and cannot operate to root out and challenge the dominance of deep heterosexist and homophobic assumptions. In this way, legislative change is a necessary but wholly insufficient objective of many progressive movements.

Yet, all in all, I celebrate the passing of Bill 7, Section 18, as a victory, however conditional. Ever critically conscious, I remain mindful that fear and hatred of lesbians and gay men will continue to steep in the guts of most.

Notes

1. The official intention of Section 18 and all other sections of Bill 7 was to make Ontario statutes conform to Section 15 of the federal Charter of Rights and Freedoms. The amendment to prohibit discrimination against lesbians and gay men was only one part of the larger bill, known officially as the Equality Rights Statute Law Amendment Act. Other areas covered in the bill include the rights of disabled persons, pregnant women, psychiatric patients, and the banning of adult-only apartment buildings and condominiums. In the federal Charter of Rights and Freedoms, there is no explicit protection against the discrimination of lesbians and gay men.

2. CGRO's first brief to the Ontario Legislature, "The Ontario Human Rights Omission: A Brief to the Members of the Ontario Legislature," was released in June 1981 in response to the exclusion of lesbians and gay men from protection under the new Ontario Human Rights Code, introduced in the Ontario Legislature on April 24, 1981.

3. See Coalition for Gay Rights in Ontario (CGRO), "Discrimination Against

Lesbians and Gay Men: The Ontario Human Rights Omission: A Brief to the Members of the Ontario Legislature," Toronto, October 1986, p. 4. Here, I would like to register that the under-representation of lesbians in the Coalition (as well as the invisibility of lesbians more generally) is reflected in the abundance of materials documenting gay male experience.

4. CGRO, "Discrimination," p. 4. For a more detailed history of gay male organizing in Canada, see Gary Kinsman, *The Regulation of Desire: Sexuality in Canada* (Montreal: Black Rose Books, 1987).

5. On the second day of open House debate, Noble Villeneuve, PC member from Stormont-Dundas-Glengarry, argued strongly against the passage of Bill 7 Section 18, stating that a ban on discrimination against homosexuals in Quebec had precipitated a fall in the province's birthrate, once the highest in Canada. This remark provoked snickers from the Liberal and New Democratic Party benches, among other constituencies.

6. These quotes were all recorded during the debate in the legislature and can be found in the *Instant Hansards*: George McCague, L-1620-1 Dec. 1, 1986; Nicolas Leluk, L-1505-1 Dec. 2, 1986 and L-1520-1 Dec. 2, 1986; Cam Jackson, L-1635-1 Dec. 2, 1986; Jack Pierce, L-1635-1 Dec. 1, 1986; David Peterson, L-1750-1, Dec. 2, 1986.

7. For a fuller discussion of compulsory heterosexuality as a powerful political institution and a cornerstone of patriarchal social organization, see Adrienne Rich's essay, "Compulsory Heterosexuality and Lesbian Existence," *Signs*, Vol. 5, No. 4, Summer 1980, pp. 631-660. Also see Carole Vance (ed.), *Pleasure and Danger: Exploring Female Sexuality* (Boston: Routledge and Kegan Paul, 1984), and Ann Snitow, Christine Stansell and Sharon Thompson (eds.), *Powers of Desire: The Politics of Sexuality* (New York: Monthly Review Press, 1983); and Howard Buchbinder et al., *Who's on Top? The Politics of Heterosexuality* (Toronto: Garamond Press, 1987), pp. 13-46.

8. See Susan Fish's statement to the legislature, *Instant Hansard*: L-1750-1, Dec. 1, 1986.

9. See Anne Jones, *Women Who Kill* (New York: Holt, Rinehart and Winston, 1980), p. 287.

10. See Luce Irigaray, *Ce sexe qui n'en est pas un* (Paris: Minuit, 1977), translated by Catherine Porter as *This Sex Which is Not One* (Ithaca, New York: Cornell University Press, 1985).

11. See Annabel Faraday, "Liberating Lesbian Research." Kenneth Plummer, (ed.), *The Making of the Modern Homosexual* (London: Hutchinson, 1981), pp. 112-129.

12. To learn about the character of these differences, turn to Audre Lorde, *Sister Outsider: Essays and Speeches* (Trumansburg, New York: The

Crossing Press, 1984); Cherie Moraga and Gloria Anzaldua (eds.), *This Bridge Called My Back: Writings by Radical Women of Color* (Watertown, Massachusetts: Persephone Press, 1981); Mary Adelman (ed.), *Long Time Passing: The Lives of Older Lesbians* (Boston: Alyson Publications, 1986); Evelyn Torton Beck (ed.), *Nice Jewish Girls: A Lesbian Anthology* (Watertown, Massachusetts: Persephone Press, 1982); the collection of writings and graphics on lesbian s / m, *Coming To Power*, edited by members of Samois (Boston: Alyson Publications, 1987); and Lorna Weir and Eve Zaremba, "Boys and Girls Together: Feminism and Gay Liberation," *Broadside*, Vol. 4, No. 1, October 1982, pp. 6-7.

13. These "slogans" appeared on the placards carried by people at various anti-lesbian / gay demonstrations across the United States, and were filmed for the collectively produced u.s. video on lesbian violence, *Just Because of Who We Are* (1986). For more discussion of the video, see Mary Louise Adams's interview with collective member Abigail Norman in the July / August, 1987 issue of *Rites: for Lesbian and Gay Liberation*, p. 9.

14. This line is borrowed from Virginia Woolf's *Three Guineas* (New York: Harcourt, Brace and World, 1938; reprinted London: Penguin Books, 1977), pp. 70-71.

15. State regulation of lesbian printed and visual materials is explored more comprehensively in my article, "Launching Lesbian Cultural Offensives," *Resources for Feminist Research / Documentation sur la recherche feministe*, Vol. 17, No. 2, Spring 1988, pp. 15-19; and Marusia Bociurkiw, "Territories of the Forbidden: Lesbian Culture, Sex and Censorship," *Fuse*, No. 49, April 1988, pp. 27-32.

16. In July 1987, Manitoba's NDP government finally passed legislation to include sexual orientation protection in its Human Rights Code.

17. For instance, see, "Grossman Shows He is No Captive Leader," *Toronto Star*, Dec. 3, 1986.

18. Karen Andrews is a lesbian, Toronto library worker and union member who became embroiled in a legal battle to obtain Ontario health insurance coverage (OHIP) for her lover. With the emotional (but no longer financial) support of her union, the Canadian Union of Public Employees (CUPE), she appealed a February 1988 Ontario Supreme Court decision declaring that lesbian and gay couples have no legal right to equality in health care. For more information about Andrews's case, see articles in *Rites*, March, Vol. 4, No. 9 and April, Vol. 4, No. 10, 1988.

19. In an open letter to the Prime Minister, Alliance Against Abortion member Joe Borowski penned this statement: "The Homosexual version of a social order is unfettered lust, selfishness and unrestricted, perverted sexual orgies. They are the breeders and messengers of an incurable disease that is

as deadly as the bubonic plague." (Quoted in the CGRO brief to the Ontario Legislature, 1986.)

In the Toronto-published magazine *Contrast*, the "Dear Vera" columnist responded to a woman who was curious about the possibility of her lesbianism. "Vera" replied, "You are not mentally sick but some counselling from a psychiatrist or sex therapist would help. Tell your family doctor about what you feel and ask him or her to recommend one.... Try to enjoy your family more, as well. *The love of a good man would cure you quickly.*" (My emphasis.) *Contrast*, Jan. 28, 1987, p. 17.

A morally conservative sexual agenda that peddles (heterosexual) monogamy and celibacy as solutions to AIDS has been most coercively exercised in the quarantine legislation proposed in British Columbia (see the November / December 1987 issue of *Rites*, p. 6), in the tear-gassing of a man with AIDS by the police in Toronto, and the statement made by the Canadian Medical Association that confidentiality can be broken in AIDS cases (see the September 1987 issue of *Rites*, p. 4 and p. 5).

In England, Section 28 of an omnibus bill passed by the House of Lords in May 1988 prohibits any local authority from "the intentional promotion of homosexuality." For more discussion of the implications of this law, see Gillian Rodgerson, "Forward to Yesteryear," in *X-Tra!*, No. 95, February 26, 1988. In Canada, the Secretary of State's Women's Program introduced official funding guidelines that render ineligible all individuals and groups who intend to promote a view on sexual orientation. For an analysis of this legislation, see Becki Ross, "The Secretary of State's Regulation of Lesbian Existence," *Resources for Feminist Research / Documentation sur la recherche feministe*, Vol. 17, No. 3, December 1988, pp. 21-24.

20. Hostility and oppression are not automatically erased by legal protection, as evident in the ongoing battles of those people oppressed by the conditions of white supremacy and religious intolerance.

10

Aristotle, Sex, and a Three-Legged Dog

The Naturalness of Lesbian Sex

Joan Blackwood

THOSE WHO TRY to discredit lesbian sex most often use one of two types of arguments. They claim that lesbian sex is not real (that is, natural) sex at all and that real sex involves, almost by definition, a male and a female; or that lesbian sex is real sex, but it is immoral. Each of these arguments, I believe, is manifestly weak. Indeed, lesbian sex not only fulfils the criteria for real sex, but there is also very little that can be said in its moral condemnation.

I concentrate on lesbianism rather than homosexuality in general for two reasons. First, lesbian sexual activity need not involve any of the female reproductive organs, whereas male sexual activity necessarily involves the male reproductive organ. This difference poses interesting problems as well as powerful support for my position.

My second reason for concentrating on the lesbian issue is less philosophical. It is simply that the vast majority of information written about homosexuality is written about men. Even in a time of supposed increasing awareness of women's issues, the average "person on the street" understands little about lesbianism. This is, perhaps, accounted for by the masculinist assumptions of our society and the concomitant belief that the norm is always male. Certainly the social construction of sexuality privileges men as subjects and relegates women to objects, primarily of the male sexual gaze.

Much has been written, of late, about the social construction of sexuality. As a result, the practice of some philosophers of beginning an analysis of an idea or concept by examining the way we talk about it is seen by many as at best quaint, at worst self-defeatingly ideological. Though in many respects I agree with this criticism, I am also convinced through my own lived experience that it is not only sticks and stones that can do me an injury; but words can also hurt me, particularly words that can be used by hostile groups or individuals to justify harassing me at work or on the street, jeopardizing my peace of mind, or even threatening my possibilities for employment or accommodation in places where those basic rights are not protected by law (or even where they are). For these reasons it is important to examine the way words such as "unnatural," "abnormal," and "immoral" are used against lesbians, and to try to find ways of countering the damage that such words can do.

In dealing with the arguments against lesbian sex, I deal primarily with arguments from nature, since most people turn to nature in one of its many forms to try to discount lesbian activity. This is true for both the conceptual and moral arguments.

A: Lesbian Sex is not Real Sex

When saying that lesbian sex is not real sex, people usually mean that there is something inherent in what we call sex that precludes lesbian activity; that by its very nature, sex is heterosexual.[1] A strong support for this idea comes from Aristotle's treatment of nature in the *Metaphysics*, and although Aristotle's ideas are not the basis of all my arguments, they do offer a good beginning.

According to Aristotle's fifth definition of nature, anything that is made of natural matter but does not have the appropriate form cannot be natural. Because he uses the example of "animals and their parts," a dog is a good example of what he has in mind.[2] A dog is made up of parts: legs, head, body, tail, various internal organs, and so on. It is not enough, however, for the animal to possess these parts. The parts must be in a particular order; the animal must have a particular form. Thus it is in the *nature* of a dog to have four legs. Although four-leggedness does not adequately and completely describe the nature of dog (that is, it is not a sufficient condition), still it is generally conceded that being four-legged is part of the nature of that creature called dog. That there are dogs with only three legs does not mean that four-leggedness ceases to be a criterion of dog, or that "or three-legged" should be added to the definition.

To find out what form is appropriate to a "natural object," Aristotle looks to the particular instances of that object, arguing that the forms are perceivable only in the particulars. In the case of the dog, after observing a certain number of creatures called dogs, one notices that, on the whole, they have four legs. A three-legged dog, because it has only three legs, deviates from the nature of dog.

A similar argument can be applied to sexual activity. Modern sex research tells us that approximately 90 per cent of the population *identify* as heterosexual, and so heterosexual sex is taken to be natural. This puts lesbian sex in an analogous (though not identical) position to the three-legged dog: it deviates from the nature of sex. Thus, sex is spoken of as *heterosexual* sex. That there are instances of lesbian sex does not change the "fact" that, on this theory, sex is, by nature, *hetero*sexual.

There are problems with this sort of argument when it is used to deny lesbian sex its identity as real sex. First, it is not clear that *natural* is the same as *real* (note that I am talking about what constitutes *sex*, not what constitutes *sexual intercourse*). In terms of the dog analogy, I am interested in what constitutes the concept *dog*, not what constitutes the concept *Cocker Spaniel*. Although it is reasonable to say of a Schnauzer to whom long silky ears have been attached, "That's not a real Cocker Spaniel," it makes much less sense to say of a three-legged canine, "That's not a real dog." By the same token, we can be perfectly willing to agree that lesbian sex is not "real sexual intercourse" without conceding the necessity to deny that it is "real sex." Just as a three-legged dog does not become a milking stool simply because it has three legs, or give up any identity it may have and become a nothing, so lesbian sex retains its identity as real sex.

We can now ask whether the fact that lesbian sex is *different* from heterosexual sex has moral implications.

B: Lesbian Sex is Immoral

There lingers in contemporary society an intuition that lesbian sex is deviant and, because deviant, immoral. Thus, the arguments against lesbianism on moral grounds often depend on some notion of *nature* or what is *natural*.

There is, in much ethical thinking, a distrust of the attempt to derive ought from is and a denial that it can be done. However, the unnatural-therefore-bad argument is so prevalent in the popular culture that I am going to take it seriously. The first step is to determine what is meant by *nature* and whether this can be used as the basis for a moral judgment.

Christine Pierce in "Natural Law Language and Women" distinguished four different senses of the concept nature:

(1) Nature is that which is untouched by human intervention.
(2) Nature in the sense of *human* nature is everything that human beings do.
(3) Nature in the sense of *human* nature is that which we have in common with animals.
(4) Nature in the sense of *human* nature is that which distinguishes us from animals.[3]

On the basis of the first definition of nature as "untouched by human intervention," those who oppose lesbian sex judge it to be unnatural since, they claim, it does not occur where human beings have not intervened, and anything that does not occur in a state free from human intervention is unnatural and by extension (they say) immoral. This is a contentious argument based on the outdated claim that homosexual activity between animals occurs only in captivity (that is, where humans have intervened). More and more, however, we are presented with evidence that points to the occurrence in the wild of homosexual behaviour in animals (for example, lesbian relationships among seagulls). As well, the argument as presented puts us in the position of calling into moral question many things necessary for or conducive to our continued (comfortable) existence. An umbrella, something that does not occur in a state free from human intervention, thus becomes unnatural. Can what is unnatural based on this definition also be judged immoral?

Many things are not natural in this first sense of the term, but are at least morally neutral and often morally good. For example, umbrellas and furniture are morally neutral, yet they are the result of human intervention in "nature." Also, writing and, by extension, reading, other examples of human intervention, are generally considered to be morally good. The first definition of *nature*, therefore, does not present "a coherent basis for normative judgments."[4]

The second definition of (human) nature as "everything that human beings do" poses no problem for lesbianism. With this definition, lesbian sex is quite natural. This definition also provides no basis for moral judgment of human behaviour, because it justifies any human action.

Consideration of the third and fourth definitions of *nature* produces two questions: Is lesbian sex unnatural based on either of these definitions, and are these definitions sufficient to justify a moral judgment?

Definition (3), nature as that which we have in common with animals, forms the basis of one of the most common arguments against lesbianism – the reproductive model of sexuality. With this model, the natural end of sexual activity is reproduction. Therefore, any sexual activity that is not of the reproductive sort is unnatural. There are two problems with this. The first is the vagueness of the expression "the natural end of sexual activity," which could be interpreted in two ways:

(a) Nature intends sex to be reproductive;
(b) Sex is the only activity that ends in reproduction; therefore we can assume that sex is, by nature, reproductive.

As Christine Pierce points out, it is difficult to know the meaning of the claim that nature intends something to happen. "We know what it means to say that 'I intend to pack my suitcase,' but what sense can it make to say that nature intends for us to do one thing rather than another?"[5]

If nature cannot easily be said to *intend* sexual activity to be reproductive, then perhaps I can turn to the more Aristotelian second interpretation, which says that it is in the nature of sexual activity to be reproductive. Therefore, any sexual activity that is not reproductive is unnatural. But this raises a second problem (quite apart from the problems discussed with respect to the Aristotelian concept of nature).

First, developments in reproductive technology have made it possible for us to accomplish the reproductive function without engaging in the mechanics of heterosexual sex. Technologies such as artificial insemination and *in vitro* fertilization have in our time made false the claim that only sexual activity ends in reproduction. However, to base a defence of lesbian sex on the grounds of reproductive technology means that only latter-day lesbians have their sexuality justified. If we are not to abandon lesbians of earlier times, we must look for a broader-based argument.

To that end, let us examine the claim that sex that is not reproductive is unnatural. On the strictest interpretation, this means that any instance of sexual activity which does not, as a matter of fact, prove to be reproductive can be considered unnatural. This means that not even those engaging in the so-called "natural" act of heterosexual intercourse can know *beforehand* whether a *particular* sex act will be "natural." As well, heterosexual intercourse using some form of birth control is deemed unnatural, because birth control interferes with the "natural end" of sexuality. (Of course, there are those who *do* think that birth control is unnatural, and for them this last statement will not have the ring of absurdity that I intend it to have.)

To counter this objection, it is possible to make the criterion for the naturalness of sex the *potential* for reproduction. This, however, comes equipped with its own problems. This view requires dismissing as unnatural heterosexual intercourse by or with a woman past childbearing age. Even the staunchest supporter of the reproductive model of sexual activity would be hard pressed to accept the consequences of the consistent application of this view.

If these criticisms are acknowledged, then those who still wish to prevent lesbian sex from being accepted as natural on a biological basis are forced into one of two positions: first, of arguing that heterosexual sex is natural simply because it involves a male and a female participant, which begs the question and amounts to saying that heterosexual sex is natural simply because it is heterosexual (where the issue is: *what makes heterosexuality natural?*); or, second, of saying that "non-reproductive sex could still be 'natural' provided it is the sort of intercourse that could lead to procreation *were conditions normal.*"[6] Russell Vannoy points out in *Sex Without Love* that this is more difficult to counter because, on these terms, lesbian activity can never be "normal" in this way. Vannoy explains, however, that this is not a telling criticism of non-reproductive heterosexual activity because "It would mean that a female who is in a temporarily non-reproductive cycle is somehow abnormal."[7] Also, he says, a woman's fertile periods are really quite brief when compared to the years of her life when she cannot bear children. The *were conditions normal* argument means that a woman is abnormal for the majority of her life.

If this argument does not hold up in a heterosexual context, it is hard to see how (or why) it can be used tellingly against lesbian sexuality. To argue the unnaturalness of lesbian sex on these grounds means agreeing that a woman is abnormal most of her life.

Although the charges of unnaturalness leveled against lesbian sexual activity cannot be supported by an appeal to a reproductive model of sexuality, we can still ask what relevance arguments about this sort of naturalness have to the moral realm.

Suppose that moral judgments *can* be made on the basis of naturalness, and that naturalness is defined as that which we hold in common with animals. What follows? In the first place, homosexual behaviour has been observed in the animal kingdom all the way from apes to guinea pigs (I have kept guinea pigs and can attest to this from personal observations).[8] The inference is either that homosexual activity is thereby justified, or that animals are acting immorally, which is an odd assessment to make of "a realm to which moral vocabulary does not [ordinarily] apply."[9]

Christine Pierce explains the second difficulty with this argument from nature:

> [This] use of "natural" reduces to saying "this is what most animals do." To the extent that this is the meaning of the term, it will be hard to get a notion of value out of it. The fact that something happens a lot does not argue for or against it.[10]

The tendency to ascribe a positive value to that which "most people do" simply "illustrates a prejudice for the statistically prevalent as opposed to the unusual.... The unusual *qua* unusual cannot be ruled out as bad; it can be alternately described as 'deviant' or 'original,' depending on whether or not we like it."[11]

Finally, one can call into question the very practice of evaluating human behaviour by what animals do. There are many animal behaviours which, if practised by humans, would be distinctly odd. One thinks, for instance, of the habits some dogs have of baying at the moon or eating excrement. Though quite natural behaviours for the dogs, such behaviour in humans would be distressing indeed.

It seems that no argument involving this claim – that what is natural is what we as human beings share with the animal kingdom – will support the ideas either that lesbianism is unnatural or that it is immoral. I now turn to the fourth definition of nature: that which distinguishes us from animals.

Traditionally, the human capacity to reason is thought to separate human beings from animals. How does human reason impact on the realm of human sexuality? Our human capacity to reason makes it possible for us to distinguish between *reproduction* and *sexuality* and to act on a variety of stimuli and motivations. As a broad generalization, people tend to engage in certain actions (or refrain from engaging) because these actions produce consequences that they want to maximize (or minimize). Thus, people engage in voluntary sexual activity because it produces consequences that they want to maximize. Sometimes these consequences are reproductive, but not all sexual activity is undertaken with a view to reproduction. Another consequence of sexual activity is pleasure.

Much traditional philosophy has held that pleasure is a passion that human beings hold in common with animals and, therefore, pleasure does not distinguish human behaviour from animal behaviour. Concerning sexuality, however, it is not merely the experience of pleasure that is the distinguishing feature of human sexual expression. At issue is the human capacity to seek out and engage in sexual activity solely for the sake of pleasure. The maximization of pleasure is the *reason* to engage in sexual activity, not simply a by-product of it. And where sex is engaged in for pleasure, the degree and quality of the pleasure produced becomes a criterion for the evaluation of the activity itself.

Before dealing with the concept of pleasure as applied to lesbian sexual relations, I will examine pleasure as it relates to so-called "natural" heterosexual activity. For men, the reproductive organ and the sexual organ (that is, the organ whose stimulation produces sexual pleasure) are one and the same: the penis. Therefore, heterosexual intercourse serves men as both a reproductive and a pleasurable activity. In women, however, the reproductive organs (vagina, uterus, ovaries) and the sexual organ (clitoris) are separate. Heterosexual intercourse, though adequate for reproduction, may be completely inadequate for producing sexual pleasure in women. To the extent that women engage in sexual behaviour to maximize sexual pleasure, heterosexual intercourse, where it does not produce (or produces less) pleasure for women, is a failed activity, in that the intentions of one of the participants were not accomplished. (This situation *can* be remedied within a heterosexual context but suffice it to say here that, in our patriarchal world, women's sexual pleasure is not taken seriously enough by enough men to warrant a reorganization of heterosexual relations.)[12]

When the pleasure component of sexual relations is taken seriously and women's experience of sex is focused on, it becomes clear, as Karen Rotkin explains:

> Since the clitoris is the centre of female sexual response, the phallus is less relevant to female sexuality than is a finger or a tongue, either of which is a more effective stimulator of the clitoris than a penis could possibly be.... We can stimulate ourselves or be stimulated by other

women *as well as* men can stimulate us because that unique male offering, the phallus, is of peripheral importance, or may even be irrelevant, to our sexual satisfaction.[13]

In other words, on the grounds of pleasure, lesbian sex, with its emphasis on clitoral stimulation as the focus of "the act," is at least as rational and, therefore, natural (in the human sense) as heterosexual sex. It may, in fact, be more so.

This reasoning is disconcerting to those who find lesbianism puzzling or offensive. Though acknowledging that pleasure is an important motivation for sexual activity, some people take up a modified reproductive position that widespread acceptance of lesbianism would threaten the continuation of the species. Michael Levin uses this concern as the basis for arguing that the traditional mode of male/active-female/passive sexual behaviour be retained. He claims that if neither men nor women were aggressive, there would be no sexual activity. But:

> If both were [aggressors] either nothing but mating would happen, or, more probably, the similarity of the mating behaviour of the sexes would deprive members of one sex of the grounds for pursuing the opposite sex rather than their own, and homosexuality would wipe the species out.[14]

It is flattering to lesbians that some people think lesbianism is sufficiently attractive to all women to win everyone over (why hasn't it, then?), but this shows a lack of understanding of the issues. To argue, as I have, that lesbian sexuality is conceptually and morally legitimate is not to recommend that all women become lesbians. Nor is the prospect of more women coming out as lesbians in the face of the growing legitimacy of that lifestyle any threat to the continuation of the species. Even if all women became lesbians, there are, after all, lesbian mothers.

The disentanglement of human sexuality from reproduction makes possible the acceptance of lesbian sex as real (or conceptually legitimate) sex, opening the door to a consideration of other criteria for naturalness in sexuality, including, but not limited to, pleasure.

The two major objections to the acceptance of lesbian sex – that it is not real sex, and that it is immoral – are often based on some moral concept of *natural*. Yet the *nature* of human sexuality – like the nature of most other things in the world – is sufficiently flexible to accommodate variations in the number and sex of the participants.[15]

The question of the morality of lesbian sex is more complicated, especially when approached from a naturalistic perspective. Though it has long been recognized that there is no particular connection between "naturalness" and moral goodness, many critics persist in believing that what is "unnatural" is immoral. "Unnatural acts" – an expression that in contemporary society has an almost exclusively sexual connotation – thus become "bad acts." Therefore there is a component of pleasure in the nature of human sexual interaction that both motivates sexual interaction and acts as a criterion for judging it. On these grounds, a sexual interaction that produces more (or more intense) sexual pleasure is better than an interaction that produces less, or better than an interaction that produces pleasure for one participant and pain or harm to another. Regarding women's sexual pleasure, lesbian sex produces (or has the potential to produce) as much (and perhaps more) pleasure for women as heterosexual intercourse. On the grounds of pleasure, therefore, lesbian sex is, or can be, *at least as good* as heterosexual sex.

Some will find my reasoning unpersuasive. Some hold ethical theories that find pleasure, or the lack thereof, morally extraneous. Where sex is concerned, I disagree fundamentally and, probably, irremediably with them. Others might admit that sexual pleasure is *desirable* but hesitate to say that it is *morally* good. This presents no practical problem since they can be persuaded of the legitimacy of lesbian sex on the grounds that it promotes the satisfaction of (harmless) human desires. Still others may be hostile to the use of reason to decide moral issues, feeling that intuition or divine guidance is the preferred method for deciding moral issues. I have not written this for them. But for those who are interested in countering everyday objections to lesbian sexuality and lifestyle, I hope I have offered something practical and useful.

Notes

1. Many people are clear about the meaning and use of the term *homosexuality* but are puzzled by the term *heterosexuality*. It took me a little while to realize that the puzzlement resulted from a world view in which heterosexuality just *is* sex.

2. Aristotle, *Metaphysics*, trans. W.D. Ross (Oxford: The Clarendon Press, 1960), 1014b 35-1015a 10.
3. Christine Pierce, "Natural Law Language and Women" in Jane English (ed.), *Sex Equality* (Englewood Cliffs, N.J.: Prentice Hall, 1977), p. 133.
4. Ibid.
5. Ibid.
6. Russell Vannoy, *Sex Without Love: A Philosophical Inquiry* (Buffalo: Prometheus, 1980), p. 35.
7. Ibid.
8. Del Martin and Phyllis Lyon, *Lesbian / Woman* (New York: Bantam Books, 1972), p. 86.
9. Pierce, p. 133.
10. Ibid., pp. 133-134.
11. Ibid.
12. See Karen Rotkin, "The Phallacy of our Sexual Norm," in *RT: A Journal of Radical Therapy*, Vol. 3, No. 1, September 1972, for a perceptive treatment of this issue.
13. Rotkin, "The Phallacy," p. 157.
14. Michael Levin, "Vs. Ms.," in English (ed.), *Sex Equality*, p. 218.
15. For a more in-depth treatment of the nature of human sexuality, see: Thomas Nagel, "Sexual Perversion," and Sara Ruddick, "Better Sex," both in Robert Baker and Frederick Elliston (eds.), *Philosophy and Sex*, 2nd ed. (Buffalo: Prometheus, 1984); also Alan Goldman, "Plain Sex," Robert Solomon, "Sexual Paradigms," and Sara Ann Ketchum, "The Good, the Bad and the Perverted: Sexual Paradigms Revisited," all in Alan Soble (ed.), *Philosophy of Sex* (Totowa, N.J.: Rowman and Allanheld, 1980).

I I

Outsiders on The Inside

Lesbians in Canadian Academe

Jeri Dawn Wine

LESBIANS ARE, by definition, marginal beings. Their experience is denied and erased by the assumptions that underlie malestream "knowledge." In the academic environment lesbians encounter a tension between instances of silencing and prejudice on the one hand and, on the other, positive possibilities offered by feminist and gay-positive professors and courses.

I am intrigued by the unique dialectic of problems and possibilities presented by the academic environment, partly because I am going through the terrifying yet profoundly exciting process of "coming out" as a lesbian in academia – a process that has occurred in tandem with my developing feminist consciousness. I don't wish to be overly optimistic about the positive potential for lesbians in academia. Feminist scholars have amply documented its androcentrism and lesbian scholars its heterosexism. There does exist there, however, at least a pocket of potential that does not exist elsewhere in the world, with the possible exceptions of some feminist organizations and some areas of the arts. In order to explore these issues I interviewed twenty-one women who were either students or instructors in Canadian post-secondary institutions.[1]

In this work I make no claims for being "objective" and "unbiased." Indeed, I am extremely suspicious of research on lesbian and gay issues that does purport to be. I might most accurately be considered not just the researcher but the twenty-second participant in the study. My aim is to give voice to these women, but my own voice is clearly woven throughout.

The experiences of these women are quite varied. They came to see themselves as lesbian at ages ranging from thirteen to thirty-eight years old, and they arrived at their lesbian identities by very different paths. Several had experienced periods of being intimately involved with women, interspersed with involvements with men. They differ in whether they had a loving, sensual relationship with another woman before or after coming to describe themselves as lesbian. Several had two or three such relationships before coming to accept the label. Others came to the realization that seeing themselves as lesbian helped to make sense of their lives personally and politically prior to any sexually loving relationship with another woman. Almost all of them had felt deep attraction to women, sometimes for many years, before they identified as lesbian. Many have had considerable sexual experience with men, including marriage, which in some cases has reflected genuine heterosexual attraction. Often, their experiences with men were a desperate bid to cling to heterosexual privilege, to avoid self-labelling and societal (family, friends, school, work) disapproval.

Common to most of them is that this has been a very difficult, painful process; most have gone through a private hell while coming to terms with their lesbian identity and with their existence as lesbians in the world. The sources of that pain and difficulty are heterosexist society's almost total silence around lesbian existence, and complete lack of supports for women going through this difficult process. Paradoxically, as that identity was accepted and they entered into the coming out process by revealing their lesbian identities to other people, the potential for integrating their personal, intimate existence and their public self became possible. That experience was simultaneously profoundly exciting, joyful, and terrifying.

A variety of features of the academic setting bear on this process. Some negative ones are the almost seamless heterosexist assumptions permeating academic knowledge and the accompanying silence around lesbian existence. When the silence is lifted homophobia may be revealed, even in academe. Positive features are those that lift the veil of silence and do so in a supportive manner; in academe this occurs especially in the context of feminist studies. The women reported that they have been able to integrate their private and public selves as a result of the supports provided by exposure to lesbians secure and positive in their own identity, by connecting with other lesbians as supports, especially other students grappling with the same issues, by being exposed to positive lesbian literature whether in or out of academic course content, by exposure to feminist studies, especially with lesbian-positive feminist professors, whether they be lesbian or heterosexual.

Problems

Lesbians encounter a variety of problems in academe, perhaps the most pervasive and formidable being its intense heterosexism. For most of the students academia has been almost entirely silent on lesbian and gay issues. With the exception of women's studies courses, none of the students could recall more than one or two instances of lesbian and gay topics being included in course content or class discussion. The omnipresence of the heterosexist assumptions that everyone is and should be heterosexual and the consequent erasure of lesbian and gay experience are evident in these statements:

I would say that the silence is really profound.

Nothing ever. Zero.

It wasn't an issue in any of the classes that I was in. It didn't come up.

It [the sexual orientation of authors] was not raised; it never is. You find out later, if at all.

Explicit and active prejudice against lesbians and gays was infrequently experienced in the academic setting, though there were some exceptions. Perhaps the most extreme set of experiences with homophobia was reported by one of the students who had been an undergraduate in a small denominational college on a large campus. She had revealed her lesbian identity in a sociology class in which homosexuality was under discussion. She was subsequently subjected to considerable verbal harassment by male students both in and out of the classroom. This was accompanied by more subtle devaluation by the male instructor in the class; for instance, a failure to see her raised hand in class discussions, or dismissal of her contributions as inappropriate or invalid. This was a stressful period in her life and she began seeing a psychiatrist for therapy at the university health services. After several sessions, she revealed her lesbian identity to the psychiatrist and was promptly psychiatrically hospitalized.

Another student described the instructor of a course on sexuality that she had taken before her perception of herself as lesbian:

> He was very bad and he was a homophobic and he told us right at the beginning he couldn't deal with it, and that if we wanted to deal with it in the course then he would have to get somebody in to guest lecture.

More frequently than outright homophobia, the attitude students have encountered when gay or lesbian issues are discussed in classes is that of the apparently well-meaning, but ill-informed and heterosexist professor: he mentions homosexuality but negates any positive potential through heterosexist assumptions such as attempting to explain homosexuality but not heterosexuality. For example, one of the students entered a prolonged discussion in a psychology class about the causes of homosexuality:

> So I pointed out that if it was perfectly okay what our sexual orientation was why should there be all this hubbub? Why are people so concerned that if you do this you might turn out with someone who is homosexual? If we really thought it was a good thing, or at least as good a thing as being heterosexual we wouldn't be so concerned about it. Why are we looking at it that way?

Other apparently well-meaning professors negate potentially gay or lesbian-positive statements by disassociating themselves from their content. For example:

> ... making sure that she's not personally identified as a lesbian. Don't you even *dare* think that!

Or by mentioning a lesbian / gay issue briefly and inappropriately, such as the professor who in a lecture on sexuality brought up male homosexuality in the last five minutes of the class, and lesbianism in the last two minutes in the context only of lesbian sadomasochism.

Among the instructors, only one had concrete knowledge of an incident in which her lesbianism almost resulted in a negative consequence to her academic career. She had been out of the country on study leave when her dean:

> was told by someone who purported to have read my mail that I was a lesbian.... he called the recruitment committee and said, "Professor —— is a lesbian so we have to think about getting a replacement for her." ... The issue didn't really ripen because one of the members of the faculty took strong exception to this whole line and confronted the dean, told him that he thought it was an unacceptable reaction. So that by the time I got back there was nothing done and nothing said.

She would never have learned of the incident had the male colleague who defended her not chosen to tell her. Though the other instructors did not have concrete knowledge of specific incidents in which knowledge of their lesbianism had negative repercussions on their careers, several did not have their contracts renewed or were not granted tenure. One of them stated:

> If they think that "We don't want her here because she's a queer," they can think of other reasons. That's the level on which that kind of thing operates. If people don't want you they can get rid of you. They would never say that was the reason.

The four women who now have tenure are certain that they would not have gotten it had they been doing academic work at the time of their tenure applications that obviously reflected a lesbian and, in some cases, even feminist vision. To one of the part-time instructors who is completing her Ph.D., the prospects do not appear to be good:

> We – as lesbians and feminists – more than other groups are in danger of losing or not getting jobs, because of who we are. Being lesbian feminist is a double-barrelled threat. So you ought to be prepared to dichotomize yourself and be something at work and something else at home, which isn't very satisfactory, or you reconcile yourself, as I think I have, to either very low participation in the university system or none at all.

Several women pointed to the academic environment's liberal-ism, which provides partial protection, but they also noted problems inherent in academic liberalism. Though liberalism does not describe the politics of all members of the academic community, it is shared by enough faculty to provide some protection for differing "lifestyles" and freedom of expression:

> People in academe tend to be of the sort of self-conscious lib-eral variety where they would rather die than actually admit that they were sexist or homophobic or anything like that. But they're being frightfully liberal through clenched teeth all the time.

The liberal attitude is "what you do in the privacy of your own bed-room is of no interest to me," an attitude resulting again in the silencing of lesbian experience. Lesbian experience is thus seen from the liberal viewpoint as entirely sexualized. It isn't recognized that being lesbian permeates one's entire existence, just as does being heterosexual. Several women pointed out that heterosexual liberals don't seem to realize how very frequently they "come out" as heterosexual in their interactions with other people, from the most informal interactions to the more public arena of the classroom.

One of the instructors spoke of academia's "mad liberalism," which treats every position as precisely equal and deserving. She referred to a *Body Politic* article by Marianna Valverde that devel-oped some of the implications of an extreme liberal position:

> It's perfectly all right for me to say, "I'm a human being, let me live like a human being. I don't want to be mistreated. I don't want to be ostracized." It's also all right for someone else to say, "But you're evil and you're awful, and you're terrible and you should be beaten up." The extreme liberal position is, "Now let's all be terribly liberal and discuss all of this in a sane manner." And presumably we'll all arrive at a compromise where I'm only half beaten up. That is the lunacy of the logic and of the kind of problem that arises.

In other words, the extreme liberal view is one that renders it impos-sible to examine the injustice of positions, to name oppressors and the oppressed.

Most of the instructors have, for at least a period of time, attempted to protect themselves and conceal their lesbian identities by keeping their private intimate lives and public academic lives separate. Most of them are aware of the immense personal toll taken by the secretiveness and deception involved in leading a closeted existence. One of the instructors who is most "closeted" in her academic position described her precarious existence as "One foot in the closet, the other on a banana peel." As well as involving a continuously high level of anxiety and fracturing the sense of self, leading such an existence grants tremendous power to anyone who might discover the truth:

> I feel that the more people are secretive, the more you seal your own self into those box cars for them to take you away.

Most feel that the liberalism of their academic settings will provide some protection for their "lifestyles" *if* they do not allow their lesbian experience to inform their teaching and productive work in obvious ways. Most of the instructors have occupied, at least for a time early in their academic careers, a position that might be called the "safe niche":

> I am careful to be out but not out, do you know what I mean? There's a sort of a little niche. You don't have to go around always protecting yourself because that's really uncomfortable, but you also aren't so visible that you rock any boats. In the safe niche, one is "out" to a circle of friends, to a few trusted colleagues, perhaps involved in feminist political work outside the academic environment. One may even cautiously introduce lesbian / gay content in the classroom. For example, I'd just do a sort of a balancing thing, like if you were talking about households, I'd point out that there were all kinds of households ... it could be any kind of people living together, women and women, men and men, married and not married. That kind of thing.

When occupying the safe niche one is not challenging the essential androcentrism and heterosexism of academia in a direct way. But simply introducing lesbian / gay content in the classroom in any fashion provides a chink in the heterosexist armour and may allow an opportunity to explore forbidden territory.

Six of the students had confronted lesbian / gay issues in the classroom, primarily in response to negative, inaccurate, or limited information presented by professors. For example, the student who described a homophobic professor of a sexuality course engaged in verbal battle with him throughout the course and wrote her course papers on lesbian sexuality. This was an important set of events in her lesbian identity process:

> It wasn't that I was defending anybody in the class, I was defending myself in some way. And then I started to think that that made sense of my life. It made sense of my experience. It made sense about my self, about people, about women. It made sense about feminist attitudes that I had, it just made sense. It was like the last piece of a jigsaw and all of a sudden it makes sense to you and there you are: of course, why didn't I think of this before?

The student who entered the psychology class discussion about the causes of homosexuality found that identification with an outsider position, especially in the conservative atmosphere of a typical psychology class, strengthened her sense of self. The effect that these actions had on their self-perceptions and on others' reactions to them was quite consistent. Taking a lesbian-positive stand was self-affirming, and often helped the student to make sense of her own life. In the case of the two examples of student confrontations, their actions in the classroom occurred *before* they had realized a lesbian identity, but were important events in that process.

Student-initiated classroom confrontations were rare among these students, even among those who had shown some courage in doing so. Most reacted to missing or negative information with silence. They sense that their experience is not legitimated in academe; they fear the possible consequences; and they are aware of the enormous power that professors exert in the classroom:

> It's very dangerous in the setup in the classroom; the professor has all the power. Even though they're only one person, they can lead the discussion any way they want.

Both students and instructors expressed fears that one of the consequences of appearing to be pro-gay was that others would be likely to view them as lesbian:

Any time that you deal with homosexuality in any way, especially in a positive way or take it into account as an example of prejudice or something like that you're biasing people to wonder if you're gay because most people won't talk about it.

Once they were believed to be gay by other people there was a sense of loss of credibility. One of the instructors was concerned that:

They can just dismiss it. Oh well, what do you expect from a dyke? Of course you'd defend them, you're one of them.

Several students expressed fear that with such invalidation professors might view them differently and their academic marks and futures might be negatively affected. Some of the instructors were concerned that they would be invalidated as sources of information about women, especially by heterosexual female students:

Once they categorize you they can say, "Oh, her problem is that she just never found a good man ... or she's anti-male," so that what it does is, it sort of sets you up in a certain place as "other" and lets them not really look at the issues in their own lives.

Possibilities

It is a far simpler task to delineate some of the difficulties facing lesbians in academe than it is to describe the potential for mediating the personal and political, the private and public existences of lesbian students and instructors. I've suggested that any reference to lesbian / gay issues in course content and in classroom discussion, however misguided, breaks the silence and creates some potential for mediation. The extent to which such potential is realized is very much dependent on the instructor, the atmosphere of the class, and the self-confidence and strength of the individual student. I had hoped to find that courses with gay male professors would provide a supportive atmosphere, but the students who had taken courses with identified gay male professors (only two) felt that the teachers had been quite anti-woman:

He *does not* like women and this is a known fact.... He wouldn't listen to us and he wouldn't recognize the women when they had their hands up.

The most consistently positive experiences were described in the context of women's studies courses and instructors, though until recent years the students' experience in women's studies has also been characterized by the erasure of lesbian existence. One of the women who had struggled with wanting to know more about lesbianism before identifying herself as lesbian said:

> I tentatively raised the topic of lesbianism at different points in one of the women's studies courses I took and I distinctly remember a very tense silence. I've come to associate a tense silence with bringing that up in the academic setting.... It was disappointing because it's what I really needed at the time.

Their experience in the last few years has been that women's studies courses are more consistently offering at least some opportunity for discussion of lesbian content in courses taught by both lesbian and heterosexual feminists. Reading lesbian-positive material was important to several women in developing an understanding of lesbianism as an option for them, and in beginning to integrate their private with their academic experiences. Most often, this happened in the context of feminist studies courses. The most frequently mentioned single piece of feminist pro-lesbian literature was Adrienne Rich's "Compulsory heterosexuality and lesbian existence." Another student mentioned being assigned Marge Piercy's *Woman on the Edge of Time* as a reading in a women's studies course:

> Lesbian relationships were completely validated; in fact, the teacher would talk about it in class. She was straight but she was really comfortable. Definitely that book and that class gave me a chance to even think of lesbianism as an option, as a real option in some way.

Six of the students had taken feminist courses taught by "out" lesbian professors (two professors) and the experience had been profoundly positive for them. One of the lesbian students described her reaction to her first experience with an "out" lesbian instructor:

> I'm so grateful for having a feminist professor and I'm quite amazed at having a lesbian professor.... I identify myself not just as a feminist, but as a lesbian and that's another part of my

identity that is added to it some way.... Similarly, it's not until you see Blacks in advertising that you realize Blacks have been omitted ... It's the discrimination by omission that you don't understand until you start to have it and then — wow! where have you been? I've been waiting for you!... One of the things that happens at university is ... presenting things as though somehow white males are objective, they're a clean slate and it's real information. Somehow when you have feminists and lesbians come in and talk ... you start to see the dynamic of who is telling you this and how that works into what's being said.

Most of the students and instructors have some supports in academe. With few exceptions their support systems are comprised almost entirely of other women. The students' supports are most frequently other lesbian and heterosexual feminist students. Especially helpful was exposure to lesbians who were comfortable and positive about their own identity. This was important to them early in their own lesbian identity process:

> We had one who was just very free and open and positive. She was wonderful about it in class, accepted it herself. There wasn't anger or sort of trauma for her. Oh, it was wonderful for me.

Heterosexual feminist students are also important supports, especially when they are willing to break the silence surrounding lesbian existence:

> It seems important to a number of women I know who are straight, as well ... that doesn't put the pressure on me to confront, to do it constantly, or struggle on whether to say anything or not because there are other women who are also doing that. And that feels good.

In some cases, especially among the graduate students, they have formed supportive connections with pro-lesbian professors, both female and male.

Most of the instructors are "out" to a few trusted colleagues and those who are fortunate enough to teach in universities where there are women's studies programs usually have feminist colleagues as supports. Most of them also have solid support systems in the community outside academe. These support systems are typically made up of women, both lesbian and heterosexual:

> I live in largely a woman's world. It's not only a lesbian world. A lot of them are straight women. But they are women and basically women on their own that make up a large majority of them. So I live in a woman's world and part of that is lesbian women.

Most of these women, both students and instructors, have some commitment to the feminist movement; their work is most accurately described as identified with the general feminist movement rather than focused directly on lesbian feminism or gay liberation. The graduate students were all doing research from a feminist perspective, though none were researching explicitly lesbian topics. One of the undergraduate students was completing an honours thesis on a lesbian topic. Two of the instructors are involved in feminist publishing, one in creative feminist writing, the other in scholarly feminist work. Some of the women believed that one's lesbian identity inevitably informs feminist work. One of them stated:

> I think as a lesbian you are more clear about the implications of patriarchy and the radical feminist critique than you would have been otherwise. That informs your work – that insight informs your work even though it isn't focused squarely on the lesbian experience at all.

The instructors are at various stages of the complex multi-layered process that is coming out in academe, involving as it does colleagues, students, publishing, and other work. Most are beyond the completely closeted existence and its immense personal tolls. Though few are fully and publicly out in every aspect of their academic existence, all of them make some attempt to deal with lesbian and gay issues in their teaching. In general, their productive work and personal commitment is to the feminist movement and to the empowerment of all women, whether they are lesbian or heterosexual.

Most of the lesbian students have a positive lesbian identity and many of them are learning to break the silence, with some fear of loss of credibility, but a consequent strengthening of their sense of self. On the whole, they don't have much hope for academe in general to meet the needs of lesbian students, but as feminists they expect more from women's studies and they often get it. In recent years, the silence surrounding lesbian existence has been lifted in many women's studies courses by feminist scholars, whether heterosexual or lesbian, though there are still far too many exceptions. A number of the students recall that their most positive experiences were in courses with pro-lesbian heterosexual feminist professors.

The academic environment provides unique possibilities that most other settings in the public sphere do not provide. It is hardly a benign environment. Academe provides, however, a setting that is, at least nominally, explicitly devoted to the production of knowledge and its understanding; a liberal attitude that is frequently present and exemplified by the term "academic freedom." These features of academe provide a measure of opportunity to explore forbidden areas; to examine relationships between one's experience of the world and what is academically "known." A stigmatized outsider position is often an excellent vantage point for stimulating creative re-vision of existing knowledge. The growth of feminist studies has provided a home within the academic environment for work to flourish that reflects the lesbian identities and associated woman-identification of these women, whether they are students or teachers.

Notes

1. This paper was presented as part of a symposium entitled "Toward a Sociology of Lesbianism" at the conference of the Canadian Sociology and Anthropology Association, the Learned Societies, Winnipeg, 1986.

   The interview data has also been published in *Atlantis* 13, No. 2, Spring 1989. I interviewed thirteen university students and eleven teachers (three were both students and teachers). Of the students, seven were undergraduates and six were graduate students, ranging in age from twenty-one to forty-one years. Most were from universities in Ontario, with Quebec and British Columbia also represented. The eleven instructors were all in their thirties or forties and, with only two exceptions, were all academics in Ontario. All but one of the instructors were white; two of the students were women of colour.

   All but two identified themselves as lesbian: one student described herself as bisexual, and one instructor, though involved in a long-term relationship with a woman, felt strongly that sexual orientation classifications are derived from a norm of heterosexuality and resisted such classification.

With the above two exceptions, all have identified as lesbian for periods ranging from a few months to over twenty years. The students were "out" to at least a small group of trusted friends. Six of them had "come out" in the context of classroom interactions or in their academic work. Most of the instructors were "out" to at least a few friends and / or colleagues. Three of the instructors were fully and publicly "out" in their academic environments. "Closeted" lesbian instructors, who are likely to be the largest proportion of lesbian instructors in academe, are underrepresented here. However, one of the instructors was quite concealed, two others were not out in their academic environments, and others were out to only a few colleagues.

12

The Mind-Drifting Islands

Micheline Grimard-Leduc

THIS PAPER IS part of a book, *L'île des amantes (Lesbian Lovers' Island)*, half essay, half poetry, I originally wrote in French about the island as a basic symbol in lesbian culture.[1] The main argument of the book runs as follows: the Amazons existed; their tribes were a basic primitive pattern of female society; and if there are so many legends of female-only islands, it is because the Amazon tribes often lived on islands. When these Amazon societies were destroyed by male supremacist societies, lesbians became the heirs of an ever-menaced culture that had to move from islands of stone and sand to psycho-spiritual shelters, or "mind-drifting islands."

I am aware that a North American white middle-class education, which in my generation (1950-60) translated into Quebec Catholic classical studies, limits my perspective.[2] As with any research that is deeply motivated, I know that mine is not over, and I do hope that it will contribute to a further knowledge of our multi-faceted culture.

Lesbians as Exiles

The uprooting of lesbians is an historical fact that breeds its sequels well into our contemporary individual lives. We no longer tap from our roots and this shows in our behaviour and attitudes, to the great satisfaction of male supremacists. Furthermore, we have forgotten where our oppression has come from; we have forgotten that the cause is exterior to ourselves.

In her book *Sappho*, Edith Mora writes that Sappho participated in the political feuds that arose between Lesbos' noble families and the merchants and shipowners.[3] Her pamphlets against the new "democracy" caused her to be exiled twice in her lifetime. My interest is not so much in these oligarchic quarrels as in the geography of these exiles. The most historically acknowledged exile is the second one, the one to Syracuse (Sicily); it is worthwhile noting that here we are dealing with banishment to an island. But her first exile, less well-known, was to a small village named Pyrrha a few kilometres from Mytilini. This exile at first seemed strange to my electronic-age mind accustomed to transatlantic flights: what was the fuss, how could one feel exiled when banished from one's city to what might be called a suburb? Exiled to one's own island ...

Here one could play with the word itself, "ex-isle," "cast out of one's isle." But my main purpose is to examine the concept of exile, a notion that reaches far beyond geographic dimensions, as shown by Sappho's ostracism to Pyrrha.

For me, the idea of exile includes two elements:

1) the banishment is imposed and not decided by the person herself;
2) a rooting out of the social self, a wandering situation where one no longer shares a collective system of values.

Patriarchal history has resorted to exile to solve unwanted political or legal situations by casting out used-up emperors, criminals, "progressive" elements, and sometimes even entire communities (the Acadian population).[4] Each of these was sent far away from their native country, often to inhospitable islands. And this uprooting inevitably had a profound impact. For Sappho in Pyrrha, exile meant precisely this uprooting: she lost contact with her own collectivity, she was no longer part of the social flow of mutual acknowledgement, she no longer partook in collective values. In her time, a few kilometres sufficed. This "de-possession" of one's social self fits well into Marx's and Hegel's definition of alienation: one is alienated because one is deprived of oneself by outside forces; no longer possessing oneself, one becomes the plaything of conquerors and events.

As lesbians, our collective and individual story has been one of estrangement since the breaking-up of the Amazon tribes by male supremacy. Collectively, we have been deprived of our Amazon structures; even considering that the Amazons were nomadic, they nevertheless constituted a social canvas into which individuals could weave their collective identity, the kind of collective identity that is necessary for strong ego sanity. As lesbians we are left out, and we are left – with this paralysing fear, this ontological uneasiness, this dread of being. This kind of oppression induces choking instead of anger and revolt; such oppression splits the personality. Indeed, without any collective identity, forced into cultural wandering, and without being able to determine the external causes for this exile, what choices are there for a lesbian to maintain minimal sanity?

A first solution is to blot out the feeling of estrangement and assign it to one's overly sensitive imagination, to think that the whole thing will straighten out by itself, as long as one conforms to the norms and adapts to this strange land. Women (I go on to differentiate "women" from "lesbians" later) adopt these alien values and go so far as to estrange themselves with the stranger. As spouses, women do receive a few social and economic benefits, and some "well-adapted" lesbians manage to carve out for themselves nice pieces of the socio-economic pie. But since lesbians have not crossed the ultimate threshold of submission to male ownership in their private lives, their situation remains precarious. Indeed, since a lesbian does not intimately belong to a man, she is a "graft" that will be rejected by the male system at any sign of crisis: "What is not mine, is against me." Bitter deception lurks behind the "melting" stance. We shall never be able to melt into a male-dominated society because of its heterosexist political mechanisms, in which heterosexual choice does not really exist.

There is the self-destructive solution that runs the gamut from drugs, alcohol, smoking, to suicide, not to mention conventional psychotherapy and various psychosomatic illnesses resulting from the uneasiness of being "different." This "difference" is epitomized by the notion of a "third sex," where sexual marginality is interpreted as a biological fatality.[5] When supposedly embedded in the genes, this "difference" cannot act as a potential subversion of sexual polarity (which is a social phenomenon), but is felt as a dead-end, and thus reinforces self-destructive behaviour. How far will such a schizophrenic scenario take us? The set-up is remarkably appropriate for ghettos, couples in hiding, closet cases, and all the alienated souls that think of themselves as being alone of their kind in the world.

Presumably, I am forgetting other solutions. But there is one other

I think of: a solution that often coexists with others and has its own little schizoid tinge, that is, to seek shelter in a fictitious inner world. To build, by imagining, an island inhabited by lesbian lovers and to hold onto it mentally. I am creating a fantasy where I can forego the distress that arises from my "strange" condition. Am I trading my first estrangement for another one in fantasyland?

Freudian goblins are laughing sarcastically all around.... Yes indeed, I am fleeing. Running away is symptomatic of any situation where one is deprived of one's self as a social being. I build my own land of refuge. And I have come to think that every lesbian, through the ages and throughout continents, has built, be it for no more than a short moment, some sort of a shelter. I am also convinced that this refuge has most often taken the shape of an island. The flight to the island is a symptom of uneasiness, a sane reaction to the restlessness caused by a destructive social environment.

The Wise of the past and of today "spin a spiral," as Mary Daly would say.[6] Perhaps this spinning comes from our continual moving, at least in our minds. We have been spinning a spiral, a circle that generates itself by its displacement in time and space.

Since the time Amazon tribes were chased into oblivion, we survived by continuing to draw this revolving spiral in time-space. The width of the spiral was narrowed each time male aggression intensified and destroyed many of us; but it kept moving further in the dimension of time, where figures are not important, as long as the movement continues.

A Place to Land: Island as Autonomy

If we try and shed our passive attitude towards this exile, I think we can turn this prison-island upside down into autonomy, into at least psycho-social autarky. This would mean a first step towards overthrowing the established order. One of the devices that holds this order together functions like this: since each of us is deprived of collective points of reference by which to "plug" into a collective reality, we tend to develop negative mental attitudes, which in turn impede the building of this reality!

This is the kind of vicious circle we must break through. It is important indeed for male society that we be crazies, whether cute or tough crazies; so each of us reassures herself by secretly thinking about others who are "even crazier." The system relies on our schizophrenic "abilities" to ensure an isolation that it does not even have to enforce since it comes from ourselves: the detachment from our own selves and from others. Of course, as long as my dream-island is known only to myself, I actually live on a prison-island, in sheer isolation. In Italian, "isola" means island ...

But as soon as I share my dream with another lesbian, I start breaking through the alien circle. This single act of communication materializes the dream. By this exchange we build reality. Communication and schizophrenia are antitheses; I am no schizophrenic if I am actually able to communicate.

Psychiatric diagnoses are meaningless when crazies, "lost minds," start sharing their dreams and, most of all, start to mould them into reality. Who then is going to send us off in exile to an island we call our own land? Who will impose banishment on us when we are already elsewhere?

If our exchanges enable us to rebuild a social fabric, collective values, an economy (wow! what a dreamer!), who would still talk of uprooting? Perhaps one of the causes of confusion around lesbian separatism (as I view it) is a conception of the "island" as a ghetto instead of as autonomy. The ghetto-island stays in the closet, providing short-term security; the autonomy-island means the building of a community, with a collective visibility.[7] It means a positive choice, a long-term bet on a different society. There is a qualitative leap between these two conceptions of our "island."

I admit that to choose autonomy and visibility is no piece of cake: fear and insecurity do not vanish, but are transformed. Fear that arises from isolation and internalized oppression, paralysing fear, is replaced by the more objective fear of socio-economic repression, which political lesbian analysis readily calls a political repression. Even with the inevitable phantasms that pervade any kind of fear – most of all the fears we have plenty of time to contemplate – fear of repression is based on concrete situations that can eventually happen and that one will either have to confront or, better, try to prevent: homophobic jokes, mail opening, loss of job, denying of parenthood, and in some cases worse forms of censorship. One is then concerned about the consequences of one's own actions in the course of affirming oneself. Quite different from the fear of being!

Fear of repression does not make for easy living, even when we try to establish a network of communication, and sometimes *because* we try to do so. Each of us is not necessarily ready to take chances and risk visibility to the same degree as her sister; communication between us acts as a stimulus as well as a frustration or a deterrent. "Why is she still in the closet? Why is she bullying me so soon into visibility? Should I involve my lover in my deeds? I am not allowing her to be vocal," and so on.

Couples, groups, friendships are sometimes torn apart by this shadowy fear that is not so easy to pinpoint. But there is still a longing, something that lingers between nostalgia and hope.

We wish our island could materialize in a flash, somewhere, and we would rush there to organize our own society. But the unleashed demography of male societies would soon find us, be it by plane, boat, or what have you; according to the values of these societies, there is no possibility for the existence of independent females, for the existence of a lesbian society. Female autonomy cannot and must not be. So, we create small islands, we are small islands. Each time a lesbian reveals herself to another lesbian, she is this island, a place to land. From countryside to city, from city to city, from continent to continent, across generations, couples, and groups, overcoming the fear, each time we become visible to one another, we create the island. We are an archipelago, one that drifts through time and geography and allows us mutual recognition and the support of the social fabric.

That is the whole meaning of lesbian works, magazines, videos, movies, research, all of which shape our collectivity into reality. A collectivity becomes flesh and bone each time one of us thinks of herself as partaking in an actual lesbian community.

I realize that in addition to our individual security investments in male society, there still are racial and social clashes between us, conflicts that seriously slow down the building of our community. Ours is not always "a rose garden."

I even happen to think of our island as a swamp when I am fed up and pessimistic. But I still prefer it to the islands that bloom on TV commercials, with male voice-over. Our island is inhabited by real females, by lesbians. Instead of the voice-over, I would rather imagine Ioanna's voice through her letter: "I am now sitting in our small garden, at Glyfada; it is awfully hot, but I have just watered the flowers, everything is wet, and I am feeling good. I am happy to know that you are doing fine, that you are content with your surroundings. That is something. Perhaps, near the end of our lives, many of us will gather on an island. At least, let us dream about it."[8]

In a corner of their living room, Betty and Ioanna have built a small-scale lesbian village. The little houses are waiting. I can fancy them. There are red ones ...

"Lesbians Are Not Women"

In the preceding pages, I have tried to avoid the use of the word "woman," except in those cases where I wanted to describe a social entity altered by his-story. Among the various possible verbal compromises, I chose the word "female" for its biological semantics: a biological entity deriving from a certain chromosomic organization, characterized by genes xx, displaying a certain hormonal and morphological configuration, blah, blah, blah. Far from being adequate, this term still makes me feel clumsy; for I am once more trying to name — hence to think of — our own identities with an alien language, the male language.

"Lesbians are not women" ("Les lesbiennes ne sont pas des femmes"). In these words Monique Wittig summed up her paper on the straight way of thinking, "La pensée straight," a work that contributed to bringing out into the open the ideological conflict that had been latent amongst the editorial staff of the French feminist magazine, *Questions féministes.*[9] Conflicts over this question about the meaning of "lesbian" and "woman" have since been sprouting in almost every feminist and / or lesbian circle with more or less hostility. Monique Wittig has aptly shown that the conception of "woman," which apparently refers to a natural entity, actually is a camouflage for negative, downgrading socio-cultural semantics.[10] The downgrading mechanism itself is no longer decipherable — and so less easy to confront — since the resulting hierarchy is attributed to "nature." If the word "woman" has received phallocratic consent, if its use is current, it is because it is politically useful for male society. Through a biological smokescreen, "woman" actually refers to a social entity, an ancillary, downgraded entity at that.

If I do conceive of myself as an autonomous entity, if I am not privately dependent on a man, if I have stopped focusing on the male show and I now focus on what it has always tried to hide, how shall I call myself? "Woman" perpetuates the erasure of my autonomous self, pushes my intimate life back to nothingness; it blots out a way of living that generates my whole vision of the world, a way of living that is eroticism with / for my sister, eroticism that fuels my will to live. Then, how shall I call myself?

I call myself a "lesbian." My "reality" is indeed invisible to male society. In the view of men, a Lesbian is a "monster." As if to reassure themselves, men make pornography of the "monster": they reduce "it" to utilitarian fantasies, such as David Hamilton's teens or Nazi "kapos." In pornography lesbians are fantasy robots programmed by and for men.

Many lesbians refuse the "label": in doing so, are they assuming for themselves the male fantasy, or have they been "crushed" by it? Does the word "woman" allow one to "pass" and feel less vulnerable? I agree that in a straight environment it seems less complicated to use the "wo-man" password than to try to demonstrate one's lesbian reality. But when we are together, expressing our intimate selves to one another, assuming our reality among ourselves, what is the point in refusing to call oneself a lesbian?

For the time being, I have not found any other word that is understood in many languages and that also holds up so well the meaning of our autonomy, of our radical rupture from this man's world. Since our intimate life roots itself elswhere than in male "reality," we, and only we, can give ourselves a reality visible to us, through the words we choose. In this way, we de-sign reality, we send signs to each other, positive signals that in turn transform our way of thinking. This simple word "lesbian" brings forth the vision of the island; in spite of the mirages, this word draws the contours of our collectivity to reveal the shape of our island.

Coming Out to Land on One's Island

In the *Coming Out Stories*, Sarah Hoagland compares "coming out" with "coming home."[11] It has been such a long exile away from our island that when we do at last realize our lesbian identity, it is like reaching a longed-for country.

This is at least the strong impression I got from my first night of love with a woman. If I write "night of love" it is not meant in terms of technique, but in terms of my perception of the event. The fact is, that night almost ended in a rebuff. Yet I felt thoroughly at peace with myself in the morning: I knew that I had come to my coherent self, mind, heart, body, all of them merging into one emotion. I felt I had reached the land I had been travelling towards, delayed by so many detours. At last, I was coming home! I even remember the physical feeling of landing on an island. There would be a lot yet to discover on this island, but, after all, there I was! The wandering had come to an end.

Indeed I have been discovering many things since this first landing. With quite a few years behind me, I can see now that claiming and living my lesbian identity was not and is still not a "sideline" in my life, but it is a growth process involving my whole personality. Seemingly, what started it all was being infatuated and then learning the pleasure of the senses, but at no moment was this process confined to the individual level. As Audre Lorde has so beautifully written, erotics inform and fuel our whole life.[12] Pleasure and intimacy, instead of closing me off in secrecy, gave me the curiosity and boldness that visibility demands and helped me expand into collective awareness. Private growth and social interactions are interlocked.

I cannot help noticing that for many of us coming out has to take place at least a few kilometres away from our family or from the social environment that represents it. Is not "family" the main transmitter of the so-called "heterosexual" patriarchal values? When I first came out I was studying abroad. Very often lesbians are actual travellers who dare to confront crosswinds only once we are away from our familiar surroundings, coming back later when we have acquired self-confidence in our own way of sailing through life.

A question still remains. How is it that so many lesbians have been travelling across oceans, through book shelves or through feminist discussions, and have never reached their island? If coming out can be an agonizing process, it must mean that there are not only implacable determinisms driving us, shaping us in or out of lesbianism; but there must also be a tiny thread of free will, somewhere, that we can hold onto. I was told once that will is an emotion, an emotion that drives us to action. Are some of us more emotional than others? Emotional enough to walk through all the supposedly insurmountable barriers of taboos and meet our authentic selves?

I have found no rational answer yet. But the answer might have something to do with true love for oneself: a strong, untamed love in which one's very first move is to insist that her life no longer be constricted. As if to merge with this thought, the image of Morrigan comes to my mind.[13] Morrigan, from "mor-gen," meaning both "morning" and "strength-generating." In Celtic legends, Morrigan (Morgane) was a druidic priestess; she was also a fairy, living on an island with other priestesses, and a mare stomping the seashore with her surf-like hooves. Morrigan, the wild mare, celtic morn, Morrigan the strength-giver, is dawning on our island.

Notes

I am greatly indebted to Ariane Brunet for the friendly but thorough critical discussions she shared with me in the course of this work. Diana B. helped me with the translation from French to English.

1. Micheline Grimard-Leduc, *L'île des amantes* (Montreal, 1982).
2. At that time, classical studies were offered at the "collèges classiques," a private system of education extending from secondary to college level.
3. Edith Mora, *Sappho* (Paris: Flammarion, 1966).
4. In the 18th century, the Acadian population inhabited areas of the Maritimes. In 1755, families were split apart by the British military authorities and were chased away on small craft. Those who landed somewhere ended up on the Boston coast, in North Carolina, even in Louisiana, others in the Magdalen Islands and elsewhere in the gulf of St. Lawrence.
5. See Radclyffe Hall's *The Well of Loneliness*. The idea of a "third sex" reminds me of a lobotomy without a scalpel.
6. Mary Daly, *Gyn / Ecology: The Metaethics of Radical Feminism* (Boston: Beacon Press, 1978).
7. J. Steakly makes an interesting distinction between "ghetto" and "community" in an interview in *Gay Community News*, Vol. 9, No. 48, June 26, 1982.
8. Letter from Ioanna Kouklakis, July 1981. Glyfada is an Athenian suburb.
9. Monique Wittig, "La pensée straight," *Questions féministes*, No. 7, February 1980.
10. The magazine *Amazones d'hier / Lesbiennes d'aujourd'hui* (Montreal) ran a series of papers on this debate in its June 1982 issue (Vol. 1, No. 1).
11. Julia Penelope Stanley, Susan J. Wolfe (eds.), *The Coming Out Stories* (Watertown, Mass.: Persephone Press, 1980).
12. Audre Lorde, *Uses of the Erotic: The Erotic as Power* (New York: Out and Out Books, 1978).
13. Merlin Stone, *Ancient Mirrors of Womanhood*, Vol. I (New York: New Sybilline Books, 1979).

Part III
Lesbians Organizing for Survival

13

A Test of Unity

Lesbian Visibility in the
British Columbia Federation of Women

M. Julia Creet

IN 1974 AND 1975 A crucial debate focusing on the issue of lesbianism took place within the British Columbia women's movement.[1]
Is lesbianism a personal issue best kept in the closet, or does it have
profound social and political implications? Do lesbian issues have an
integral place in the women's movement? This highly charged
debate had the potential to split the movement, as it had almost
done in the United States.[2] Instead, out of it came what would
become an important feminist element in British Columbia: lesbian
feminist praxis.

The debate took place when a new lesbian feminist consciousness
was developing, during the early days of B.C.'s first and largest organization of women's groups, the British Columbia Federation of
Women (BCFW).[3] The birth of the BCFW coincided with an emerging
lesbian feminist consciousness. The formation of the Lesbian Caucus of the BCFW in the context of the 1974-75 debate regarding lesbianism and the women's movement resulted in a conflict that precipitated an identity crisis in the nascent movement.

The lesbian issue produced fear in some women, who then
attempted to silence lesbians, arguing that visible lesbians would
hurt the credibility of the movement. The issue also served to delineate the differences between radical and conservative politics (for
example, revolution versus reform), differences that fell roughly
along sexual lines. In their own lives lesbians were facing contradictions and tensions caused by general social attitudes, fear of losing

their children, and internalized myths and images that kept them silent and invisible. Lesbians argued that they faced greater discrimination than heterosexual women, and that since the movement was concerned with the needs of all women, their needs were important too. Before the first year of the debate was over, lesbians were arguing for the necessity of lesbian feminist politics including a critique of heterosexuality as a cornerstone of male supremacy.

Lesbianism was a new thing not only for many heterosexual women in BCFW, but also for many lesbians in BCFW. Though there was a lesbian underground culture with a history of its own, the combination of visible lesbianism with politics was a very new phenomenon. Many lesbians who were also feminists had become both at around the same time, and were struggling to find an identity that resolved the contradictions between lifestyle and politics, without denying the history of their subculture or separating entirely from society. There were tangible differences and tensions between women who belonged to the "old gay" culture, the new lesbian feminists, and the separatists who no longer wanted anything to do with men at all. Yet these three groups of women, plus others who were less visible, shared a lesbian identity that had been primarily defined by society. With the growth in consciousness that came from feminism came also the need for self-definition on a personal and political level. Lesbians in the feminist movement found themselves in uncharted territory.

It was hard for the new lesbian feminists to appreciate the political struggles that had already taken place in working-class bars. It had not been long since lesbian sexuality, in itself, was a criminal offence (it was decriminalized in 1969). The code of the bars was to be "butch" or "femme," which for many women was a statement that they did not accept a traditional female role. But the visibility afforded by the roles also brought with it the dangers of public and police harassment. By the 1970s a new lesbian ethic arose, which censored "butch / femme" roles because they were seen as mimicking heterosexuality.

The politics of the "old gay" community were hard for the new lesbians to appreciate, since they had fundamental differences in attitudes towards sexuality. The external appearance of the butch / femme roles *seemed* to embody the very power imbalance and affirmation of male roles that the feminist movement sought to redress.[4] As the first generation of their kind, the new lesbians wanted to create role models for themselves. They wanted to redefine lesbianism, so that they would be more acceptable to other women and at the same time could present a radical challenge to normalized gender roles.

The Umbrella Opens: The How and Why of BCFW

In the early 1970s the women's movement in British Columbia was expanding exponentially. In 1969 there were two established groups; in 1970, five. Seven more were established the following year and the number doubled again in 1972. By 1974, seventy-two new groups had been formed in the province, bringing the total to nearly a hundred. The movement, however, was diverse and unorganized, and many women were becoming frustrated by government inaction on feminist issues.

The idea of an umbrella federation of women's groups emerged at a conference of women in education held in British Columbia in August 1973. In the October 1973 issue of the Vancouver women's newspaper, Pedestal, the "Mothers of Confederation" issued a call to arms, noting "a great need for a confederation of all feminist women's groups in the province so that women can get their due share of the power."[5] They asked B.C. women to submit ideas regarding the structure and purpose of a federation to the Interim Coordinating Committee so that a large meeting could be planned "before the snow flies."

Winter came and went, and though no concrete work was done on the formation of a federation, the idea was taking hold. Cynthia Flood, a member of the NDP Women's Committee, attributed the growing attractiveness of creating a united women's group to three causes: 1) NDP government inaction on election promises concerning women's rights; 2) recognition of a remarkable degree of unanimity among women's groups during government hearings on Legislative Priorities for Women's Rights; and 3) several exceptionally well-attended women's conferences in early 1974.[6]

In April 1974, representatives of the NDP Women's Committee made another call for a major strategy conference of the B.C. women's movement. This time the response was positive and a loose steering committee of representatives began working on the project. On May 25, three hundred women attended the Action for Women Strategy Conference in North Vancouver. "Nobody knew exactly what would or could come out of the conference ... the vague idea of some sort of umbrella group was in the air, but no one had a clear idea of what that could mean, and no group came prepared to make such a proposal."[7]

As various groups at the conference described strategies for trying to win governmental action, it became apparent that clever strategy was far more likely to be effective if it had broad-based support. By the end of the day, there was virtually unanimous recognition of the need for a federation of women's groups. The women's movement, delegates felt, needed to clearly demonstrate its strength and unity to the government.

Representatives from about twenty groups volunteered to work on a steering committee to organize a founding convention for the federation.[8] By its second meeting the steering committee had found a name for the infant organization – the British Columbia Federation of Women – but the problem of inventing a structure that could meet the infinite needs of women with extremely varied political experience, ideology, and geography was to occupy committee members throughout the summer.

In discussions to define the major responsibilities and objectives of the Federation, representatives repeatedly expressed concerns for the autonomy of individuals and groups within the umbrella. They recognized the diversity of groups and were concerned that the Federation, if it was to have broad-based support, not alienate hesitant potential members. In the words of the Kamloops representative, the Federation "must be non-threatening to 'Missus Joe Smith'."[9]

While almost everyone present expressed the desire and vision of a united front, committee members proposed two distinct approaches to conflict resolution within the Federation. One representative, articulating the need for autonomy, suggested that the membership should not be required to support all issues. Another representative stated that the "umbrella group would have to risk the loss of those who can't or won't agree with someone else in the group."[10] Clearly, the structure would have to accommodate the diversity of the movement while providing a united political front. The first year of the Federation would strain this tenuous fusion to the limit.

The founding convention of the BCFW – a historic event – was held September 13-15, 1974, with 350 women attending. Women's groups and individuals represented virtually every area of the province. They made decisions and proposed policy in the areas of health, education, childcare, and employment, and elected a Standing Committee with twenty-two positions.

Much ground had been covered, but there was one serious oversight that would become a major issue in short order. At the close of the convention, a group of women stood at the back of the hall talking. One of them, Pat Smith, articulated her concern in a simple question: "Why no lesbian policy?"[11] Others concurred. The needs of lesbians had been overlooked; lesbians had overlooked their own needs. They decided to form an interest group and call a meeting. Smith went to the front of the hall and wrote a notice on the board. The first meeting of the Lesbian Caucus of the BCFW would be held the following Sunday at the Vancouver Ms. Club.

The convention had been successful, but as Cynthia Flood wrote a day later, "Now comes the hard part – making it work."[12] Making it work would take a commitment to working on personal issues as much as political issues; Pat Smith's question was fundamental. Lesbian visibility in BCFW would become a backdrop for many issues: autonomy and unity; the nature of what is personal and what is political; organizational structure; the gap between radical and conservative politics; rural / urban differences; and, most fundamentally, the connection between lesbianism and feminism. It was the responsibility of the Standing Committee to keep their heterogeneous group united around basic aims. This would be hard work indeed.

Coming Out in BCFW

Yvonne Johnson was working at the Ms. Club the weekend of the BCFW Founding Convention. She got the news as she talked to the women coming in:

> My strongest recollections of that weekend are of women coming in after the conference and talking and the underlying theme, in fact, almost the sole topic of conversation among the women I knew, was how bizarre they felt, how strange it was, that with the large number of very strong lesbians present at the convention, when policy decisions were being made and platforms were being voted on, not once was lesbianism mentioned, not one piece of lesbian policy was brought forth.[13]

Woman after woman would say, in a tone of disbelief, "Do you realize, that with all of us there, not one of us stood up and proposed any lesbian policy or even the inclusion of lesbianism in the confines of other policies?"[14]

The following Sunday about thirty lesbians met to discuss what had happened, what to do about it, and what they might want to present in the way of policy to the Federation. Many of them were already involved in other feminist groups and wanted to continue their work in those groups. They did not see lesbianism as a separate issue.

Years later, three members of the Lesbian Caucus described their optimism and political naivety:

> We were energetic, idealistic and convinced that we had merely to bring this regrettable oversight in policy to the attention of our sisters and the women's movement in B.C. would unite in revolutionary fervor and we would achieve the liberation of women almost immediately.[15]

They added, with tongue-in-cheek hindsight, "It is taking somewhat longer than we anticipated."

News of the formation of the Lesbian Caucus was brought to the first Standing Committee meeting in October. There was no indication in the Co-ordinator's report that the formation of the Caucus was seen as a problem or that it invoked hostility from other members.[16]

The following month the first issue of the *BCFW Newsletter* carried an announcement from the Lesbian Caucus. It said, in part:

> The policies instated at the founding convention of the B.C.F.W. completely overlooked the rights of lesbians. We feel omissions were not intended but occurred due to a lack of consciousness about lesbian oppression. Those of us who were aware were hesitant to articulate our feelings of how present laws and attitudes oppress lesbians. Hence a lesbian caucus formed to raise consciousness and to collectively draft policy amendments and proposals for discussion at the next convention.[17]

Lesbians at the convention had been hesitant to articulate their concerns due to a fear of reaction and repercussions, and due to a lack of a conscious formulation of the exact nature of their concerns. Thus they sought not only to raise the consciousness of other women in BCFW but also to clarify for themselves why they remained silent. They wanted to show how lesbian oppression was carried out, why it was the concern of all women, what policy could be formulated, and what action could be taken to address specific needs and concrete demands for change.

Caucus members listed a number of concerns: rights of lesbian mothers; ending employment discrimination; changing immigration laws; inclusion of sexual orientation in the human rights code; and positive counselling in schools on women's sexuality, including lesbianism and celibacy. They called on other women to see the connections between these concerns and the concerns of all women:

> These issues are not the isolated concerns of lesbians. Laws and attitudes oppressive to lesbians are used to threaten and control all women. Every woman must have the right to choose for herself a lifestyle suitable to her needs as an individual.[18]

The strength and clarity of their analysis faltered, however, when it came to the reality of women identifying themselves publicly as lesbians. The Caucus refused to have its own members' names printed and could only be contacted by letter or in person at the lesbian drop-in.

Yvonne Johnson volunteered to be the identified representative of the Caucus at the Interim Standing Committee meeting in mid-November. She had very little experience with political organizing, but representing the Caucus seemed fairly straightforward. At the meeting she was astonished to see that a discussion of the newsletter and the article from the Lesbian Caucus was on the agenda. When the discussion began the hostility and anger towards the Caucus was, in her words, "quite phenomenal." She remembered:

> One woman said that she had to hide her copy of the newsletter under her mattress so that nobody would see it. Another woman said that she had to burn hers for fear that the garbage man would see it when he picked up her garbage and would see the word "lesbian" right there in the paper.

The Caucus had taken the critical step of making the lesbian presence in BCFW public. Most women could tolerate lesbianism as long as it was discreet, but demanding rights and recognition launched it from the private into the political sphere, and into the lives of all women in BCFW.

Fear of and misconceptions about lesbians surfaced: it was easy for lesbians to be political, they had no families to take care of or jobs or responsibilities, they had nothing to do but go to meetings and infiltrate the women's movement. They had stereotypical ideas of what lesbians were, and could not take lesbian concerns seriously.

Cy-Thea Sand (formerly Nancy Ryan) and Linda Hancock, two lesbian members of the editorial collective for the newsletter, were shocked by the hostility. Their policy was to publish whatever articles were sent in that were appropriate and in keeping with guidelines. The newsletter was for internal communication within BCFW. They pointed out that the Lesbian Caucus had not made a public statement.

Johnson, as the only identified member of the Caucus, did her best to defend the lesbian position, but with little success. She went home in a "state of complete emotional upheaval," overwhelmed by the intensity and not understanding the complexity of what had happened.

The next meeting of the Lesbian Caucus decided that no Caucus member would ever go to a meeting alone again. In fact, members decided to send as many women as possible. They began to formulate strategy, theorizing that greater exposure to lesbians would quiet the fears of others who were reacting to myths. An open lesbian presence would serve to demystify lesbian existence and promote understanding as well as a sense of personal and political unity.

Organizational meetings for the next two months, on the whole, went smoothly and there appeared to be support for lesbian issues. Hostilities were put aside and the organization moved forward, strategizing actions and structuring the Federation. The second issue of the *BCFW Newsletter* came out in late January 1975 with all the news of the Federation, a centre-page article on rape, and a full page on lesbian issues.

The Caucus printed letters sent to *Time* magazine challenging the bigotry of its description of Kingston's prison for women as "a 'hell-pit' that assembles around 160 of the worst women in Canada, most of whom are lesbians, heroin pushers and other drug-related offenders."[19] A lesbian mother wrote of her fear of exposure, "Lesbian Paranoia??" She, justifiably, envisioned that she would lose her children if she were open about her sexuality.

Child custody was a major issue for members of the Lesbian Caucus, since most had children or lovers with children. Politically it was an issue that crossed sexual boundaries, since any mother could be declared unfit if she engaged in socially unacceptable activities — even feminist activity.

In 1974 Yvonne Johnson had just left her husband and three-year-old son and was "head-over-heels" in love with another woman. She had left her son behind, knowing her husband would win a custody battle in the courts. Had she not been involved in political organizing, she might have had a chance at securing custody of her son, but as it was her visibility worked against her. The courts enforced invisibility for lesbian mothers [see the chapter by Mary Eaton in this book] and showed little respect for women who expressed a need for a community of other women.

At an Interim Standing Committee meeting in February 1975, lesbian visibility again became a major issue. Lesbians were accused of creating controversy and sensationalism with their articles. It was argued that the newsletter was giving BCFW an anti-male image.

At the next two Lesbian Caucus meetings, strategy was the main agenda item. There were differences about how far they should push the issue of lesbian visibility, which was threatening to split the Standing Committee. Was there a way to compromise? They decided not to print the Preamble to the Lesbian Policy Proposals in the next newsletter, in case it caused a split or resignations.

The Preamble was a reflection of the experiences of Caucus members, who saw the conflict within BCFW as a reflection of common attitudes towards lesbians in society as a whole. The conflict in the BCFW had served as a catalyst for the distillation of lesbian feminist identity and politics. According to the Preamble:

> Society defines women in relation to men. Women who choose not to relate to men in traditional ways, or who choose not to relate to men at all, are regarded with contempt and fear. All women who do not fit the "approved" stereotypes suffer severe consequences, especially those who deviate the furthest, i.e. lesbians.
>
> Women's fear of themselves and each other clearly divides our strength as a group. Until such fear is no longer used to control and manipulate us, women will not be free to choose alternative lifestyles.[20]

Anticipating ratification of policy proposals, the Preamble continued:

> The BCFW therefore recognizes and fully affirms lesbianism as one of the variety of strong and free life choices for women and recognizes that the struggle for acceptance of lesbianism as a valid lifestyle is the struggle for the right of any woman to define her life.
>
> The goal of the BCFW is to create a society where women are free, full human beings without being defined in relation to men; sexually, economically, politically or socially.

In the Lesbian Policy Proposals, printed in the next newsletter without the Preamble, there were nine areas of concern. They included: the right of lesbian mothers to live openly and not be declared unfit; the removal of the distinction between "legitimate" (that is, male-owned) children and "illegitimate" children; an end to discrimination against lesbians in childcare, housing, health, education, and employment; recognition of lesbianism as an alternative lifestyle and the inclusion of sexual preference in anti-discrimination clauses; the removal of homosexuals from the Immigration Act as a class of persons not allowed to enter the country; and that the age of consent for homosexuals be the same as for heterosexuals.

Without the Preamble, however, the policy rationale was not clear. The Preamble spelled out the crucial links between feminism and lesbianism that had to be made clear if lesbians were to win support from the entire organization. The Caucus therefore took the Preamble to the next General Standing Committee meeting, which decided to print it in the next newsletter.

The Caucus had won the right to publicize views within BCFW, but those in charge of external communication were not willing to pass on policy statements on lesbian issues to the press.[21]

The debate raged over the next few months. There were few who did not have feelings about the issue. At meetings BCFW members left chairs empty beside known lesbians, out of fear of association. There were fears that lesbianism could be used to discredit BCFW.

The Lesbian Caucus, determined to win public support for lesbian concerns, learned to function in spite of hostility. Feeling hurt and embattled, they focused on knowing the rules and articulating themselves better than others. They manipulated agendas, dominated meetings, and outvoted their opponents. It became a win or lose situation, one of the most difficult that many within the movement had ever experienced.

As members of a group under fire in BCFW, lesbians were being closely scrutinized and were more visible than they were comfortable with. Clothes became a symbol of politics. Lesbian Caucus members thought about what clothes to wear to meetings; although jeans and plaid shirts were worn by lesbians and heterosexual feminists alike, it did not help to look too much like a "dyke." As the conflict intensified, one woman who usually dressed in jeans and plaid shirts came in skirt and makeup; she did not want to be identified with the lesbians. For some lesbians, dressing in comfortable, rugged clothes was an inheritance from working-class backgrounds, as well as a symbol of sexuality.[22]

Lesbians in the Caucus, aware that their behaviour was of political import, tried not to be overt in their sexuality. They did not want to perpetuate common myths about lesbians, like lesbians being sex-crazed, always ready to leap into bed with another woman, or always exhibiting their sexuality. They became very careful not to touch each other at meetings so that they could not be accused of "flaunting it."

The issue came to a head at a general meeting of the Standing Committee in March 1975. There was a motion calling for representation of interest groups on the Standing Committee (the Lesbian Caucus was one of several interest groups). After that motion passed, four members opposed to it resigned from the Committee.

Those who could not agree with lesbian visibility had by then left BCFW, which meant that the immediate battle had been won; but the struggle was far from over. For example, the Committee had received a letter from Terrace which addressed lesbians as "green slime who should go back to the bars where you came from." Left unchecked, it said, lesbians would "bring the organization down to their gutter level."[23]

The struggle was not just one for political rights for lesbians, but was, perhaps more importantly, for a sense of acceptance and self-worth. Nym Hughes described it this way in *Stepping Out of Line*:

For years I worked as a feminist and as a lesbian in the women's movement, struggling to have lesbianism validated. The most blatant homophobic reactions I have ever experienced were from other feminists. My most painful struggles for self-worth and acceptance were within the women's movement.[24]

The Caucus had articulated the links between lesbianism and feminism as clearly as it could. Its members had presented their relationships in the best light possible, but they could not ignore the contradictions they felt in their own lives and identification with other lesbians who had different politics. To be a visible lesbian in society meant many different images and some lesbians seemed to feed the very myths that made them unacceptable as a group. What did it mean to be "out" in society as a lesbian feminist or a separatist or, maybe, a "bar dyke?" The Lesbian Caucus members were not just dealing with how they were perceived in BCFW, but with how lesbians were seen, and how they saw themselves, in society in general. The struggle for self-acceptance and self-definition was inseparable from their political battles.

Visible and Invisible: Growing Pains for BCFW

The Lesbian Caucus had won a major battle with the Standing Committee, but it had been costly. The conflict had reduced the number of Caucus members to about eight. No longer faced with opposition, the Caucus began to question its own basis of unity.

Deciding it could not do both political activism and formulate theory at the same time, the Lesbian Caucus announced the formation of the Rights of Lesbians Sub-Committee of the BCFW. This new group took on working with BCFW, while the Caucus, which then consisted of a closely knit group of six, began to focus on educational issues and developing theory. That fall the Lesbian Caucus began a series of educational workshops on the topics of lesbian feminism, lesbians and mental health, lesbian mothers, lesbians and employment, lesbians and the media, and lesbians and the community.[25]

The second annual BCFW convention was held on the last weekend of October 1975. About eighty women came from several regions of British Columbia to ratify the constitution, pass new policy, and elect a new Standing Committee. The convention unanimously passed the constitution, including sections on childcare policy, rights of lesbian women, rights of women in prison, education, and general actions. The BCFW had developed a unified base. But, as the outgoing Standing Committee made clear in the statement it handed out, that base had not been easy to find.

The BCFW had survived its first year. It had connected women province-wide and provided political experience for many. But the diversity of the movement and differences among the women had strained this tenuous fusion to the limit. Many of the differences had been fought out over the lesbian issue. The Lesbian Caucus had been the target for a good deal of scapegoating. At the time, the inability of BCFW to move forward or encourage participation was blamed on the lesbian presence.

For feminists in British Columbia the first year of BCFW was the beginning of the process of dealing with visible difference and anger between women in a public way. Difference and anger were not things that had been dealt with by many consciousness-raising groups or women's groups until that point. Conflict was, in fact, a test for support and unity.

For lesbians in British Columbia the struggle within BCFW gave rise to a theory of lesbian feminism and the incorporation of lesbianism within the feminist movement. Both are irrefutable and strengthening. In 1984 the remaining members of the Lesbian Caucus published a workbook on the connections between lesbianism and feminism.[26] It was the first book of its kind in Canada and has at its core the concepts that began at the 1974 founding convention of BCFW.

For some women the BCFW was their first political experience. For others it was the first contact with the realities of lesbianism or recognition of lesbianism within themselves. For all, it was a time of expansion of feminist consciousness and analysis.

Notes

1. This article is an abridged version of a much more detailed study, researched and written in 1985-86. Information was gathered by examining a mixture of oral sources, published materials, and unpublished documents. The original paper is available at the Canadian Women's Movement Archives, Toronto.

   Thank you to the following people for their histories and documents: Cy-Thea Sand, Esther Phillips, Nym Hughes, Yvonne Johnson, Cynthia Flood, Alice Ages, Gillian Smith, Linda Hancock, Ellen Frank, Jacquie Denage, Miriam Azreal, Donna Lee, Coral, and Rob Joyce. For personal and academic support, thank you to Phyllis Tatum, Rowena Hunnisett, Indianna Matters, Dr. Paddy Tsurumi, Dr. Christine St. Peter, and Dr. Angus McLaren.

2. See Sidney Abbott and Barbara Love, *Sappho Was a Right On Woman* (Toronto: Stein and Day, 1972). Chapter 5 gives a history of the lesbian-heterosexual feminist confrontation that took place in the New York chapter of the National Organization of Women.

3. BCFW warrants a history of its own; it was an essential and illuminating attempt at the mass mobilization of women in British Columbia. This article gives only a partial account.

4. For a re-examination of "butch" and "femme" and an excellent use of oral history see Madeline Davis and Elizabeth Lapovsky Kennedy, "Oral History and the Study of Sexuality in the Lesbian Community: Buffalo, New York, 1940-1960," *Feminist Studies*, Vol. 12, No. 1 (Spring 1986), pp. 7-26.

5. Letter from the "Mothers of Confederation," *Pedestal: The Vancouver Women's Liberation Newspaper*, Vol. 5, No. 6 (October 1973), p. 12.

6. Cynthia Flood, "BCFW Herstory," *BCFW Newsletter*, Vol. 1, No. 1 (November 1974), p. 5.

7. Ibid.

8. They also wanted, but were unable, to organize a women's parliament, as a show of the collective power and insight of the women's movement. This was a direct inheritance from the suffragists at the beginning of the century, when women's parliaments were a high profile feature of the movement in Canada. See Catharine Lyle Cleverdon, *The Woman Suffrage Movement in Canada: The Start of Liberation 1900-20* (Toronto: University of Toronto Press, 1950), pp. 59-70.

9. General Steering Committee meeting minutes, Board Room, YMCA, Vancouver, June 15, 1974. Alice Ages chair.

10. Ibid.

11. Esther Phillips, group interview, March 22, 1986.

12. Cynthia Flood, "BCFW Founding Convention," *Priorities*, Vol. 2, No. 9 (September 1974), p. 36.

13. Yvonne Johnson, oral history, recorded by the author on February 7, 1986, San Francisco.

14. Ibid.

15. Nym Hughes, Yvonne Johnson, Yvette Perreault, *Stepping Out of Line: A Workbook on Lesbianism and Feminism* (Vancouver: Press Gang, 1984), p. 7.

16. Kate Swann, "BCFW Standing Committee Meets," *BCFW Newsletter*, Vol. 1, No. 1 (November 1974), p. 2.

17. "Lesbian Caucus," *BCFW Newsletter*, Vol. 1, No. 1 (November 1974), p. 9.

18. Ibid.

19. "Inside Canada's prisons," *Time*, December 9, 1974.

20. "Lesbian Caucus," *BCFW Newsletter*, Vol. 1, No. 4 (March 1975), p. 9.

21. Jacquie Denage, telephone interview, April 2, 1986.

22. For Lesbian Caucus members, class would have been a major issue had anyone thought to address it. Almost all in the Caucus came from working-class backgrounds, although they tended not to recognize this until several years later. Differences in clothes and behaviour were not just rooted in sexual differences but in class backgrounds too.

23. Esther Phillips, collective interview, Vancouver, February 9, 1986, tape 1-1, and Nym Hughes, personal interview, Vancouver, December 7, 1985.

24. Hughes, Johnson, and Perreault, *Stepping Out of Line*. There is another explanation of the hostility. In *Sappho Was a Right On Woman* Sidney Abbott and Barbara Love write of the lesbian-heterosexual hostilities that almost split the National Organization of Women (NOW) in the United States:

> Hostility within a group of like-minded people is more bitterly felt than when it arises between separate entities.... The many shared similarities among feminists – goals, interests and feelings – heighten the importance of any discrepancies and sharpen the antagonisms. Thus, people who have many common features often do to each other worse harm than they would to complete strangers.

25. These workshops were the beginning of what would become an important part of B.C. lesbian feminist theory and culture: the "Stepping Out of Line" workshops.

26. Hughes, Johnson, and Perreault, *Stepping Out of Line*.

14

Lesbian Mothers Organizing

Sharon Dale Stone

On International Women's Day, 1978, the Lesbian Mothers' Defence Fund (LMDF) launched its efforts to put lesbian mothers' and our children's needs high on the agendas of the gay and women's movements. Our services have included financial help for women's custody struggles, peer counselling, our newsletter (the *Grapevine*), monthly pot-lucks and an information and referral phone line. Nine years later, on Lesbian and Gay Pride Day, 1987, we're announcing the closing of the LMDF.

We have spread the word to our communities and to the public that lesbian mothers exist and will no longer pay the penalty of forced childlessness or separation from their children for the "crime" of loving the wrong person. The LMDF has helped many women keep or win custody of their children and has brought many more into contact with each other.

We have no sense of completion, only one of having run out of steam for now, and of being unable to meet demands on time and energy we don't have.

Thank you for your help and friendship.

THIS ANNOUNCEMENT, signed by the women of the LMDF in Toronto, appeared in the September 1987 issue of the lesbian and gay newsmagazine, *Rites*. Tragically, another lesbian organization was unable to keep going.[1] LMDF folded for much the same reasons that many organizations depending on volunteer labour fold. Yet those who worked to keep it going faced an added pressure: they were not engaged in work that was acceptable in a wider social context. Had they been doing "respectable" work, they might have been able to count on donations from wealthy patrons, government grants, and new volunteers. But LMDF was engaged in publicizing something that most people don't like to acknowledge – the existence of lesbian mothers – and was helping them to feel good about who they were.

In 1984, when LMDF was relatively strong, I interviewed twenty women who were involved with the organization.[2] I thought it was important to document the experiences of the women who got involved with LMDF, what they did, their motivations, hopes, and dreams.

LMDF was originally conceptualized in the mid-1970s by a small group of non-mothers who had, as one of the founders said, "grandiose" ideas about what they could do to improve the position of lesbian mothers in society. They believed that if they could do something to change the fate of lesbian mothers, all lesbians would benefit. As one of them saw it, the right to mother was a fundamental human rights issue, as important as the right to choose to remain childless.

In 1976 the group, still just a loose collection of friends, organized a lesbian conference that included a session on lesbian mothers and child custody. To advertise the conference they put up posters in various places, including a Children's Aid office. A lesbian mother, Mrs. X who was "in the first throes of a custody fight for her three kids," saw the poster there and contacted the group.

They then became involved with the first of what would be many custody battles, working for the next year with Mrs. X and her lawyer to find as much legal and psychological material on the issue as possible. They helped her out financially by raising money at a benefit dance, and publicized her case to raise consciousness around the issue. Finally, in November 1977, Mrs. X's husband dropped his suit and she won unconditional custody. Feeling victorious, the group was inspired to continue this kind of work, joined by Mrs. X who wanted to help other lesbian mothers facing difficulties. In March 1978 members formally founded LMDF as a resource organization for lesbian mothers fighting for child custody. As one of the founders put it:

> We wanted to highlight the obstacles to lesbian mothers keeping their kids, such as the prejudice against lesbians, women's poverty which prevented women from leaving marriages which

were miserable, and the shroud around the existence of lesbian mothers which meant that every lesbian mother who contemplated fighting for her kids felt she was the only one. If we could first of all begin to publicize these events, generally without using any woman's name, we could begin to raise the consciousness of people in legal and psychological fields who work with these women.... And if we could do the public education successfully then we would be able to do a whole set of other things like put together networks of lawyers and psychologists who were interested in this issue. We could begin to effect changes from the point of view of judges and the Official Guardian and even people in the schools who were working with kids.

The first year of LMDF was a busy one. With the help of a grant, LMDF printed two thousand brochures and mailed them across Canada. Posters advertising its resources were delivered to local church groups, community centres, women's services, and legal and social service agencies. As they delivered the posters, the women talked to staff about the importance of displaying the material. Only two places, both social service agencies, were reluctant to display it, arguing that they had no lesbian clients. Later, an early LMDF newsletter commented: "Because of the need for concealment, especially in dealings with welfare and legal aid workers, it is not surprising that these two agencies have remained ignorant of the existence of lesbian mothers among their clientele."[3]

During the first year there were also media interviews, meetings with lawyers, law students, and women's groups, and speaking engagements in schools and various other organizations. Lesbian mothers began hearing about LMDF and telephoning for information. Soon LMDF was receiving calls daily and meeting with many lesbian mothers.

The numerous meetings with individual mothers soon became too much to handle and group members got the idea of having monthly potluck lunch meetings. This was suggested by Mrs. X, who felt that in addition to help with custody battles, lesbian mothers needed contact with each other. The first potluck meeting was early in 1979. An LMDF report described the event:

> There were nine mothers gathered, all meeting each other for the first time, and about a dozen other women who were friends of the mothers, or women working with the Defence Fund ... ,

We planned our first issue of our newsletter and scheduled the next monthly meeting, so we could tell new women about it. Through the afternoon we all marvelled at being together. Those of us who have been building the Defence Fund for three years, from a single contact with Mrs. X, felt tremendous pride and excitement. But the mothers, who have been absolutely alone, had suddenly found themselves. The Lesbian Mothers' Defence Fund is now all of these women. Each of them has something in mind that she wants to do to help.[4]

By 1984 LMDF was made up of lesbians in a variety of situations. Some mothers were open about their lesbianism even before contacting LMDF; some were coming secretly to meetings while still living with their husbands; some came only after leaving a marriage to find help with a custody battle; some never had to worry about custody; some had told their children about their lesbianism, while others had not. There were also lesbian mothers who had never been married, refusing to believe that lesbianism was a barrier to having and raising children. And there were childless lesbians who came to support the rights of lesbian mothers.

Within two years of the founding of LMDF, all but one of the original non-mothers had left. The one who stayed explained why she remained committed:

In some ways I think it's been a strain. It's not a real natural place for me to be. In other ways it has felt natural because I've never wanted to make a decision not to have a child, and it's been on my mind ever since I started thinking about the issue. It's been part of the personal stake. The other part would be just that I've always felt that the lesbian world is a lot bigger than it was represented to be a couple of years ago – that concerns were much more miscellaneous and wide-ranging ...

It used to appear that lesbians were mainly young and childless and footloose and homogeneous and that the concerns of lesbians were largely with building a lesbian culture that reflected our independence from men.... I feel we've really expanded the picture.

Other lesbians who were not biological mothers came into LMDF over the years. Some of them came simply because they believed that LMDF was engaged in important work. Others came to accompany lovers with children, and to get some support themselves in the role of co-parent. In the first issue of *Grapevine,* for example, one wrote:

> I feel a lot of the time at a total loss as to the way to approach my lover's son.... But I know now that there are other women in similar positions. Through the Defence Fund for Lesbian Mothers I do not feel as alone.

For lesbian mothers the motivations behind the decision to become involved with LMDF were varied. Without exception, however, the mothers interviewed mentioned a desire to know other lesbian mothers. One explained:

> When a mother who is in the position that I was in, where you feel like you've got no friends, nobody else is in your position with children ... it helps a lot just meeting other mothers too.

Another valued the support of other lesbian mothers because:

> I didn't have to first convince people why I wanted my children. You don't have to sit down with a woman who's in the same situation as you and justify loving them. Some women ... make you wonder whether having children is seen as a valid thing to be doing and they're not the people you're going to want to go to for support on the issue of keeping your kids.

Other mothers expressed the desire to be with other lesbian mothers, as opposed to being with childless lesbians:

> Just being a mother separates you automatically from one that does not have a child, if only in that there's a better understanding, a sympathy there, that you can communicate with.

Another said:

> I guess I'm afraid that other lesbians who don't have kids are not going to understand, or they're going to come over and want to spend time with me but reject my children.

Also:

Just on the mothering side of it, it's important to me to be able to share experiences with other women who are raising their kids in lesbian households.

Mothers often said that they felt relief after attending their first LMDF meeting. They were relieved to discover that they were not the only lesbians in the world to have married and had children, that there was not a contradiction between being a lesbian and being a mother, and that one did not have to fit a stereotype to be a lesbian. Many came to LMDF looking for a place to discuss their concerns as single parents or issues unique to lesbian mothers, such as what was the best way to tell their children about their sexuality, whether the children should be told, and how to deal with a homophobic school system.

Those worried about the custody of their children were often prompted to call LMDF in the first place simply for information. One mother, who lived just outside the city, said:

All I wanted to do was plan my case. What was great was that any time I needed information I could call them and I did that over and over again. I got vast amounts of photocopied information. I would have been obliged to go up to a library in Toronto and research it myself in the middle of a custody action. It would have been just impossible.

Before LMDF began to plan regular social events such as camping trips and a monthly night out (called Cameo night), it was difficult to make friends with others. One woman reflected:

When I first came to the group, not knowing any other lesbians at all, the potlucks being once a month, I found it not enough. I didn't really know anybody – I'd only met them once ... I left the first potluck meeting thinking I can't wait another month, you know, it's too long.

As it turned out, it was largely due to this member's insistence that a regular night out became institutionalized. On this, she commented:

Now it doesn't go a whole month because there is the Cameo

night ... so there's two regular things a month now which I think helps a lot.

According to another:

I like the Cameo nights because they are something that are very clearly just social. One of the problems with the potlucks is that there are just too many things, too many agendas. Cameo nights give an opportunity to socialize, to take off some of the pressure to get everything done at a potluck, including making new friends.

Another valued Cameo night because:

I feel very isolated a lot of the time. I don't have the opportunity for much of a social life at this point. So the LMDF gives me the opportunity to get out to ... their Cameo nights and start establishing a social life.

The mothers I interviewed were concerned about the emotional well-being of their children. Several said that one reason they valued LMDF was because it allowed the children to realize that others were in their situation. Mothers believed that it helped their children, just "seeing that they're not the only ones." One mother wanted LMDF to become like an extended family for both herself and her children, while another noted:

Just as it was important for me to know that there were other people like me out there, I think it's really important for [my son] to know that he's not the only one with a lesbian mother. And if he has problems with that as he grows up there will be friends that he can talk to or complain with or whatever he wants to do with them. There are other kids his age who are in the same situation.

Few lesbian mothers, when they first became involved, were able to see beyond their own personal situations. Most simply looked for support of one kind or another. With the passage of time, however, including time to grow more secure about their identities, many began to think about helping to make it easier for other lesbian mothers. One reflected:

I think you change. After a while you want to get involved and feel that maybe you've got something to offer.

Additionally:

> Before I would have said LMDF was important to me for emotional support. Now I want to inform other people about who we are and what we do ... I will probably be with LMDF for a long time and that comes primarily because of the solitude that I thought I was sort of wallowing in when I was alone. I didn't have any resources available to call on, and I'd like to offer that over the next I don't care how many years.

Another woman said, "It's not the kind of thing you can walk away from," while another did not see how one could "forget about all the other women who are dealing with the reality of threats and custody cases." For reasons such as these, all enthusiastically supported and contributed to LMDF's attempts to reach out to others.

Most restricted their outreach activities to helping with the production of *Grapevine*. The advantage of working on *Grapevine* as opposed to other types of outreach work was that it could be worked on anonymously. All considered *Grapevine* to be of inestimable value. It was a means of making contact with people who lived far away and it carried the potential of reaching lesbian mothers who were alone.

Grapevine stood as a tangible expression of LMDF's views. Produced two or three times a year, it reported on North American custody battles and commented on implications for other lesbian mothers. Sometimes in *Grapevine* lesbian mothers told their own stories about their fights for child custody. Other articles discussed LMDF activities. Each issue also reiterated both the goals of LMDF and the resources available to lesbian mothers.

Other types of outreach activities, such as media interviews or public speaking, were taken on by relatively few LMDF women. They travelled to various Ontario towns and cities, and other Canadian cities such as Calgary, Montreal, and Halifax, to promote LMDF. Yet, they felt unable to accomplish all that they wanted. One commented in 1984:

> We've probably had the most speaks, the most opportunities, in the past year, that we've ever had, and it's growing more and

more. However, what we're finding a problem with is that there's not enough people within the organization who can afford to come out publicly, so we're missing some opportunities too.

When LMDF first started, public speaking was done almost exclusively by non-mothers. When mothers did speak, it was anonymously. Mrs. X spoke at a demonstration in 1978 with a paper bag over her head. In 1979 two LMDF mothers were interviewed on television, but were disguised. By 1983 public speaking was done almost exclusively by lesbian mothers. This added considerable credibility to the message that LMDF was trying to get across.

Most of those I interviewed stressed the need to reach lesbian mothers who were isolated in their homes, mothers who believed that no one had ever gone through what they were experiencing. It was important to the women at LMDF to break the barrier of silence surrounding lesbian motherhood, and to let others know that they were not alone. This was why they believed it was important to talk to the mainstream media. Publishing *Grapevine* was not enough. One woman estimated that 50 per cent of those who got involved with LMDF first heard about the group by reading a newspaper or magazine article, listening to the radio, or watching television.

Aside from reaching other lesbian mothers, the women at LMDF were interested in educating the public about the existence of lesbian mothers and what kind of people they were. As one said:

> One of the things we have to fight against is ... getting people to realize that we are people – multi-faceted individuals. Our lifestyles are varied, our attitudes are varied, we're all individuals. I think it's important for people to start realizing that just because we're lesbians, we're not automatically pushed into one category of child-molesting monsters who are demented and twisted.... We're still the same people that we always were. It suddenly doesn't turn us from good mothers into monsters because all of a sudden the word lesbian is connected with us. I think that's the major thing that has to be broken through.

Several mothers pointed out the necessity of educating other lesbians and gay men. Many of them had found out for themselves that lesbians don't always welcome or support other lesbians who are different from them. For example, one mother related the following anecdote:

> At International Women's Day last year, we were carrying the LMDF banner and two lesbians were walking in front of us. They were walking along and all of a sudden they looked up and they realized what banner they were marching under. And they said, "Oh my God! Do you realize where we're marching?" I just looked at them and said, "Don't worry, it doesn't bother us." And they just looked at me!

Another mother once spoke on behalf of LMDF to a gay men's group, only to hear one of them say, "Well, I guess it's okay for lesbians to be mothers." She pointed out to them that it was not a question of whether or not it was okay, because she *already was* a lesbian mother. The comment, she felt, was symptomatic of the widespread ignorance about the existence of lesbian mothers.

Others believed that public education should be done within the public school system. This led some LMDF women to enter into discussions with the Toronto Board of Education in 1980 and by 1984 LMDF was part of a coalition working to change the guidelines on sex education and family life curricula for both the Toronto Board of Education and the Ontario Ministry of Education. The coalition presented a brief recommending that homosexuality be included as a standard topic of discussion in schools. As one woman wrote in *Grapevine*:

> Women in the LMDF have an intense interest in this issue, both on behalf of their children, who are made to feel there's something bad in a subject that never seems to see the light of day in school, and in remembrance of their own experience as children and teenagers, when a few unbiased words about lesbianism might have made a difference in the choices they made.[5]

Finally, one mother told me that in breaking the silence about the existence of lesbian mothers, LMDF was breaking the silence about motherhood. She said:

> LMDF is breaking new ground in that the issues were never addressed before. The issue of motherhood is really a primary

issue.... I think the whole issue of motherhood is being addressed in the work that the LMDF does. LMDF is making us talk about mothering and what that means.

How successful was LMDF in changing life for lesbian mothers? Certainly, it made a difference for those who became involved in LMDF activities. Equally certain, LMDF forced a lot of people to acknowledge the existence of lesbian mothers. The courts no longer automatically consider lesbianism per se as a barrier to granting custody. How much the work of LMDF had to do with this is questionable. Perhaps the courts would have become more tolerant anyway. Two mothers from LMDF, though, believed that their husbands did not even try for custody of their children because they felt threatened by LMDF's existence.

The very existence of LMDF challenged conventional ideas not only about what it is to be a lesbian, but also about what it is to be a mother. Those who spoke out and supported lesbian mothers deserve credit for breaking the silence. They have made it easier for all to recognize that lesbians truly are a diverse group of women.

Notes
1. Another LMDF, in Calgary, continued to meet.
2. This article is based on those interviews and on LMDF documents. The women I interviewed included four non-mothers, five mothers in the midst of child custody battles, six mothers who feared they might be sued for custody, and five mothers who had never faced or feared a custody battle. Their ages ranged from twenty to forty and the ages of their children ranged from less than one year to fifteen years old. All women were white and most had low incomes. I believe my sample was representative of those who attended LMDF meetings in all respects except race (occasionally, lesbians of colour attended meetings but not in large numbers or frequently). I thank these women for allowing me to interview them.
3. Lesbian Mothers' Defence Fund, *Interim Report of the Activities of the LMDF*, Nov. 15, 1978.
4. Lesbian Mothers' Defence Fund, *Calendar of Recent Activities of the Lesbian Mothers' Defence Fund*, February 1979.
5. Lesbian Mothers' Defence Fund, *Grapevine*, No. 4, 1984, p. 4.

15

Organizing Lesbian Studies
at Concordia

Carolyn Gammon et al.[1]

BEHIND EVERY ORGANIZATION there are personal histories that answer the question – why? Why get involved? Why organize? Why this particular focus? Each member of the Lesbian Studies Coalition of Concordia (LSCC) answers these questions in a different way. Altogether the stories create a mosaic of how one organization came into being.

The LSCC was formed in spring 1987 and soon began to take shape, to plan and realize projects. Because we are a relatively young organization it seems appropriate to outline the "whys" of our organization, which we hope might serve as inspiration for other student groups across Canada. To document how the LSCC came into being, Coalition members were asked to write on why they joined, or why they saw a need for the group. Following are the responses.

Susan

Last Wednesday afternoon during a meeting of the Lesbian Studies Coalition, I found myself looking around the room wondering what on earth brought me together with such a diverse group of people every week – and loving it. The answer goes back to a time almost thirty years ago.

When I was a little girl and grown-ups would ask me what I was going to be when I grew up, I would never answer. I had a recurring nightmare of being in a box with no escape and had assumed that when I grew up I would be buried alive. It was only many years later that I read a book by Marilyn Frye, *The Politics of Reality*, that gave me a different explanation for my boxed-in dreams.

Oppression is like a birdcage, she said. If you look very closely at just one wire in the cage, you cannot see the other wires. No matter how hard you look, you just cannot see why a bird would have any trouble getting past the wire to fly away. It is only when you stand back and see the whole cage that you can understand why the bird cannot go anywhere. The wires, like the strands of oppression, are a network of systematically related barriers which together are as confining as the solid walls of a dungeon.

In the years before I fully understood the implications of my oppression as a woman and as a lesbian, the educational system and I were continually at odds. In my last year of public school, angry at being forced to wear a skirt during the biting Ottawa winters, I organized a group action with the other girls after discussions with my teachers had proved futile. We all appeared at school one day in slacks. Our teachers were outraged and made us change back into skirts immediately. I was the only student who hadn't brought a skirt in her schoolbag to change into and therefore was the only one punished. Being detained after school for two weeks meant that I missed my school bus and had to walk the two miles home – in a skirt.

The incident was just the start of a series of clashes with school authorities. In high school, after my repeated questions about the relevance of some of the course material went unheeded, I gave up and stopped going to many of my classes. When I was sixteen I left school altogether. I managed to find work and later went to community college to learn a trade, but always dreamed of obtaining a "higher" education.

In my late twenties I was accepted as a mature student by the University of Ottawa, where I wanted to major in philosophy. The first term I was fortunate to take a course called "Philosophical Issues in Women's Studies." I was ecstatic. It was the first time I remembered being in a classroom learning about issues that were clearly relevant to my life. Disappointed to learn that the course was not a regular one – it was taught by a part-timer – I naively sought out the head of the philosophy department in the hope of getting more such courses offered on a regular basis.

I pointed out to him that his department, the largest in the Arts faculty, had twenty-nine men and one anti-feminist woman, teaching undergraduate courses to mostly women students. I expressed surprise that there was only one occasional course that dealt directly with women's issues, and all the other courses had reading lists of books written by men only. Couldn't something be changed, I asked?

His answer shocked me. If I was interested in learning things from a women's perspective, he said, I was in the wrong department. Perhaps I should investigate the Women's Studies Program, he suggested as he ushered me out of his office.

After a few other such incidents in "mainstream" courses, Women's Studies was indeed where I ended up. Taking Women's Studies courses proved exciting and rewarding, but there were limitations. I was just coming out as a lesbian and found that my shaky questions about lesbianism were dealt with as abruptly as my questions about women were dismissed by mainstream professors. It was only in my final year that I took a seminar course that offered books by lesbians on the reading list. I was validated for whom I was by the course content, and by the contribution that other lesbians and myself could bring to the discussions. I learned more in that one course than in any other I had taken during my three years at that university.

When I moved to Montreal I zeroed in on Concordia because of the Simone de Beauvoir Institute, but quickly realized that lesbians were marginalized in courses here as well. I joined the Lesbian Studies Coalition to try to change that situation. Since becoming active in the group and feeling the support of the other lesbians with me, I find I am able to be more open in my classes. Now that my self-repression has lifted somewhat I feel more energetic and enthusiastic about my academic work. For example, I am taking a studio art course where I recently presented a performance piece which I felt was the first artistic work I had done that came from me and not from outside. I was very proud of it and it was well received by the audience.

Interestingly enough, the work itself had no specifically lesbian content but dealt with the constricting nature of social etiquette. I am quite sure that on a deeper level that artwork represents my first real attempt to escape from the cage I have been in since I was a little girl. I intend to continue both my artwork and my theoretical work as a way of bringing myself and others trapped in their cages out into the open. Once we're free, who knows where we'll fly?

Monica

I joined the LSCC for two very distinct reasons. The first was entirely personal. I am just now beginning the process of "coming out" as a lesbian, even to myself. I'm searching for other lesbians with whom I can relate, who can understand what I'm feeling and who are asking some of the same questions as I am. Such women are not easy to find.

Until you are an established member of it, and maybe even after that, the lesbian "community" is a very nebulous concept. The most concrete manifestations of it are probably the bars. That makes it awkward to approach if you're a lesbian who doesn't drink. The Lesbian Studies Coalition at Concordia was the first group I found where lesbians were getting together to discuss ideas and were active in having those ideas, and who they were, recognized and affirmed by the broader community.

The second reason I have for joining relates to my own experience as a lesbian student. I have been a women-loving woman for as long as I can remember but I didn't even know such a thing as a lesbian existed until a few years ago. If homosexuality had shared equal status with heterosexuality in my high school and college curricula, reading material, and as a basis for discussion, I would have been spared a lot of unnecessary pain. If I can, I would like to spare other young lesbians that pain.

School, along with family and peers, is a young person's major source of values and personal identity. Not only is lesbianism never mentioned within it, but so-called "queers," "fags," "dykes" are actively degraded and humiliated. A university is a good place to start influencing the educational system because of its avowed commitment to academic freedom. But eventually we must work for the elimination of homophobia and heterosexism from nursery school right up through graduate school.

Ina

Last Wednesday afternoon Carolyn marched into our weekly Lesbian Studies Coalition meeting with a copy of *How to Stay Out of the Gynecologist's Office* and said loudly: "I've photocopied the relevant pages for you, here, they'll tell you all you'll ever need to know about vaginitis." I gave her a look that was meant to freeze her in her tracks but had no effect whatsoever.

Then we got down to serious business.

On the agenda was the info packet we plan to make up for faculty. We decided that we'd like to invite faculty involved in Lesbian Studies in universities near us to a Round Table, to discuss the info packet and steps to implement Lesbian Studies here at Concordia. It was suggested we'd have to bribe them here with the promise of something besides alcohol. I suggested girls. Utter, dead silence. Then someone said: "I can't believe someone said that."

Well, if this doesn't document the need for Lesbian Studies, I don't know what could.

Renel

Education is about freedom. How can we have freedom for ourselves and with others? How can there be any sharing of ideas, of beauty between people who have learnt to hate one another? Who have learnt not to listen to one another? Freedom is a product of growth and personal growth requires an expansion of thoughts and perspectives to move us to more sensitive and sensible actions.

I feel a keen sense of salvation when I think of lesbians and the perspective of lesbians. Think of a society undergoing the same realizations about women as lesbians have undergone ... celebrating our strength, our tenderness, our sternness, our softness. Think of recognizing our power, of greeting our thoughts, mind, and body, and all the perspectives and talents we own.

I think it is essential that the voices of lesbians are not just considered vaguely but recognized as a force and source of power which, in its very nature, may prove to be the lever needed to swing things over to a new and better level of consciousness.

Being a lesbian is far too marvelous a thing to keep hidden.

Claudette

DE LA NECESSITE D'UNE PERSPECTIVE LESBIENNE; OU COMMENT J'AI SURVECUE A UNE EDUCATION HETERO-SEXISTE

La question concernant la pertinence d'intégrer une perspective lesbienne à l'école ayant été démontrée de façon assez convaincante, il nous reste tout de même à élucider un mystère. Je m'explique: comment une personne "normalement" constituée, ayant vécue dans une famille "normale," dotée d'une intelligence "normale," passant normalement du primaire au secondaire puis, du secondaire au cegep, etc. ... comment dis-je bien une telle personne peut-elle survivre "normalement" à une éducation si normalement hétérosexuelle et se découvrir lesbienne au cours du processus???

Voici donc quelques étapes de ce processus hétérosexualisant à travers lequel j'ai si admirablement survécu:

PRIMAIRE:
Cours: Dictée
"Jean et Jeannette s'aiment. Jean et Jeannette sont mariée depuis cinq ans. Jean et Jeannette ont deux beaux enfants, Yves et Yvette. Yves joue aux camions. Yvette joue à la poupée."
Récréation: cour d'école:
"– On joue aux gars qui attrappent les filles"

SECONDAIRE:
Cours: Mathématiques
$1 + 1$ = beaucoup d'enfants, une maison, une voiture, le bonheur assuré avant la fin de vos jours.
Elémentaire ma chère!
Cours: Biologie
"Voici l'appareil reproducteur mâle ... et femelle. Voici "la" sexualité.

CEGEP
Cours: psychologie du comportement sexual
"– Nous savons que deux personnes sur dix sont homosexuelles, logiquement nous devrions donc retrouver quelques spécimens parmi nous. Nous reparlerons de ce problème au chapitre dix de votre livre, chapitre traitant des dysfonctions sexuelles chez l'être humain."
J'abandonne le cours.

UNIVERSITE:
Cours: Sexualités et Sociétés
Je soumet, timidement, un essai sur les tendances politiques du lesbianisme, on remarque: "Travail très intéressant, malheureusement, vous êtes trop près de votre sujet d'étude, en locurence, vous manquez d'objectivité."
HA!?

J'ai, comme vous l'avez sûrement remarqué, simplifié de beaucoup le "dit" Processus hétérosexualisant. Sous cette forme, il ne consiste qu'en un échantillon non-aléatoire et trés subjectif. Mais, qu'importe la scientificité puisque, devant un tel phénomène, nous ne pouvons qu'en arriver à une conclusion: celles d'entre nous qui avons survécues à ce processus, sommes, et je le dit sans fausse modestie, nous sommes des héroïnes. Comme toutes les héroïnes, l'histoire ne peut se passer de nous plus longtemps. Entrons dans l'histoire, re-faisons l'histoire.

Ming

I was born in Vietnam, where I lived to the age of five when my parents and I emigrated. Since, I have done most of my growing up in Canada, where I have had the experience of belonging to minorities, both in terms of race and sexual orientation.

I found the two experiences to have some things in common, like invisibility in the media, segregation into low-income brackets and / or unskilled labour pools, covert discrimination in the form of jokes and stereotypical caricatures, as well as more overt forms of discrimination like heckling and physical violence. However, I must admit that I find it much less nerve-racking to be Vietnamese than to be lesbian in this society.

For one thing, no one ever asks me to justify myself as a Vietnamese. I've never been asked to explain how I became Vietnamese, or to try to remember when I had my first Vietnamese experience. These types of questions are the first things I hear when I come out to the average heterosexual. I've even been told to "reconsider" my sexual identity, lest it cause me or my children pain and unhappiness in the future. I doubt this person has ever considered changing her Vietnamese identity and cultural values to save herself and her children the unhappiness of being different from the North American "norm."

Along the same lines, I find it quite easy to find information, scarce as it is, about Vietnam, its history, its culture, and its people. I only need to ask my relatives, or I can go to any library or bookstore in search of the available literature. The Vietnamese people have community centres, businesses, and schools that are quite easy to find because they are prominently advertised.

By comparison, I found my quest for information about anything lesbian or gay, begun at age sixteen, to be much more problematic. At the time I was fortunate enough to be living in Vancouver where there are lesbian listings in the phone book and a large and active lesbian community. Even so, it took me years to feel that I knew the community and that I belonged in it. One of my first attempts to come out was in university, at the local women's centre. It was met with hostility and disapproval by the collective members who were lesbians themselves, but who didn't want the word "lesbian" associated with the women's centre.

Years later, when I came in contact with the Lesbian Studies Coalition of Concordia, I was struck by how novel the idea of Lesbian Studies seemed to me. Over the years, I had come to take lesbian invisibility as a fact of life. Lesbian material was marginal in the women's studies classes I had attended, and completely absent from any other course I've ever taken. Having lesbian material available at a university level would have been so helpful to me when I was coming out. I'm sure it would be for many other lesbians who are struggling to come out. They deserve to have information available to them. Isn't it about time they got it?

Carolyn
I grew up in Fredericton, New Brunswick, and took my undergraduate degree there in physical education. I was a regular alienated adolescent who was lucky enough to vent her frustrations on the basketball court and field hockey pitch. I never felt I fit in on those teams. I would often remain silent for the seven-hour drives back from Nova Scotia when the "girls" discussed their boyfriends, who was sleeping with whom, what contraceptive they used, and "Didn't Julie make so much noise with Paul in the next room last night!" I did not date; I had no desire to, except maybe to have something to talk about during the long van trips. Then, in third year, I managed to "get a boyfriend" in what I see now as an act of proving my "normality," my heterosexuality.

I have since learned about myself that heterosexuality never interested me except as a way of conforming. My emotional, affective, political, and sexual life-driving forces I find in other women. Some lesbians might say they "knew at age seven" or easily chose their sexuality. Unfortunately I had a lot of internalized homophobia, and therefore self-hatred, to work through before I could realize my choice.

Growing up white, middle-class, without handicap and with education-oriented parents, I had no reason to live oppression as many do. I lived for sports, I didn't see that "politics" had anything to do with my life. That the men's sports teams had four times our budget or that I was constantly hassled while hitching I took as a natural status quo between females and males. Among my peers, lesbian was so dirty a word I virtually never heard it. Once I remember a teammate would not get on an elevator because she had heard that another player was "one of them." There were numerous jokes and slanders without the word ever being spoken. At university I studied homosexuality under the Sociology of Deviance.

A few years later, visiting Fredericton with my lover woke me up. Suddenly I could no longer take her hand; I felt embarrassed by our partnership in public. This censorship came from within. I had often felt oppressed as a woman but never identified it. But now I felt oppressed for what I considered most vital to my well-being, for whom I chose to spend my time with, for whom I loved.

I have since learned the politics. How the capitalist patriarchy needs women's exploited labour as housewives; how lesbians do not fit the plan of oppression for women; how, if girls and women were taught choice in their sexuality, lifestyles, lifelong partnerships, more and more women might actually choose lesbianism, lessening the grip of individual men over individual women. I have learnt a lot. But it doesn't make me less angry. I am angry that I grew up anti-lesbian and had to go through self-hatred and self-psychoanalysis to become lesbian. I am angry that for years I was forced to deny very positive and loving feelings I held for so many women. And I am angry that my elementary, junior, high school, and university totally failed me in this "education." I don't think it should happen anymore.

When I came to Concordia to study creative writing, I was naively expecting something better – it was 1986, and not Fredericton, after all. I censored myself in applying, selecting non-lesbian poems for submission, but since entering the program I have not. I often say in the first class that I work from a lesbian feminist analysis; my scholarship and thesis proposal stated the exact nature of my work. I have been told by advisors that my viewpoint is limited. In the game of academic freedom this is the ultimate insult and the only way they know to put down my work. When I open my lesbian mouth in class I am accused of bringing sexuality into a debate where it has no place. I educate, then I educate some more. I'm spending my time at university educating.

One year of this taught me that not my lesbian poetry, nor my openness in class, nor gaining one more enlightened prof was going to change the heterosexism in education at Concordia. In the spring of 1987, as a part of Gynergy Day in the wake of International Women's Week, I proposed a workshop: "Lesbian Studies at Concordia: Making it a Reality." Although I am not in Women's Studies, I had sat in on a few classes and once again had been dismayed at the commitment to only heterosexual studies there. I felt that collective action was needed from all lesbians and women to change this. The women coming out of that workshop felt that an ongoing group was necessary to keep the gynergy or lesergy going all year.

Our first action was a questionnaire about the need for Lesbian Studies, distributed through the student newspaper. It was accompanied by an article explaining what was meant by lesbian studies and why we perceived a need for it. We felt the article was necessary because censorship of lesbian education material has been so complete, that without some explanation it would be like asking a white person who had never seen a person of colour to comment on racism. We did not claim scientific "objectivity" but aimed at testing the field, accomplishing some consciousness-raising and gaining publicity for our newly formed group. The majority of responses were very positive so that was encouraging, but some wrote comments like "I am not in the least bit willing to be subjected to this junky attitude" (female respondent, student); or "All of this has *nothing* to do with university curriculum – except perhaps health education" (male, professor).

The negative responses helped us see what we were up against and how "academic freedom" are throw-away words to some. It was also interesting that 95 per cent of the respondents believed that professors were unwilling to deal with lesbian subject matter. One of our focuses as a group is to work with faculty to help them overcome their own homophobia, to realize they are eliminating a valid and valuable part of education when they teach heterosexism, and to give them tools to begin the process of integrating lesbian studies into university education.

In the fall of 1987 the Lesbian Studies Coalition of Concordia developed a constitution to accompany a budget request from our Student Union Association. Following is the preamble of the constitution.

Traditionally, education has reflected male experience as is seen in the overwhelming number of male professors and authors, the teaching of men's role in society (wars, business, politics, etc.) while devaluing women's role. This is a sexist education. A *heterosexist* education likewise provides only a partial world view. It offers only heterosexual models / realities / authors and teaches us to think and be heterosexual to the exclusion of all other choices.

Women especially are discriminated against by a sexist / heterosexist education. Sexism teaches women that their role in life is secondary; heterosexism in education further promotes male privilege by teaching women that their social, emotional and erotic commitment must be to men at all costs. With this teaching, women fit better into an economic system which needs their free labour as housewives and mothers. A lesbian political perspective points out the compulsory nature of heterosexuality and suggests that women should be able to freely choose their partners in life, for work, intellectually, emotionally and sexually. Our education should reflect the many life choices available to women and men.

We would not think to define "heterosexual" only in terms of sexuality; it is a social system, a politics, a way of life. So too, lesbianism is not just a matter of sexual preference but a perspective which informs all aspects of society. Lesbian studies can be brought to bear on such disciplines as: English – literature by lesbian authors or books which treat the subject of women-identified women; History – the treatment of "independent" women who did not fit male criteria for "woman" i.e. the burning of "witches" or the internment and execution of tens of thousands of lesbians and gay men in Nazi war camps; Anthropology – the study of matriarchies, of African women secret sororities, Chinese marriage resistance sisterhoods; Sociology – why lesbians have been perceived as "deviant," to serve what purpose, to maintain which social systems; Education – how children are taught to assume fixed female-male sex roles, how children are indoctrinated with exclusively heterosexual values. These are just a few examples of how Lesbian Studies could be integrated into mainstream coursework. Other applicable disciplines might be: Religious Studies, Psychology, Art, Women's Studies, Political Science, Journalism, Law, Philosophy, etc. Lesbian Studies should be seen as *one of many* critical approaches to these disciplines.

If education is to inform us about all aspects of ourselves and other's lives, it must include a lesbian studies perspective. To discourage any perspective by classist, racist, sexist, or heterosexist attitudes defeats the purpose of education. No student should feel ostracized in our university environment for her or his point of view or choice of scholarship.

Currently there is much heterosexism at our university; a curriculum which integrated Lesbian Studies as one of many possible perspectives would do much to cut away at the prejudices which now exist. We believe that *all* students, women and men, would profit from such an education.

The LSCC is made up of women who, as Adrienne Rich put it, know they need to "claim," not "receive" an education.[2] The integration of lesbian studies has been happening for years in many institutions in the United States and Europe. We feel it's high time to make a consolidated attack on the heterosexism in our Canadian universities. Why get involved? Why organize? If you have your own personal / political reasons, please join us.

Notes
1. Contributors include: Ming Dinh, Claudette Lambert, Monica McQueen, Renel Mitchell, Susan O'Donnell, and Ina Rimpau. Edited by Carolyn Gammon.
2. Adrienne Rich, *On Lies, Secrets, and Silence* (New York: W.W. Norton & Company, 1979).

16

Personal Reflections on Lesbian Organizing in Ottawa

Carmen Paquette

ON MARCH 3, 1987, John Oostrom, MP for Willowdale, stood up in the House of Commons and declared:

> Ottawa is hosting the International Women's Week ... and over 10 lesbian groups will be sponsoring seminars. This conference ... has applied for a $20,000 grant this year. Yet, the Secretary of State (Mr. Crombie) stopped payment of an $8,000 cheque for the Alberta Federation of Women United for Families, which is an anti-abortion group, and the conference has excluded REAL Women who represent a pro-family viewpoint. Why is the double standard being applied by the Secretary of State? The views of pro-life groups are far more important than the anti-life lesbian rights.[1]

So this is what happens when lesbians occupy 3 per cent of the agenda during International Women's Week. For the first time in the House of Commons, lesbianism was specifically mentioned. On this historic occasion, the six lesbian workshops out of the total 222 events organized during International Women's Week in March 1987 were denounced, and it was asked whether public funds had been directed to them.

These six lesbian workshops attracted much attention locally and nationally. Workshops for lesbians with allergies ("What are lesbians allergic to – men?") and for lesbian mothers ("How can a lesbian be a mother?") perplexed some and were the butt of jokes for others. As organizers of the workshops, we were unprepared for this ridiculous attack in the House of Commons and in the media.

The incident represented some key obstacles to lesbian visibility: lesbians in the women's movement as a threat to funding, and REAL Women's right to funding as they pursue their lesbian-bashing. It became clear to us that lesbophobia was alive and well in Canada. Lesbophobia focuses on denying and ignoring the presence of lesbians in society. This denial piggybacks on a general denial of women and women's sexuality, and the seeming impossibility of women's sexuality if no man is involved. When society is confronted with the reality that lesbians do exist, there is a strange flip flop: we are then seen as dominating every event we are involved in.

Many of us were scared or disillusioned by the excessive reactions to the lesbian workshops. Some decided to retreat from active lesbian organizing. Others, like myself, felt energized. We felt that the time had come for lesbians to take their fair share of the agenda. We were determined to have more instead of fewer lesbian workshops the following year – a commitment we followed through on.

Lesbian Groups in Ottawa

Ottawa lesbians have been getting more organized for more than a decade. In the mid-seventies LOON (Lesbians of Ottawa Now) was the first Ottawa group to organize activities such as dances, drop-ins, and coming-out groups for lesbians.

According to LOON co-founder Rose Stanton, LOON had been created by lesbians who attended the Canadian Gay Rights Coalition conference in Kingston in 1975, and who went on to organize national lesbian conferences in Ottawa in 1976 and 1978. LOON lasted until 1979, when it disbanded. It disbanded for practical reasons, including the exhaustion of organizers from working on national conferences, running weekly dances, and finding a place to hold the dances. But the coup de grace was the ideological issue of separatism. Lesbian separatism is a stance taken by lesbians who choose to devote their energy to lesbians only, refusing to work with or attend events with men. Lesbian separatists, for example, are not interested in working with gay men on issues such as sexual orientation, and see little similarity between themselves and gay men. Discussions about separatism polarized LOON to the extent that it ceased to exist as an organization. Ten years later, the wounds caused by the split have still not healed for some of LOON's members.

The gay organization with the longest continuing existence in Canada is Gays of Ottawa (GO). Created in 1971, GO has remained active ever since. In the 1970s GO was more active on national efforts to end discrimination against gays than in local activities. Over the years, GO has acquired a reputation as an organization where lesbians and their concerns are taken seriously. In the early 1980s, for example, 50 per cent of GO's board was constitutionally reserved for lesbians. Some former LOON members became active in GO during that time.

Another gay rights organization with a significant lesbian presence is the national organization EGALE (Equality for Gays and Lesbians Everywhere). Formed in 1986 and operating out of Ottawa, EGALE is lobbying to have discrimination on the basis of sexual orientation made illegal.

Since the 1970s there have been activities for lesbians at Ottawa's two universities (Carleton and Ottawa), such as coming-out groups, discussion groups, dances, and even a Lesbian Film Festival at the University of Ottawa in 1983. As well, the Ottawa Women's Bookstore has continued to be a place where lesbians can connect with each other. Since 1984, *Lesbian Fury / Furie lesbienne* has published a quarterly newsletter. Since 1985, the International Women's Week collective has been organizing regular women's dances. Other lesbian groups such as ADLIB (Association Dedicated to Lesbians in Business), Sporty Dykes, and Lesbian Daughters of Alcoholics have also sprung up in recent years.

The catalyst year for lesbian political organizing in Ottawa was 1986. In March 1986, International Women's Week (IWW) included official and unofficial lesbian workshops. That spring, those who organized and attended the IWW lesbian workshops created Lesbian Amazons, a radical lesbian collective for political action. In June plans began for an International Lesbian Week in Ottawa, similar to one being planned in Vancouver. The plans came to fruition as the first Ottawa International Lesbian Week was successfully held in October 1986.

During IWW in 1987 lesbians were more visible than ever, thanks not only to the publicity generated in the House of Commons, but also to the presence of three lesbian booths at IWW's Information Fair. The controversy over IWW's lesbian workshops strengthened commitment to organizing the second International Lesbian Week in October 1987. But by the time it was held, the initial elation over making lesbians more visible had begun to dissipate. There was, and continues to be, less clarity or concensus on the direction to take in lesbian organizing in Ottawa.

Like LOON a decade earlier, lesbians in Ottawa were once again polarized by the issue of lesbian separatism. Other differences also came to the forefront, as illustrated by the debate over whether to serve alcohol at the 1986 International Lesbian Week dance. This impassioned debate lasted for three hours, with some arguing that lesbians are responsible for their own behaviour (and therefore alcohol should be served) and others arguing that lesbians should not be encouraged to use potentially dangerous substances. In the end a compromise was reached: it was agreed to serve both alcoholic and non-alcoholic drinks. The compromise satisfied no one. This debate, trivial as it may seem in light of the oppression of lesbians in the larger society, is nevertheless indicative of the many differences between lesbians – differences that can make the dream of lesbian unity seem like a naive illusion.

My Struggle Against Lesbophobia

In a world with little love for women, I am doing the unforgivable: loving women totally and committing my life to improving our situation. That my commitment to women has branded me as a feminist for many years is a source of pride. Now that I wish to celebrate my love for women as a lesbian, I face a new challenge. I must struggle with myself, other lesbians, and other feminists to confront our lesbophobia. Lesbophobia prevents me and other lesbians from speaking up, and it prevents our heterosexual feminist sisters from looking at us realistically and supporting us in our struggles. Yet, overcoming lesbophobia is what I am striving for with other lesbians.

I've been organizing community groups long enough to know that some of our struggles as lesbians are similar to my struggles within the Franco-Ontarian community and the feminist community. There too, we had difficulty taking ourselves seriously enough to feel we had the right to identify and state our issues. We were encouraged to think of others first and not be divisive. As francophones, we were to think of national unity, and as women to think of family unity. The feminist movement taught me once and for all that a society must not maintain a unity based on the silence and oppression of some of its members. I've learned my lesson well, and base my lesbian affirmation on it. And I will not accept any implicit or explicit repression.

Being in a francophone group does not mean I'm anti-English; the same applies to women's groups and lesbian groups. People have a right to get together. As a francophone lesbian, I often find myself having to decide where it would be best to put my energy. Should I go into a mostly English organization which is already large and relatively powerful (such as the National Action Committee on the Status of Women), and work at making it functionally bilingual; or should I go into a smaller, less powerful French organization (such as La Fédération des Femmes Canadiennes Françaises), where I can speak in my own language and reach other francophone women. In the large but English-dominated groups I have a better chance of being heard by the government, although I often find that being bilingual means I am used as the token francophone. This makes it difficult for me to concentrate on issues other than language. In the French groups, on the other hand, I can feel comfortable working in French, but I am not sure that at this point in time these smaller groups can make a significant impact on society. It is a difficult choice to make.

For now, I am following a similar process to my evolution as a feminist. That is, I became a feminist in English and then went to work in the Franco-Ontarian community because I felt my community deserved to be exposed to feminism. Similarly, I became a lesbian feminist in English, and might continue that involvement in French. But I will no longer be active in any group which will not legitimize lesbianism as a collective issue.

I agree with Audre Lorde that our silence will not protect us.[2] Over the long haul our increased visibility and recognition can only be of benefit to us, to the feminist movement, and to society at large. Keeping quiet about lesbianism will not prevent attacks on lesbians or attacks on women who are branded as lesbians because they stand up for their rights. For my own survival, for the survival of other lesbians, and for the survival of all women who choose to live their lives with self-respect, lesbians need to speak up and be supported by all women. Lesbianism is more than a sexual preference to be tolerated by open-minded feminists. It is the source of our commitment to improving the lives of all women. It is our source of joy and celebration.

I am fortunate that I can afford to be visible as a lesbian. Not all lesbians feel safe in making their identity known to non-lesbians. There continues to be real oppression associated with more visibility. This is why I am working to affirm lesbianism as a viable life choice, for myself and for other lesbians. I would like all lesbians to be able to take pride in a lesbian identity, as I do. Yet this will not happen magically. We have to work to make it happen.

In lesbian groups I have reached new heights of solidarity and depths of anger. I once joined a lesbian separatist group but was uneasy about the dogmatism and pressures not to work within gay or certain women's organizations. My own stance was clarified in that process, as I recognized that I like to bridge groups by identifying lesbian-positive people in each. It is this logic which is behind my involvement in organizations such as EGALE. I first adopted this stance as a francophone feminist who did not want to have to choose between French and English groups. I have chosen to be active in French groups that respect women and feminist groups that respect francophones.

In 1987 I helped to found the National Lesbian Forum (NLF). The idea for the NLF began at a lesbian caucus meeting at the Canadian Research Institute for the Advancement of Women annual conference in 1987. Those of us who attended felt the time was ripe for a national lesbian organization, to work for increasing lesbian visibility and ensure that lesbian issues were discussed in both the feminist and the gay rights movements. We immediately applied for membership in the National Action Committee on the Status of Women (NAC), the umbrella group of over five hundred Canadian women's groups. What exhilaration to finally see the "L" word in the membership list of the national organization working to improve the situation of all Canadian women!

In May 1988, the NLF was asked to present a lesbian workshop at the NAC annual general meeting. At last, no more hastily called lesbian caucuses during lunch. At that workshop, fifty lesbians agreed to stand up in the Sunday morning plenary as an acknowledgement and celebration of lesbian energy in the feminist movement. But on Sunday, when it appeared that NAC was having serious internal problems, we self-censored our planned action. Our spokeswoman went to the microphone, announced our original intention, and so that the proceedings would not be disrupted said that lesbians should stand up internally.

I see that incident at NAC as a microcosm of where we are now. Lesbians are ready for action, but we are easily deterred for the sake of not ruining the party. Sometimes we are too willing to respond to the rise of right-wing ideology by giving more visibility to "acceptable" feminists (such as grandmothers and businesswomen) at the expense of ourselves.

I think that one reason for lesbian invisibility within the feminist movement has to do with the difficulty we have in reconciling our desire to celebrate women with the very real continued oppression of women. How can we celebrate when there is so much still to be fought for? It is also difficult to celebrate women's sexuality when the sexual liberation of the 1960s has been exploited by men within a societal context of sexual assault and restricted reproductive freedom. Within this context, sex has come to be seen in terms of negative consequences. There doesn't seem to be any room for women to talk about sexuality in positive terms, let alone for lesbians to talk about the joy we feel in our sexuality.

Sexual Orientation: A Feminist Issue

The issue of sexual orientation is about the right to love, as much as it is about the right to control one's body. It is an issue that affects women, and this makes it a feminist issue.

Feminist organizations are willing to lobby their MPs when women are unfairly discriminated against on the basis of variables such as race, marital status, economic status, or education. They are not as willing to lobby against discrimination on the basis of sexual orientation. Yet countless women are discriminated against because of their sexual orientation. For lesbians, the feminist movement seems a safer haven than society at large, but that safety is tenuous indeed if any emergence on our part is discouraged.

Lesbians have a right to expect all feminists to recognize the importance of and support lesbian organizing activities for the feminist movement in general. After all, we have been supporting women's rights to improve their heterosexual lifestyle through better birth control and sharing housework with family members, as well as issues common to all women such as equal pay and prevention of violence. Their support of our issues such as recognition of same sex spouses or prohibition of discrimination on the basis of sexual orientation just makes feminist sense of a woman's right to choose and be supported in those choices. We want the feminist movement to rejoice with us as lesbians when, like other emerging groups, we say that we are no longer satisfied with simple toleration or accommodation. We bring strength and joy to our commitment to women – not just threats to funding.

In 1988 the Canadian Advisory Council on the Status of Women held a press conference to launch their Shocking Pink Papers on women's issues in the federal election. Sexual orientation was not included as an issue. At the press conference, I raised the issue of including sexual orientation as prohibited grounds of discrimination in the Canadian Human Rights Act.

Most media representatives said that the issue was not of interest to their listeners or readers. This statement flies in the face of the daily coverage that was given during the summer of 1988 to the United Church debate on gay ordination. Mostly, though, their reaction was one of suprise: surprise that a feminist would consider sexual orientation to be a women's issue. One, after interviewing me at length, concluded that since both gay men and lesbians want to end discrimination on the basis of sexual orientation, there was no "gender gap," and therefore no story.

How Far Have We Come?

We now have a number of local lesbian groups in Ottawa and there is one national lesbian organization. Many feminist gatherings include lesbian events such as poetry readings and workshops. But there are still many gaps.

It is still hard to find lesbian groups that stay together and meet on an ongoing basis. In Ottawa the two easiest lesbian groups to contact are a coming-out group and a sports group. Unfortunately, it is the same in most cities. Surely we should be able to maintain groups for lesbians who are elsewhere on our colourful continuum.

Individual lesbians may be generally more visible, but many Ottawa groups seem to have lost much of their earlier energy. For example, as of spring 1988 plans for International Lesbian Week (ILW) in October were barely off the ground. That year there was no Co-ordinating Committee for ILW and we ended up with only one activity, instead of a week of celebration. Groups such as Lesbian Amazons, *Lesbian Fury / Furie lesbienne*, and Lesbian Mothers are hanging in and hanging on only because of the dedication of a few lesbians. The only activities that are popular are cultural in nature or sports-related. Political activities such as writing, workshopping, and strategizing seem to have gone canoe camping.

Political conferences and activities can be very intense and tiring. Maybe what we need to do is lighten up a little and have some fun. We might, for example, learn from the new group in Ottawa, Women of Note. They sing highly politicized songs, showing that there is more than one way to express political views. Also, I recently organized a lesbian lust workshop, and more than fifty lesbians attended. There was lots of fun and humour. I think Emma Goldman was on to something when she made the well-known statement: If I can't dance, it's not my revolution.

There is no doubt that more lesbians are politicized as lesbians. I myself am one of the recent converts. On the whole, though, the movement for lesbian liberation seems to be at a crossroads. We still have to clarify where we want to go beyond encouraging lesbian visibility. We need to look at the whys and hows of our alliances as lesbians in lesbian groups, as lesbians in the feminist movement, as lesbians in gay rights organizations. If we put our time and energy into feminist but not specifically lesbian groups, like some lesbians in Toronto, then we won't be able to help build a viable lesbian community. If we create and work in lesbian groups, like some lesbians in Montreal, we will be strengthening the lesbian community, but may be unable to do much for lesbian visibility outside that community. A third option would be to continue what some of us are doing in Ottawa, which is spreading our energy thin by working in both lesbian and feminist groups. It is difficult to know which of these roads to take.

We lesbians are superb when we stand proud. I don't expect the gay equivalent of bilingualism – but let's just imagine an immersion program for fun.

Notes

I would like to thank Carroll Holland and Sharon Stone for helping me to write this article.

1. *Hansard Proceedings of the House of Commons*, Ottawa, March 3, 1987.
2. Audre Lorde, "The Transformation of Silence into Language and Action," in *Sister Outsider* (Trumansburg, New York: The Crossing Press, 1984), pp. 40-44.

Contributors

Jeanette A. Auger is a lesbian feminist sociologist who teaches at Acadia University in Wolfville, Nova Scotia. For the past sixteen years she has worked with and for older persons in a variety of ways, from doing research, community development, and planning to conducting workshops and seminars and one-to-one counselling with older people and their families. Jeanette lives with her partner Dian and their two daughters.

Joan Blackwood lives in Toronto with her cats Munchkin and Callum. She has been a high school teacher, graduate student, teaching assistant, and has a not-so-secret longing to be a stand-up comic.

M. Julia Creet received her Masters degree from the Department of History and Philosophy of Education at the Ontario Institute for Studies in Education for her work on the political and mythical thought of Monique Wittig. She is studying in the History of Consciousness Program at the University of California, Santa Cruz, where she writes on the construction and theory of identity politics. The essay in this book was originally written as an honours thesis for her undergraduate degree in History at the University of Victoria.

Dian Day is a graduate student in sociology at Dalhousie University. She shares a small house in rural Nova Scotia with her partner and their two daughters.

Joanne Doucette is a freelance cartoonist and writer of English-Acadian-Native heritage. She has researched and spoken on issues of concern to lesbians, feminists, and low-income women. She is herself a disabled lesbian and a political activist.

Mary Eaton was born in Toronto and studies law at Queen's University in Kingston, where she is completing her Master of Laws degree and is involved in the lesbian feminist community. Her thesis is tentatively entitled, "Lesbian Legal Theory."

Carolyn Gammon has just completed her Mistress of Arts in Creative Writing at Concordia University. She is determined to see a degree-granting program in Lesbian Studies established in Canada by the year 2000. Carolyn also thanks the other contributors to chapter 15: **Ming Dinh** leads a boring but busy life most of the year as a harried Occupational Therapy student at McGill University. The saving graces in her life are her partner, her omnivorous puppy, and knowing that studies will be over in a few years. **Claudette Lambert**: vingt-huit ans d'experience de lesbianisme, baccalaureat en Anthropologie, maîtrise en Sociologie, et bien d'autres experiences.... **Monica McQueen**, having quit school and joined the Lesbian Studies Coalition of Concordia, moved to London, Ontario, with her lover and is now working at the Cross Cultural Learner Centre. She is constantly vigilant in battling racism, sexism, and homophobia in any work she undertakes. **Renel Mitchell** was a student at Concordia University. **Susan O'Donnell** has returned exhausted from a trip to India and Nepal where she led a search in the Himalayas for lesbian Sherpas. She is now seeking grant money for academic work on lesbian architecture. **Ina Rimpau**, after a fifteen-year absence, has returned to Canada to pursue a degree in Women's Studies and finds herself battling lesbophobia on all fronts.

Micheline Grimard-Leduc is a part-time writer, freelance translator, and a science teacher. Now in her mid-forties, she is trying to learn how to grow "old and wise."

Didi Khayatt successfully defended her Ph.D. dissertation on lesbian teachers and graduated from the University of Toronto. An academic and feminist activist, she teaches and lives in Toronto.

Carmen Paquette was born and raised in Ottawa. She has worked as a community organizer with Franco-Ontarian and English-speaking groups, focusing on women's issues, urban planning, international development, culture, consumerism, and the environment. She is a co-founder of the National Lesbian Forum and a partner in Convergence, a women's consulting firm.

Janice Ristock teaches Women's Studies at Trent University and does consulting and research with feminist and alternative social service organizations.

Becki Ross is completing a thesis at the Ontario Institute for Studies in Education, Toronto, on the social organization of lesbian political organizing in Toronto in the 1970s. She is a collective member of *Rites, for lesbian and gay liberation* magazine.

Makeda Silvera is a writer, editor, and co-founder of Sister Vision: Black Women and Women of Colour Press. She is the author of *Silenced* (Toronto: Williams Wallace, 1983), a book of oral interviews with West Indian domestic workers.

Sharon Dale Stone, who is invisibly disabled, lives in a rural area of her native Quebec. She has been involved in lesbian and feminist organizing for many years, both inside and outside academia. Her study of the Toronto group Lesbians Against the Right (in which she was active) appears in a book edited by Jeri Dawn Wine and Janice Ristock, *Feminist Community Organizing in Canada: From Activism to Academe*. She is currently completing a Ph.D. dissertation (Sociology, York University) on how feminists and feminist issues are treated in mainstream newspapers. She teaches sociology, women's studies, and lesbian studies.

Jeri Dawn Wine is a Professor in the Department of Applied Psychology, Ontario Institute for Studies in Education, where she teaches feminist studies, community psychology, and counselling psychology. She has published several articles on the experience of lesbians in Canadian academe, and was a member of the editorial collective for the "Lesbian Issue" of *Resources for Feminist Research*, published in March 1983. She is co-editor with Janice Ristock of *Feminist Community Organizing in Canada: From Activism to Academe* (Toronto: University of Toronto Press, 1990).

The Women's Survey Group has included as many as nine lesbians who work in various occupations and live in St. John's, Newfoundland.